a change of appetite

WHERE HEALTHY MEETS DELICIOUS

DIANA HENRY

MITCHELL BEAZLEY

contents

introduction 6

spring 10

summer 82

fall 160

winter 246

bibliography 328

index 330

introduction

Visit any newstand and look at the magazine covers. The advice on how to eat—to fight cancer, to lose weight, to achieve glowing skin—is all-pervasive. And a lot of it is telling you what you *can't* eat. We angst about food and health all the time, and yet there is clearly something wrong with the Western diet. Rates of obesity and type-2 diabetes are soaring; heart disease and cancer are commonplace.

Against this background, I gradually realized that friends weren't asking me for recipes for cakes any longer, but for advice on what to do with a tuna steak and how to cook quinoa. They wanted to eat more healthily, cook more vegetables, lose some weight, and cut their intake of red meat. When they told me what they were cooking—trying to think of sixteen exciting things to do with turkey breast—it sounded grim. Around about the same time, my doctor was urging me to get my blood pressure down and lose some weight. Perhaps I needed to take stock of my own eating as well.

I don't, by any stretch of the imagination, have a "bad" diet. I don't eat store-bought prepared meals or fast food, but I'll admit to the occasional Indian takeout. The only processed stuff in the house is canned tomatoes and beans and the odd package of cookies. But I love food. And I have a few weaknesses. One is sugar, particularly in pastries. There is not much I wouldn't do to get my hands on an almond croissant or a little *tarte aux pommes* at four o'clock in the afternoon. I also love bread—crusty baguette, rich, golden brioche—as well as healthier whole-grain loaves. (I may have been born in Ireland, but I'm clearly French. And refined carbohydrates are my *bêtes noires*.) So I decided to explore what a "healthy diet" actually is and come up with dishes that were so good (and good *for* you, too, but first of all delicious) that you wouldn't feel you were missing out.

My biggest problem was thinking about food in terms of "healthy" or "unhealthy." I can't think of meals as sets of nutrients. A meal is a colorful assembly of foods—many of which we don't quite understand in terms of health—that should be, first and foremost, enjoyable. The term "healthy" does negative things to me (in fact, I struggled with whether to put the word on the front of this book). It makes me think of miserable, beige food. It also smacks of preciousness. While at university, I briefly shared a house with a girl who was tremendously into "healthy" food. It was all nuts, seeds, and little bowls of iceberg lettuce. Not only was she one of the most joyless people I have known, she was also self-obsessed. (American journalist Michael Pollan uses the term "orthorexia" to describe an all-consuming and destructive interest in healthy food. He claims it's a growing problem in the USA.)

I'm much more into living life to the full than I am into thinking of my body as a temple. About ten years ago, I wrote a book about dining pubs (basically bars with restaurants), for which I traveled the length and breadth of Britain, meeting great chefs and food producers.

The joy and care with which they approached their food and work was so life-affirming that it put me on a high each day of my journey. To worry about whether you are getting enough omega-3 and vitamin B when you eat seems to me the anxious, hand-wringing opposite of this.

I settled on two terms that I liked that would guide me. First, I was going to eat food that was "accidentally healthy." It had to be delicious; healthiness was a bonus. Second, I was going to practice "considered eating": find out what fats were okay; if I should be cutting down on cheese; whether whole grains were better for me, so I would think about what I was consuming, but I wasn't going to be slavish.

My eating had already changed quite a lot, especially compared to the way I ate twenty years ago. There were a lot more vegetables and whole grains, the more robust the better. And I wasn't prepared to declare anything off-limits. Food is one of the greatest pleasures in life, so I wouldn't advise anyone to completely give up steak with béarnaise sauce or gratin dauphinoise. Just don't eat them often (they're rich anyway, so you wouldn't want to).

When I started to put together lists of "accidentally healthy" dishes, I found they were the kind I wanted to eat anyway. My love of Middle Eastern food goes way back, and that's a healthy place to start, but I also plundered the cuisines of Japan, Thailand, and Vietnam.

Because I cooked different dishes, I started to read about food and health as well. One of the frustrating things about trying to eat "healthily" (and one reason why I had largely ignored it) is the competing claims, the "superfoods," the misinformation. I read a lot of stuff that was contradictory, discovered that some "beliefs" had long since changed (I really thought eggs were bad for your cholesterol, for example, although the thinking on that altered quite a long time ago) and got angry about how much we had been misled (go and read about all those "healthy" low-fat spreads we were encouraged to eat in the 1970s, which were way worse than the butter they were designed to replace).

How did I choose what advice to follow? Common sense and my own experience. (There's an extensive bibliography in this book if you want to do your own reading.) Even my kids joined in. Telling them they had to cut down on sugar was one thing. Sitting them down in front of Robert Lustig (obesity expert and anti-sugar campaigner) on YouTube was another. They started to understand why sugar wasn't good for them and why, contrary to what they'd been taught at school (which seems to lump all carbohydrates together), you don't need the white stuff for energy. Learning about sugar, and the negative impact it's having on our diet and health *worldwide*, was the most fascinating and shocking research I did. The arguments as to why calorie counting doesn't work (I should know, I've done enough of it) were convincing, too, and I gradually understood the current thinking on fats and on phytochemicals, the compounds found in plants that may act upon our own biology.

I am not a fan of "nutritionism." Seeing foods just in terms of health—for what they can potentially do for us instead of simply being delicious—makes us all that much more anxious, and pressurizes us to buy things we don't need. Any food that has had something added, I leave on the shelf. These are "functional" foods, created in factories and sold by marketing people to take advantage of our worries. (You can't slap a sticker on a bunch of carrots, but they'll do you more good than a carton of carrot juice that has "extras" added.) But I was glad to find that some of the things I love—such as roasted tomatoes—are good for you as well. (They contain lycopene, which appears to protect against heart disease and breast cancer.) Eventually, I came up with answers about what was healthy (or at least what was probably healthy, as far as we actually *know*), as well as a collection of dishes I really loved.

The main thing you can do for good health is to eat proper home-cooked food, limit anything processed, really keep an eye on refined carbohydrates (especially sugar), switch to whole grains for at least some meals, and up your vegetable intake.

None of the recipes here are "cranky" or punishing (or I wouldn't eat them). There's a lot of olive oil and vegetables. There's some red meat, but not loads. Oily fish spring up again and again, as do whole grains. There's some sugar; it's in cakes, sorbets, and other desserts that are part of largely healthy "menus" and are meant to be kept for treats, not eaten every day. There's also sugar in some dressings, especially those from Southeast Asia that depend on the balance of hot, sour, salty, and sweet tastes. I think that's okay. The problem isn't with what you eat at one meal, but what you eat *across the board*.

Initially, I intended to put together a book of recipes to eat during the week, assuming most people would revert to less healthy eating at the weekend. Then I stopped seeing the distinction. This food was so good, I wanted to give it to friends when they came around for dinner, so I put celebratory seasonal menus into the book, too.

I have undergone a change of appetite. I'm eating better, I feel better. My way forward has been to reduce refined carbohydrates (I only eat them at the weekend) and significantly increase the range of vegetables I eat. You might use the knowledge in this book and settle on a different path. The biggest surprise for me has been how much friends and family like the food. There are a lot of big front-of-mouth flavors, such as chile, ginger, and lime, the kind of thing you want when you aren't eating starchy or rich food. It's food that makes you feel revitalized and energetic. Deprivation is not on the menu. If you cook the dishes in this book, you'll eat really well and happily and you shouldn't notice that you're eating more "healthily"; neither will your friends, on being served any of the menus, think you've become a health-food nut. This is good food for people who love eating. It's a great bonus that it's good *for* you as well.

spring

eating in spring

We feel ourselves to be part of something bigger when spring arrives. Without making any conscious decision, we find we want different foods: greener, cleaner, sprightlier flavors. Spinach, scallions, and radishes are all abundant, but I also want lime, which somehow tastes "greener" than lemon, mint, lemon grass, dill, ginger, and tangy goat cheeses.

It doesn't pay to be impatient. It's easy to rush on to summer and start buying red bell peppers… but resist and you will eat more interesting food. We're drawn to different cooking techniques in spring, too. I always feel like poaching and steaming, and turn out grilled skewers of meat with big salads and bright sauces. It's not time to crank up the barbecue yet, but getting your hands messy while eating is as liberating as the warming weather.

This kind of cooking requires more care and attention than wintry braises and roasts that are just tossed in the oven, but you're more alert in the kitchen in spring than in November. If you hold onto what your body seems to crave–bright, light food–the climb toward summer brings good eating that is also good for you.

early spring

avocado
broccoli
fennel
kale
leek
mache
scallions
watercress

blood oranges
grapefruit
kiwi fruit
lemon
oranges
pineapple
rhubarb

lamb

late spring

cucumber
peas
zucchini

gooseberries
lime
strawberries
watermelon

mid-spring

arugula
asparagus
avocado
baby turnips
fava beans
globe artichokes
mâche
peas, snap
  and snow
radishes
spinach

mango
oranges
passionfruit

persian salad

We don't think about putting herbs into salads, except as an afterthought. But, in the Middle East, they can *be* the salad. And this one is beautiful, but it depends on top-quality leaves and flowers as well as herbs. I like the flowers to be all blue and white; that way it has the same color palette, but see what you can get. Obviously, the flowers need to be unsprayed. Even some supermarkets seem to be doing various colors of radish-purple and mauve as well as pink–but, again, see what you can find; just use pink and it will still look gorgeous, as long as everything is absolutely perky and fresh.

SERVES 6

FOR THE SALAD

12 radishes (different colors if you can get them)

½ cucumber

2¾ cups salad greens (baby spinach, watercress, mâche, and any red-veined leaves you can find)

⅔ cup dill leaves

⅔ cup mint leaves

⅔ cup basil leaves

⅓ cup flat-leaf parsley leaves

edible flowers and petals

FOR THE DRESSING

¼ cup extra virgin olive oil

1 tablespoon white balsamic vinegar

good squeeze of lemon

salt and black pepper

If the radishes have really fresh leaves, remove them, wash, and pat dry. They can go into the salad, too. Either quarter or shave the radishes, whichever you think will look best. Peel the cucumber, remove the seeds, and cut the flesh into chunks.

Mix all the dressing ingredients together and season well.

Toss all the elements together and serve.

goat curd, blueberries, and watercress

Goat curd–which tastes like light, creamy, almost "unformed" goat cheese–is difficult to find unless you live near a top-notch cheese shop. However, it's a cinch to make, and it doesn't have to be made into a "proper" dish. Spread it on bread, then drizzle with olive oil or a little flower honey.

This salad is wonderful with added spelt (see page 224 for how to cook it, you'll need just ¼ cup uncooked). Toss it in some of the dressing and sprinkle in the bowl or on the plates before you add everything else. You'll need to increase the quantity of dressing a little, too. The vinegar I use for this, made by A l'Olivier, contains raspberry pulp.

The recipe for the goat curd is from my good friend, the food writer Xanthe Clay. It makes about 6 oz of goat curd.

SERVES 4

FOR THE GOAT CURD

4¼ cups whole goat milk (pasteurized is fine)

1 tablespoon rennet

2 tablespoons lemon juice

salt

FOR THE DRESSING

1 tablespoon raspberry vinegar

2 tablespoons hazelnut oil

2 tablespoons extra virgin olive oil

½ teaspoon honey (optional)

pepper

FOR THE SALAD

3 cups watercress leaves (with the coarse stems removed)

⅔ cup blueberries

5½ oz goat curd (or 1 quantity of above recipe)

3 tablespoons pistachios, or toasted hazelnuts or almonds, coarsely chopped

½ cup microgreens (red amaranth is especially beautiful), if you can get them

To make the goat curd, heat the milk to 77°F. Stir in the rennet and lemon juice, cover, and let stand for an hour.

Line a colander with cheesecloth and place it over a bowl. Strain the mixture through the cloth. Gather the corners to make a kind of bag and hang this to drip for a couple of hours (use the faucet over the sink, or a door handle where it can drip into a bowl). It should be thick, but if you'd like it thicker, just let drip for longer.

Transfer the cheese from the cheesecloth and to a bowl. Season with salt and gently mix this in. Cover and keep in the refrigerator.

Whisk all the dressing ingredients together with a fork, adding salt to taste. Toss the watercress and berries with the dressing, then put into a wide, shallow bowl (or arrange on plates) and dot with the goat curd. Sprinkle with the nuts and microgreens (if using), then serve.

another idea ... Slice 3 sweet tomatoes (mixed colors if possible) and put into a bowl with the torn leaves from a bunch of basil. Drizzle with extra virgin oil and lemon juice, season, and dot nuggets of 6 oz (or 1 quantity from recipe above) goat curd on top. This also works with cooked farro dressed with oil and lemon (see page 223, you'll need ¼ cup uncooked). Serves 4.

The curd is delicious with fruit as well. Use it instead of ricotta for the recipe on page 149.

spring menu longing for brightness

feta and orange salad | persian, saffron, and mint chicken | greek yogurt and apricot ice cream

Winter eating has its benefits. It can be rich and deep but, particularly as it gets toward the end of winter and the start of spring, I yearn for juiciness, crunch, color. I especially want greenness. This menu is an antidote to all the winter cooking and eating you're leaving behind. Feta, honey, and sprightly green leaves all shout "spring."

feta and orange salad with honeyed almonds

Fresh. Just what you want come April, although this is good in the winter as well, especially when blood oranges are around.

SERVES 4 AS AN APPETIZER,
2 AS A LIGHT MEAL

FOR THE DRESSING

1 tablespoon white wine vinegar

½ tablespoons orange juice

salt and black pepper

⅓ cup extra virgin olive oil

about ½ teaspoon honey

leaves from 1 sprig of thyme

FOR THE ALMONDS

1½ teaspoons olive oil

⅓ cup blanched almonds

1 tablespoon honey

⅛ teaspoon smoked paprika

⅛ teaspoon ground cumin

FOR THE SALAD

3 oranges

1 small or ½ large fennel bulb

½ bunch watercress

3½ oz feta (preferably barrel-aged), broken into chunks (about ⅔ cup)

¼ cup torn mint leaves

Make the dressing by whisking all the ingredients together. Taste to check the seasoning, then pour into a wide, shallow bowl.

To make the almonds, heat the olive oil in a small skillet and add the almonds. Cook over medium heat until they are toasted—keep an eye on them to make sure they don't burn—then add the honey and spices and cook until the honey is bubbling and almost caramelized. Spoon the hot honeyed almonds onto a nonstick baking sheet or some parchment paper. Let cool a little. You can chop these coarsely or leave them whole.

Cut a slice off the bottom and top of each orange so they have a flat bottom on which to sit. Using a sharp knife, cut the peel and pith off each orange, working around the fruit and cutting the peel away in wide strips from top to bottom. Slice the oranges into circles and flick out any seeds you see. Set aside.

Trim the fennel, reserving any feathery leaves, and remove the tough outer leaves. Quarter the bulb lengthwise (or cut the half bulb in half) and cut out the core. Slice finely (a mandoline slicer is best) and throw into the dressing. Finely chop any feathery leaves you pulled off and add, too. Discard any coarse watercress stems.

Put the oranges, watercress, feta, and mint into the bowl as well and toss gently. Add the almonds and serve immediately.

persian, saffron, and mint chicken with spring couscous

A pretty dish. Change the couscous according to what you have (even using fresh cherries when they're in season instead of dried ones). It just has to be fresh and green, so keep plenty of herbs in it. You can also use the marinade for whole chickens or Cornish game hens instead of thighs.

SERVES 4

FOR THE CHICKEN

about ¼ teaspoon saffron stamens

juice of 2 lemons and finely grated zest of 1

2 garlic cloves, coarsely chopped

2 red chiles, seeded and coarsely chopped

2 tablespoons olive oil

leaves from 1 small bunch of mint

8 skinless, boneless chicken thighs

FOR THE COUSCOUS

2 tablespoons dried sour cherries

1 cup couscous

1 cup boiling chicken stock or water

2 tablespoons olive oil

1 garlic clove, crushed

juice of ½ lemon and finely grated zest of 1

2 tablespoons extra virgin olive oil

salt and black pepper

2 tablespoons each chopped flat-leaf parsley and mint leaves

2 scallions, trimmed and finely chopped

¼ cup pistachios, chopped

handful of pea shoots (or other small salad greens)

FOR THE YOGURT SAUCE

1 cup Greek yogurt

3 tablespoons extra virgin olive oil

1 small garlic clove, grated

microgreens, such as amaranth, or 3 radishes, julienned

For the chicken, put the saffron and lemon juice in a small saucepan, heat gently, and stir to help the saffron stamens dissolve. Remove from the heat and mix with the zest, garlic, chiles, and olive oil. Tear the mint leaves into the pan. Put the chicken thighs into a wide, shallow nonreactive dish and pour the marinade over the thighs. Turn them over to make sure they get completely coated, then cover with plastic wrap and put in the refrigerator to marinate. Let stand for about 30 minutes.

At the same time, pour boiling water over the cherries for the couscous and let them stand for 30 minutes, until plump.

Sprinkle the couscous into a bowl, and pour the stock or water and olive oil over the grains. Let stand for 15 minutes. Fork it through to separate the grains, then add the garlic, lemon juice and zest, extra virgin oil, salt, and black pepper. Stir in the herbs, scallions, pistachios, pea shoots, and drained cherries.

To make the yogurt sauce, mix the yogurt with the extra virgin oil and garlic and place in a serving dish. Sprinkle the microgreens or radish matchsticks on top.

Heat a ridged grill pan until it is really hot. Lift the chicken out of the marinade and grill it (you will have to do it in two batches if your pan is small), turning frequently. You want to get it a good dark golden brown on each side. Make sure the chicken is cooked (cut into the underside to check—the juices should run clear with no trace of pink). Serve it with the couscous and yogurt sauce.

greek yogurt, and apricot, ice cream

It's really important to strain the apricot puree, otherwise you end up with an ice cream that has little pieces in it. (However, don't use a strainer with too fine a mesh, or you won't be able to push it through.) You can also use regular plain yogurt instead of Greek stuff, it's just slightly tarter. Don't use low-fat yogurt, because it will set hard. Even with this regular-fat version, you need to remove it from the freezer and let it defrost a little before serving.

SERVES 8 (HALVE THE QUANTITIES IF YOU PREFER)

2 cups dried apricots

1¼ cups apple juice

¼ cup granulated sugar

1¾ cups Greek yogurt

¼ cup crème fraîche (or extra Greek yogurt)

2 tablespoons honey

Put the apricots into a saucepan with the apple juice and sugar and pour in ⅓ cup of water. Set over medium heat and bring to just under a boil. Take the pan off the heat and let plump up overnight (turn the fruit over every so often to make sure all sides are getting soaked).

Put the apricots and their liquid in a food processor and blend to a puree. You need to get it as fine as you can, so keep pureeing. Push this through a strainer (with not too fine a mesh), pressing hard to get as much of the mixture through as possible. You shouldn't end up with that much left in the strainer.

Stir the apricot puree into the yogurt, completely incorporating it, then mix in the crème fraîche. Taste for sweetness.

Pour into an ice cream machine and churn according to the manufacturer's instructions. While it's churning, add the honey. If you don't have an ice cream machine, pour the mixture into a wide, shallow freezer-proof container and put into the freezer. You need to break the mixture up—the easiest way is to blend it in a food processor—three or four times during the freezing process so the ice crystals are broken down for a smooth ice cream. Add the honey during the last time you beat the mixture.

there are calories and *calories*

Most women I know can reel off the calorie count of a glass of white wine, an apple, or a bag of salted peanuts. I have even taken the decision—when young and foolish—to "treat" myself to a calorie-free cigarette instead of more wine, or another handful of those nuts. All experienced dieters—and that means most of us—number crunch. The received wisdom is, "If you eat it, you better burn it, otherwise you are going to store it." And if you've ever dieted, you'll have been hard on yourself, even when restricting your calories severely, if you don't lose weight. ("I should have done another hour at the gym.")

The battle, both in the United States and in the UK, against our spiraling weight (we are twenty five pounds heavier than we were thirty years ago) has been fought on the calories in <-> calories out principle. It has led us to believe that people who are either overweight or obese have only themselves to blame; they eat too much and don't exercise enough. Because we believe all calories are equal, we conclude that 200 calories of cola and 200 calories of fish will do the same thing to our weight. (If you've ever decided to skip dinner because you succumbed to a doughnut at 4 p.m., that will have been your reasoning.)

I know from experience that the calories in <-> calories out model doesn't work. I'll bet we could all produce anecdotal evidence against it. Now scientific research shows all calories are *not* equal. Highly processed carbohydrates and starches, such as sugar, potatoes, and white flour, are treated differently by our bodies than are green vegetables and fish. Refined carbs cause spikes both in blood sugar and the hormone insulin. Our bodies need insulin, but producing too much of it, basically, makes us fat. Protein also stimulates insulin production but to a lesser degree, and it stimulates another hormone, glucagon, which mitigates the fat-forming effects of insulin. Fat, it appears, does not stimulate insulin.

The form calories come in is important. The differing effects of the three "macronutrients"—carbs, protein, and fat—on key hormones means they have different fattening potentials. This is important to know not just to help you lose weight but, crucially, to help you maintain a healthy size once you get there.

Watching your weight has been made more complicated by the fat issue. Since the 1970s, we have been taught that fat, especially saturated fat, is bad and will lead to heart disease. Low-fat diets, low-fat spreads, we went mad for them. The net result of eating less fat—and we have successfully reduced our fat intake—is that we consume more carbohydrates, especially highly processed carbohydrates. We cut the fat and put on weight.

There are many studies where different diets have been followed—the same calories consumed but in different ratios of fat, carbs, and protein—and most of them show that low-fat diets don't help you lose weight (and don't help prevent heart disease either) and that high-protein low-carb diets (such as the Atkins diet) do help you lose weight. But as with all diets, you need the whole story. One of the most recent pieces of diet research was conducted in 2012 by Cara Ebbeling and David Ludwig of Boston's Children's Hospital.

They put three groups of people on diets with the aim of losing ten to fifteen percent of their body weight. One group followed a standard low-fat diet: sixty percent of calories from carbs (with an emphasis on fruits, vegetables, and whole grains), twenty percent from protein, and twenty percent from fat. This is the kind of diet we've been told is good for us.

The second group followed a very low-carb diet (similar to Atkins), with ten percent of calories from carbs, sixty percent from fat, and thirty percent from protein. The third diet tested was a low glycemic diet, with forty percent carbs ("good carbs," such as whole grains, beans, fruits, and vegetables), forty percent fat, and twenty percent protein.

The results were clear. Those on the low-carb Atkins-type diet burned 350 calories more each day than those on the standard low-fat diet. Those on the low-glycemic diet burned 150 calories more. So where your calories come from *does matter*. Ludwig concluded that "the low-fat diet that has been the primary approach for more than a generation is actually the worst for most outcomes." And this is what The Harvard School of Public Health says: "Over time, eating lots of 'fast carbs' can raise the risk of heart disease and diabetes as much as—or more than—eating too much saturated fat."

Let's look at the low-carb high-fat plans that "worked." Disciples of Atkins-type diets are vehement anti-carbists. They believe that even what we regard as "good carbs" (beans and whole grains) should be kept to a minimum (if eaten at all). They farther argue that, nutritionally, carbohydrates are of little value, that you can find all the nutrients you need elsewhere. They're not bothered about fiber because you get that in vegetables. They don't believe that meat, or a high intake of fat, is bad for you.

But even if they are correct, that's far from the whole story; you have to look at what else diets do to the body other than succeeding in shedding weight. In the same experiment, research showed that a low-carb high-fat diet produced problems when followed for a sustained period. It raised the stress hormone cortisol and levels of something called c-reactive protein, which is a measure of chronic inflammation. Ludwig states that both of these are "tightly linked to long-term heart risk and mortality." So the low-carb diet, although it seems the most successful for weight loss, has long-term downsides.

Pro-carb proponents only advocate "good carbs," not the refined carbs or starches found in sugar, sodas, white bread, and potatoes (because, by God, do they vary). The differences between carbs can be seen in their glycemic index (GI) scores. The glycemic index is a scaling system that rates, from zero to one hundred, how quickly a food raises blood sugar levels. The higher the GI, the more it affects blood sugar levels. An abundance of high-GI carbohydrates (and you get plenty in a plate of pasta) in the system triggers the release of insulin, which will move these carbs into cells where they can be stored as fat. Foods with lower GIs (fifty five or less) don't provoke such a high insulin response, so they don't lead to the fat deposits that high-GI foods (seventy or more) do.

High-protein, low-carb, high-fat diets work spectacularly for weight loss. (I have followed them myself.) But eating like this is hard to maintain. It's expensive, it's tough to refuse fruit (fruits contain good things but are also full of sugar), and it's difficult to stay away from grains and beans. Even without looking at the research on what this kind of diet can do, it feels unhealthy to eat a lot of meat and fat. (I'm not against it as a way of losing a lot of weight, but you have to change your way of eating afterward.)

David Ludwig concluded that the low-glycemic diet seemed to work best because you didn't eliminate an entire class of food; you could have "good" carbs. I'm with him. When I think back to my childhood—the 1970s, before we all became obsessed with saturated fat—my mom kept an eye on my dad's weight by cutting his potatoes (and dessert). We knew that sweet and starchy foods didn't do you any favors. Somehow that wisdom got lost.

I wanted to know what happens when you severely restrict calories (the kind of dieting I've done again and again). The Minnesota Experiment, conducted more than sixty years ago, is one of the most significant pieces of research in this area. It took thirty-six healthy men and examined what happened to them over fifty-six weeks, first eating "regularly," then while on a low-calorie ("semistarvation") diet, then a "restricted" eating period (calories went up slightly), and finally an unrestricted phase (they could eat whatever they wanted).

The men lost one-fifth to one-quarter of their body weight while on the low-calorie phase, but energy expenditure dropped by almost forty percent. They also became depressed, withdrawn, couldn't concentrate, and thought about food incessantly. Maybe you'll tolerate that to lose weight. But here's the sticking point. Once the Minnesota men were allowed to eat whatever they wanted—no calorie restrictions—they stuffed themselves, often eating four thousand calories a day. And the more weight the individuals had lost while dieting, the more they wanted to eat. Participants ended up with fat levels seventy-five percent higher than when they started dieting.

When we cut calories severely, our bodies fight. We hold onto our weight. Our drive to eat is not wholly determined by what's in our stomachs, but also by hormones that tell the body how well stocked it is with fat. Conventional dieting (calorie counting) might not just be ineffective, it might be worse than doing nothing at all. *It's where you get your calories from that counts.*

Forget counting calories, that only makes you grumpy (or smoke). It's refined carbs, especially sugar, that are your enemies.

asparagus, veneto style

This sounds very ordinary, but it ain't. A do-it-yourself dish for the diners, it's a real pleasure to do some mixing at the table. You can smell the olive oil as soon as it hits the warm egg and asparagus. Go easy on the vinegar, and season carefully.

SERVES 6

2¾ lb asparagus spears

6 eggs

good extra virgin olive oil

salt and black pepper

red wine vinegar

Break or cut any woody ends off the asparagus and put the eggs on to boil. When the eggs have cooked for seven minutes, drain and plunge them into cold water. Let cool a little, but only until they are cool enough to handle. Put them into a wire basket or a bowl lined with a dish towel, pulling the dish towel around the eggs to keep them warm.

Meanwhile, cook the asparagus either in an asparagus pan, or in a regular saucepan (covered) with the bottom of the stems in about 2 inches of boiling water and the rest of the stems and the tips propped up against the side. It should take four to six minutes and the spears should be just tender when pierced with the point of a knife. Lift the asparagus out of the water, briefly pat dry with a dish towel, put on a plate, and drizzle with extra virgin oil and season with salt and black pepper.

Take the bottle of oil to the table with the red wine vinegar and seasoning. Each person should peel and mash their egg, adding vinegar and extra virgin oil (about 1 teaspoon vinegar and 2 tablespoons oil per person is about right).

more spears ... asparagus with shrimp and dill Prepare and cook 3¾ lb asparagus in the same way as above. While it's cooking, melt 6 tablespoons butter in a skillet and gently warm 8 oz cooked, shelled, and deveined shrimp (ideally organic) with the chopped leaves from 6 sprigs of dill. Divide the asparagus among plates (or serve on a large plate). Spoon some shrimp and dill butter over each serving and season. Serves 8.

asparagus mimosa

"Mimosa" is the term applied to dishes garnished with hard-boiled egg pushed through a strainer. This version is a little more rustic. You can treat leeks in the same way (steam them until they are completely tender; how long that takes depends on the thickness of the leeks).

SERVES 6

2 tablespoons lemon juice, or to taste

smidgen of Dijon mustard

salt and black pepper

½ cup extra virgin olive oil, or to taste, plus extra to serve

1½ tablespoons finely chopped flat-leaf parsley leaves

1½ tablespoons capers, rinsed and chopped

4 eggs

1½ lb asparagus

Make the dressing by mixing the lemon juice, mustard, and salt and black pepper in a small bowl and whisking in the extra virgin oil. Stir in the parsley and capers and taste. You may want more lemon or oil.

Put the eggs into boiling water and cook for seven minutes, then briefly run cold water over them. Trim the bottom off each asparagus stem and finely peel off any the skin that looks tough. Boil or steam the asparagus until just tender (four to six minutes).

When the eggs are cool enough to handle but still warm, quickly remove the shells and chop the yolks and whites together.

As soon as the asparagus is cooked, drain it and divide among six plates. Season with salt and black pepper and spoon the dressing on top, then put the chopped egg across the middle of the asparagus. Drizzle with some more extra virgin oil and serve.

other ways ... Look at the ideas for broccoli on page 49; asparagus can be used in just the same ways. Also try it with Watercress pesto (see page 282)— just spoon it over—and top with a poached egg. Fantastic.

soft-boiled eggs with antipasti

An easy and splendid "bits and pieces" lunch dish. Put the egg cup in the center of a plate and surround it with a mixture of store-bought and home-cooked foods. To the selection below you can add cooked asparagus, roasted beets, smoked mackerel, shrimp … whatever you like. The idea is to eat the warm egg along with mouthfuls of the antipasti. Each diner gets his or her own feast.

Get the dishes ready in advance, then cook your soft-boiled eggs when you want to eat.

SERVES 8

FOR THE DRESSING

1 tablespoon white wine vinegar

1 teaspoon Dijon mustard

¼ cup extra virgin olive oil

pinch of superfine sugar

salt and black pepper

FOR THE LENTIL SALAD

1 cup Puy or green lentils

½ small onion, finely chopped

½ celery stick, finely chopped

2 tablespoons olive oil

2 tablespoons finely chopped flat-leaf parsley leaves

½ small red onion, cut wafer-thin

FOR THE BROCCOLI

8 oz baby broccoli

1 (2 oz) can anchovies in olive oil

1½ tablespoons extra virgin olive oil, plus extra to serve

2 garlic cloves, finely sliced

pinch of dried red pepper flakes

juice of ½ lemon

FOR THE RADISH SALAD

bunch of small, mild radishes

2 teaspoons capers, rinsed and drained

1 small garlic clove, finely chopped

2 scallions, finely chopped

leaves from 4 sprigs of mint, torn

1 tablespoon lemon juice

2 tablespoons extra virgin olive oil

handful of microgreens (optional)

lentilles en salade

Make the dressing by whisking all the ingredients together. Rinse the lentils, then cover them with cold water, bring to a boil, and cook until tender but still holding their shape (15–30 minutes, depending on their age).

Meanwhile, gently sauté the onion and celery in the oil until they are soft but not browned. Drain the lentils, add them to the onion mixture, and stir them around to coat in the cooking juices. Add the dressing and parsley and season well, then gently stir in the onion.

baby broccoli with melting anchovies

Trim the broccoli stems and steam until just tender; it will take four or five minutes.

Drain the anchovies and gently heat the extra virgin oil in a small skillet. Add the garlic and red pepper flakes and cook for a few minutes, until the garlic is a pale gold. Add the anchovies and press them with the back of a wooden spoon to break them up; the heat of the oil makes them melt into a sauce. Toss the warm broccoli with the sauce, adding lemon and pepper. Serve with a drizzle more extra virgin oil over the top.

radish and caper salad

Trim the radishes and cut them into thin slices lengthwise (a mandoline slicer is good for this). Toss with all the other ingredients and taste for seasoning.

silken tofu, shrimp, and chive soup

You might think you don't like tofu, but give it a try. Having it in a brothy soup is a good introduction, because it takes on the flavor of the stock and melts as you eat it.

SERVES 4

5 cups good chicken or fish stock

1 inch piece of ginger root, peeled and sliced

4 scallions

2 garlic cloves, chopped

small handful of cilantro stems

12 oz raw jumbo shrimp, shelled and deveined (preferably organic)

6 oz tofu, cut into bite-size cubes

salt and black pepper

juice of 1 lime, or more to taste

¼ cup chopped chives

2 tablespoons chopped cilantro leaves

Put the stock into a saucepan with the ginger. Finely slice the scallions on the diagonal and separate the green parts from the white. Reserve the green parts. Crush the white parts in a mortar and pestle with the garlic. Add to the stock with the cilantro stems. Bring the stock to a boil, then reduce the heat and simmer for about 30 minutes. If you have time, let the stock sit so that the flavors can steep. Strain.

Return the stock to a boil, then reduce the heat to a simmer. Add the shrimp, tofu, and seasoning and simmer for one minute, then squeeze in the lime juice and check for seasoning. Serve in soup bowls, dividing the chives and cilantro leaves among each bowl. This doesn't reheat wonderfully—it is much less fresh and the tofu makes the whole thing look cloudy—so it's best eaten when just made.

for something different This doesn't have to be made with just shrimp. You can also use scallops—halve them horizontally— or cubes of salmon. Or try shredded, cooked chicken. And there doesn't even have to be any meat or fish. In season, green beans and asparagus tips can be used, too; cook them in the stock for as long as it takes them to become tender, then add the tofu and cook for another minute.

peruvian chicken soup

Brothy chicken soup can be found the world over and this is the Peruvian version, although it is often eaten there for breakfast instead of dinner. Peruvians include egg noodles as well as potatoes, but I don't like the double starch. You could replace the potatoes with quinoa; it's better for you and, as a south American grain, seems totally apt. Just prepare it as on page 224 and spoon it into the soup, or serve on the side. The avocado is not authentic but it does go well.

SERVES 8

5 lb chicken

2 leeks, coarsely chopped

2 celery sticks, coarsely chopped

2 carrots, coarsely chopped

1½ inch piece of ginger root, peeled and sliced

1 bulb of garlic, halved horizontally

8 Yukon gold or white round potatoes (peeled or not, as you prefer)

6 eggs

small bunch of cilantro leaves, coarsely chopped

4 scallions, chopped

2 red chiles, seeded and finely sliced

juice of 1–2 limes, to taste, plus lime wedges to serve

slices of avocado, seasoned, with lime squeezed on top, to serve

Put the chicken into a large saucepan with the leeks, celery, carrots, ginger, and garlic. Cover completely with water and bring to a boil. Immediately reduce the heat to a gentle simmer and slowly cook for about three hours, skimming the surface every so often to remove impurities and fat. The chicken should be just tender and the broth around it golden.

Carefully lift the chicken out onto a plate and strain the stock. Skim the surface of fat (you can throw a handful of ice cubes into the soup, which will make the fat rise to the surface). Taste and reduce the stock by boiling if you want it to taste stronger.

Put the potatoes into the stock and cook for about 25 minutes, until tender. Boil the eggs for seven minutes, then cover with cold water and peel once they are cool enough to handle.

Meanwhile, take the meat off the chicken (or you can serve it whole and in the pot in which it was cooked). If you are cutting it up, you want to end up with eight nice big pieces of meat, one for each person, or the equivalent in small pieces.

When the potatoes are cooked, return the chicken pieces (or whole bird) to the broth to warm through. Take off the heat and stir in the cilantro, scallions, chiles, and lime juice to taste. Serve with the avocado. Each plate should have a halved hard-boiled egg and lime wedges.

beet, radish, and goat cheese salad

It might seem odd to put yogurt dressing on a salad that contains goat cheese, but it seems to work. Buttermilk dressing (see page 96) is good, too, and a little lighter. Use raw beet if you prefer—cut it into fine slices—and replace the mâche with arugula if it's easier. A little spelt (see page 224 for how to cook it) is good alongside.

SERVES 6 AS A LIGHT LUNCH

FOR THE SALAD

8 small raw beets

salt and black pepper

2 tablespoons olive oil

1 small red onion, finely sliced

½ cup cider vinegar

3 tablespoons sugar

4 oz radishes

3 cups mâche

small handful of mint leaves

1½ tablespoons extra virgin olive oil (use a light, fruity one)

good squeeze of lemon juice

6 oz goat cheese, crumbled

FOR THE YOGURT DRESSING

½ cup Greek yogurt

2 tablespoons extra virgin olive oil

1 garlic clove, crushed

Preheat the oven to 350°F. Cut the stems and leaves from the beets and trim the tufty tail off, too (if the leaves are nice and fresh, wash them, shred them, and add to the salad—they have a great color). Wash the beets well and put them into a double layer of aluminum foil set in a roasting pan (the foil has to be large enough to be pulled loosely up around the beets to make a "tent"). Season them and drizzle with the oil, turning them to make sure they are well coated. Pull the foil around the beets to make a package and put into the hot oven. If you have managed to get small beets, they should be tender to the point of a small sharp knife in about 30 minutes; larger ones can take as long as 1½ hours. Because you are eating them cold, you can cook the beets well in advance, so the cooking time won't be a problem.

Put the onion into a saucepan with the vinegar and sugar. Bring gently to a boil, then take off the heat and let stand for 30 minutes. The onions will lightly pickle. Drain.

Trim the radishes—take off only the longest part of the bottom end—then cut them, lengthwise, into thin slices.

To make the dressing, mix everything well with 2 tablespoons of water.

When the beets are tender and cool enough to handle, carefully peel them. Either cut them into circles or wedges. Toss the mâche, mint, and radishes with the extra virgin oil, lemon, and seasoning, then divide among six plates. Spoon on the pickled onions and arrange the beet and goat cheese on top. Drizzle with the dressing and serve immediately.

artichoke and ricotta salad with honeyed preserved lemon dressing

You can vary this by adding cooked and skinned fava beans, peas, asparagus, or roasted peppers. They would all work well with the artichokes and ricotta. You can use canned instead of the more expensive artichokes from a jar; they will need to be marinated first (see page 90).

SERVES 4

FOR THE DRESSING

2 store-bought preserved lemons (1 if homemade, because they will be larger)

1 tablespoon white wine vinegar, or to taste

1 tablespoon honey, or to taste

1½ teaspoons juice from the jar of preserved lemons

leaves from 4 sprigs of mint, torn

¼ cup extra virgin olive oil

salt and black pepper

FOR THE SALAD

1 (14 oz) jar artichoke hearts, drained of oil (about 6 per person)

2 cups salad greens (mâche, arugula, watercress, or a mixture)

8 cherry tomatoes, halved

1 cup crumbled ricotta chunks, fresh if possible

2 red chiles, seeded and cut into slivers

¼ cup blanched almonds, toasted and coarsely chopped

⅓ cup good-quality green or black ripe olives

2 tablespoons mint leaves

First make the dressing. Remove the flesh from the preserved lemons and discard it. Cut the skin into slivers. Mix the rest of the dressing ingredients together, season to taste, and add the preserved lemon. Taste for seasoning and sweet-sour balance, adding more vinegar or honey to correct it to your taste.

Put the artichokes into a bowl and pour the dressing over them (this helps their flavor and texture). Cover and set aside until you want to serve (ideally let them stand for at least an hour).

Lift the artichokes out of the dressing and shake off the excess. Arrange them on four plates with the other ingredients. Spoon the dressing over the top. Grind on some black pepper and serve.

pure and white

We go through a lot of yogurt every week in our house. I love its cleanness, its snowy whiteness, its gentle sourness. It's not just for breakfast but is also a dipper or a sauce with mint, garlic, or olive oil stirred in. I add my own fruit; that way I know how much sugar I'm adding. But is yogurt really "good" for us? Like milk, yogurt is filling, a good source of protein and calcium, and is associated with anti-inflammatory effects, immune system support, and a lower prevalence of bowel cancer. Fruit yogurts are trickier. Read the label: you may be surprised at how much sugar is added, especially to low-fat types. Plain regular yogurt made with whole cow milk isn't that high in fat anyway—it contains a meager 3.7 percent fat. I buy regular yogurt: it's filling, contains all the nutrients of the milk, and has a good flavor. And what about "live" and "probiotic"? All yogurt is "live" and has probiotics unless it's pasteurized. According to the World Health Organization, probiotics are live microorganisms that can confer health benefits. They can increase bacteria that aid digestion, boosting our natural defenses. But there are thousands of probiotics and only a handful have been shown to benefit us when eaten regularly. So yogurt is a good food (but read the label on low-fat containers) that may have extra perks. It's staying on my shopping list.

middle eastern leeks with yogurt, dill, and sumac

Somehow, for us, leeks don't exactly fit the image of sun and blue skies, but leeks are much loved in the Middle East. Delicious either warm or at room temperature.

SERVES 4

6 leeks

⅓ cup extra virgin olive oil

really good squeeze of lemon juice (almost ½ lemon)

salt and black pepper

⅓ cup Greek yogurt

2 garlic cloves, crushed

1 tablespoon chopped dill leaves

2 teaspoons Dijon mustard

ground sumac, to serve

Remove the tough outer leaves from the leeks and discard. Trim and cut into 1½-inch lengths. Wash really well, then steam over boiling water for four to six minutes. They should be completely tender to the middle; test with the tip of a sharp knife.

Transfer the leeks to a clean dish towel and gently pat them to soak up excess water. Immediately put them into a bowl and, while they are still hot, add half the olive oil and all the lemon juice. Season.

Mix the yogurt with the garlic, the rest of the oil, the dill, mustard, salt, and black pepper. You can thin the sauce by adding water or milk (I use buttermilk, if I have any in the refrigerator). Either pour the sauce onto the leeks and let stand, or gently toss the leeks in the sauce. Either way, sprinkle with sumac just before serving.

spring menu clean and hot

rice paper rolls with nuoc cham | japanese rice bowl | fruits with mint and rose

This is a particularly good menu for serving to friends who worry about their weight. It's light and bright but still filling, and has all those "front-of-mouth" zingy flavors that you really need if you are watching what you eat (the thrill comes from strong flavors, rather than the satisfaction you get from rich, starch-heavy dishes). The rice bowl has filling raw fish and "good" carbs and the whole meal is beautiful to look at. For an alternative dessert, serve Citrus compote with ginger snow (see page 200).

rice paper rolls with nuoc cham

The Vietnamese dipping sauce nuoc cham is addictive. These look wonderful but are fussy to make, although they are worth it if you have friends for dinner. Be patient as you put them together. I often eat the filling on its own as a main dish, with the dipping sauce and warm brown rice or rice noodles.

SERVES 6 (MAKES 18)

FOR THE ROLLS

18 rice paper wrappers

6 oz cooked, shelled, and deveined shrimp (ideally organic)

2 cups shredded iceberg lettuce

1 carrot, cut into matchsticks

1 half peeled green mango, cut in batons (optional)

½ cup bean sprouts

¼ cup each of mint, basil, and cilantro leaves

FOR THE NUOC CHAM

4 garlic cloves, chopped

1 red chile, seeded and chopped

2 tablespoons superfine sugar

juice of 2 limes, or as needed

⅓ cup Thai fish sauce

Put the rice papers, two or three at a time, into a bowl of water and let them soften for a few seconds. Don't leave them soaking or they will become too sticky to handle. Lift them out onto a damp dish towel. Let them dry a little and become flexible; they should look dimpled. If you try to roll them before they are ready, they will split.

Everything else for the rolls is their filling. Making sure each roll gets some of all the components, lay some filling down the center of each roll. Wet your hands so they don't stick to the paper, then roll the paper tightly around the filling, tucking in the sides as you work. Put them on a plate as you finish them, seam-side down, and cover with damp paper towels. If you're not going to serve them immediately, refrigerate for up to 12 hours.

To make the nuoc cham, put the garlic and chile into a mortar and pound them with the pestle. Gradually add the sugar, lime juice, and fish sauce, pounding as you do so.

Serve the rice paper rolls with the dipping sauce.

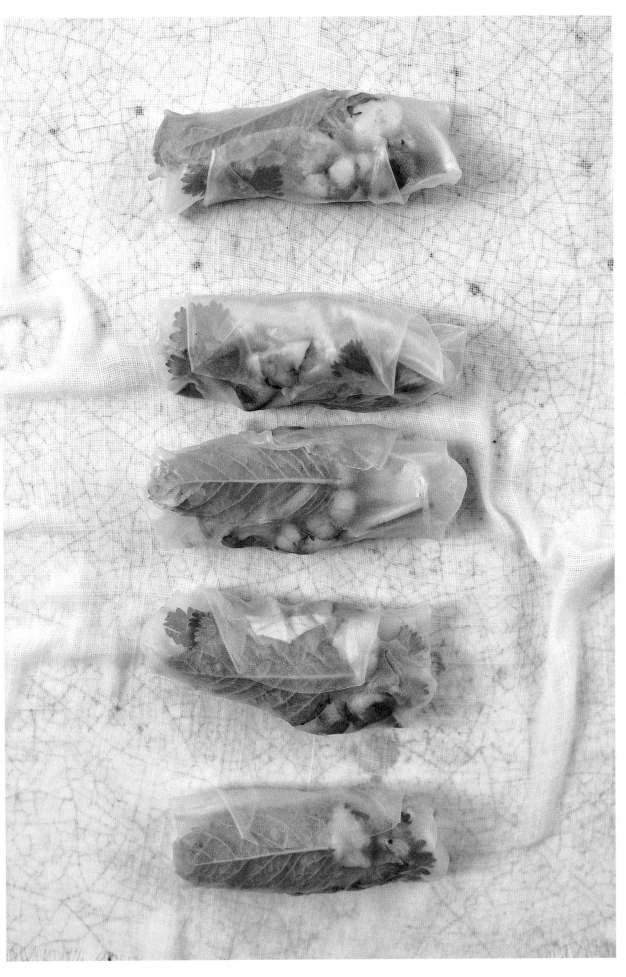

japanese rice bowl

Rice bowls are common dishes in Japan. Generally, they have warm, simmered ingredients spooned over the top, such as braised beef. They are called "donburi," which is both the name of the bowl in which they are served and also of the dish. This is a modern interpretation and a perfect recipe if you are watching both weight and health, with its whole grain rice, vegetables, and raw fish. And the flavor is satisfyingly strong because of the dressing. It also seems, perhaps because it is a beautiful dish, very centering to eat. There's nothing to cut or wrestle with. It's just you, simple food, a bowl, and some chopsticks.

Make it spicy by adding chile to the dressing, or serving wasabi on the side.

SERVES 6

FOR THE DRESSING

juice of 3 limes

3 tablespoons rice vinegar

3 tablespoons superfine sugar

1½ tablespoons tamari soy sauce

FOR THE RICE BOWL

2 cups brown rice

1 cup edamame beans

2 cups sugar snap peas

½ cucumber

1¼ lb fresh sushi-grade tuna

½ cup pea shoots

6 scallions, trimmed and chopped on the diagonal

¼ cup pickled ginger slices

2 tablespoons black sesame seeds

Make the dressing by mixing all the ingredients together.

Cook the brown rice in plenty of boiling water until it is tender (it will still have a little bite in the center of each grain), then drain and immediately stir in half the dressing. Cook the edamame and sugar snaps in boiling water for about two minutes, then drain and run cold water through them. Cut the sugar snaps in half lengthwise.

Peel half the cucumber so it has stripes down it, halve it, and scoop out the seeds. Cut the flesh into slices about ¼ inch thick.

Cut the tuna into slices about ⅛ inch thick. Divide the rice among six bowls and top with the beans and sugar snaps, the cucumber, tuna, pea shoots, and scallions. Spoon the rest of the dressing over the top and add the ginger and sesame seeds. Serve immediately.

change of pace ... The variations on this are endless and you can make really pretty combinations. Crunch is nice, so a version with matchsticks of carrots, bean sprouts, and radishes is good. You can also add fried tofu with soy sauce, baby broccoli, fried shiitake or oyster mushrooms, slivers of avocado, raw salmon or mackerel, or cooked chicken. And while it isn't authentic, I sometimes use a Southeast Asian dressing instead of a Japanese one (see page 103).

fruits with mint and rose

This is scented, but you can change the scent. Use orange flower water instead of rose, or basil or lemon thyme instead of mint (omit the flower water if using the different herbs). And, of course, use whatever fruits are in season and available. They just all have to be ripe and in perfect condition. Try to cut the fruit irregularly. A bowl of chunks looks, well, just like a bowl of chunks.

SERVES 6

FOR THE SYRUP

¾ cup granulated sugar

2 wide strips of lime zest, plus the juice of 2 limes

leaves from a small bunch of mint, plus small sprigs of mint to serve (optional)

2 teaspoons rose water, or to taste

FOR THE FRUITS

1 large orange or 1 pink grapefruit

½ small pineapple, carefully peeled, core and "eyes" removed, and cut into small pieces

½ just-ripe mango, peeled, pitted, and cut into irregular pieces

½ small Charentais or honeydew melon, skinned and seeded, cut into cubes or small slices

12 licthis, peeled and carefully pitted (or you can use drained canned fruit)

little rose petals, to serve (optional)

To make the syrup, put the sugar in a saucepan, pour in 2 cups of water, and add the lime zest. Slowly bring to a boil, stirring from time to time to help the sugar dissolve. Boil for four minutes. Remove from the heat, add the lime juice and mint leaves, and let cool. Once it's cold, add the rose water, a little at a time; they vary in strength and you don't want this too scented. Strain to remove the mint leaves.

Cut a slice off the bottom and top of the citrus fruit so it has a flat bottom on which to sit. Using a sharp knife, cut off the peel and pith, working around the fruit and cutting it away in wide strips from top to bottom. Working over a bowl, slip a sharp, thin-blade knife in between the membrane on either side of each segment and ease it out. (If you don't want to do this, just slice the citrus fruits into circles, but don't make them too thick and use a sharp knife. Flick out all the seeds you see.)

Put all the fruit into a large bowl—or individual bowls—and add enough syrup to coat it. (You don't want to drown it.) Chill before serving with sprigs of mint or rose petals, if you desire.

spring barley couscous with harissa and buttermilk sauce

A dish that is so full of young vegetables it could have come out of Mr. McGregor's garden. It is also good made with two-thirds barley couscous and one-third pearl barley (see page 223 for how to cook that). Just toss the two together once cooked or plumped up. It is excellent with a pot-roast chicken (use the cooking juices instead of the stock here as your broth and mix the harissa with it).

Try finding barley couscous, which has a slightly different flavor to the wheat version. It is one of a variety of couscous products; there is also whole-wheat couscous. For any couscous, just pour boiling water or stock over, cover, and let stand for 15 minutes (unless you are using the instant version often sold in supermarkets). As a general rule, use 1 cup of liquid to 1 cup of couscous to serve four people as a side dish, but with an important caveat: you'll need less liquid if you are adding "wet" ingredients, such as tomatoes, to the couscous. Finish with olive oil and seasoning and fork through to aerate the couscous grains.

SERVES 8 AS A SIDE DISH,
4 AS A MAIN COURSE

FOR THE COUSCOUS

1⅓ cups shelled fava beans

1½ cups barley couscous

2 tablespoons extra virgin olive oil, plus extra to serve

finely grated zest of 1 lemon, removed with a zester, plus a generous squeeze of lemon juice

salt and black pepper

8 oz baby carrots

1⅓ cups shelled peas

5–6 baby leeks

1 tablespoon coarsely chopped flat-leaf parsley leaves

1½ cups vegetable stock or chicken stock

about 1–2 teaspoons harissa

FOR THE BUTTERMILK SAUCE

½ onion, finely chopped

½ tablespoons olive oil

½ teaspoon ground cumin

1¼ cups buttermilk

2 tablespoons Greek yogurt

2 tablespoons chopped cilantro leaves

Cook the fava beans in boiling water for five to seven minutes, until just tender. Drain. When the fava beans are cool enough to handle, slip off their skins (laborious—it really is time-consuming—but worth it).

Put the barley couscous in a bowl and cover with 1¾ cups of boiling water. Add the extra virgin oil, lemon juice, and salt and black pepper. Cover with plastic wrap and let plump up in the water for 15 minutes.

Meanwhile, cook the rest of the vegetables. Simmer the carrots and peas in separate saucepans until tender; the carrots will take about 15 minutes, the peas about 7 minutes. Quickly steam the leeks for four minutes, then immediately drain them into a colander and run cold water over them to keep them a bright color.

Meanwhile, make the buttermilk sauce. Sauté the onion in the regular olive oil until soft but not browned. Add the cumin and cook for a minute, then add the buttermilk, yogurt, and seasoning. Heat but don't boil, then season and add the cilantro.

Put the fava beans in a colander and run boiling water through them to reheat. Fork through the couscous to fluff it up, add the lemon zest and parsley, and put it on a serving plate. Arrange all the hot vegetables on top and drizzle with extra virgin oil.

Bring the stock to a boil, add the harissa, and serve it in a pitcher or a bowl with a small ladle or spoon. Serve the warm buttermilk sauce on the side, too.

beautiful broccoli

Brassicas, along with watercress, are the foods there seems to be the most agreement on among nutritionists and doctors. They are—put simply—really good for you. As well as being packed full of vitamins C and K, they contain minerals and phytochemicals that are believed to have a strong anticancer action, as well as an anti-inflammatory effect that may help reduce the risk of heart disease and stroke. You can never have too many ideas for how to cook broccoli, so here's a bunch of suggestions. I prefer baby broccoli, or broccolini, to any other kind, but eat the regular type the rest of the year.

new potatoes, baby broccoli, quail eggs, anchovy cream

This is wonderful with salmon, or serve it with another vegetable dish to make a main course. (And add a bunch of radishes. This is wonderful served with radishes. Pure spring). The sauce is also great with roasted peppers; it's the salty anchovies against the sweet peppers that is so good.

SERVES 6 AS A SIDE DISH
1 tablespoon olive oil
3 shallots, finely sliced lengthwise
12 quail eggs
12 oz new potatoes
salt and black pepper
1 lb 2 oz baby broccoli
2 tablespoons extra virgin olive oil (a light one)
1 tablespoon lemon juice
2 tablespoons finely chopped flat-leaf parsley leaves

FOR THE ANCHOVY CREAM
1 (2 oz) can anchovies in olive oil
2 garlic cloves
⅓ cup pine nuts or blanched almonds
½ cup extra virgin olive oil (fruity or buttery instead of grassy)
juice of ½ lemon, or to taste

Heat the regular olive oil in a skillet and gently sauté the shallots until they are soft but not browned.

Hard boil the quail eggs for four minutes, then drain.

To make the garlic and anchovy cream, put the anchovies, garlic, and nuts into a food processor. Turn it on and start adding the extra virgin oil in a steady stream. Taste, add the lemon juice, then taste again. You want a mixture that has the texture of heavy cream, so if it seems too thick, add some water to thin it down.

Boil the new potatoes in lightly salted water until tender.

Meanwhile, trim the bottom of each stem of baby broccoli—they can be a little dry and coarse—then steam them, timing them to be ready at the same time as the potatoes.

Drain the potatoes and gently mix them in a bowl with the broccoli, extra virgin oil, lemon juice, parsley, sautéed shallots, salt, and black pepper.

Peel and halve the eggs and gently mix into the other ingredients. Drizzle on some anchovy cream (don't drown the dish, serve the rest in a pitcher or bowl with a spoon). Serve warm, as it is, or at room temperature.

broccoli, second helpings

These recipes are easy but, I hope, unexpected. When baby broccoli is not available, you can substitute regular broccoli.

FOR THE BABY BROCCOLI
WITH RICOTTA

10 oz baby broccoli

6 oz ricotta

2 oz Parmesan

finely grated zest of ½ lemon, plus
the juice of 1

salt and black pepper

½ cup extra virgin olive oil

baby broccoli with ricotta, lemon, and parmesan

Light and unfussy, so you can really taste the broccoli. You can also treat asparagus this way. Trim the broccoli stems at the bottom if they need it—they may be a little dry—and steam for four to five minutes, until just tender. Meanwhile, break the ricotta into lumps (so you have about ¾ cup) and shave the Parmesan with a vegetable peeler. Put the hot broccoli on plates and dot with the ricotta. Sprinkle on the lemon zest and spoon the juice over the top. Season. Sprinkle Parmesan over each serving, drizzle with the oil, and serve. Serves 4 as an appetizer or side dish.

FOR THE BROCCOLI STRASCINATI

3 tablespoons extra virgin olive oil,
plus extra to serve

1lb broccoli or baby broccoli

3 garlic cloves, finely chopped

½ teaspoon dried red pepper
flakes

squeeze of lemon juice

broccoli strascinati

Heat the extra virgin oil in a skillet and add the broccoli (in florets if it's regular, the whole stems if it's baby broccoli). Cook for six to eight minutes, until lightly browned. Add 3 tablespoons of water and the garlic. Cook gently until the water disappears, then add the red pepper flakes and cook until the broccoli is just tender and the garlic golden brown. Season and serve with a little more extra virgin oil and the lemon juice. Serves 6 as a side dish.

FOR THE BABY BROCCOLI WITH
CHINESE FLAVORS

1lb baby broccoli

2 garlic cloves, finely sliced

¾ inch piece of ginger root,
peeled and shredded

1 tablespoon peanut oil

2 scallions, finely chopped

⅓ cup oyster sauce

stir-fried baby broccoli with chinese flavors

Steam the broccoli until only just tender. Meanwhile, sauté the garlic and ginger in the oil until golden brown and soft. Add the broccoli, scallions, and oyster sauce. Gently heat through and serve with brown rice. Serves 6 as a side dish.

also try ... Toss cooked broccoli with green lentils or strips of roasted red bell pepper and drizzle with Anchovy cream or Tahini dressing (see opposite and page 135).

Stir steamed broccoli into Kale pesto with whole-wheat linguine (see page 282) for a double hit of brilliant brassicas.

Add a little more chile to Calabrian pesto (see page 282) and serve steamed broccoli with it, or toss both with whole-wheat linguine.

crab with chile and garlic

Of course, you can eat crab cold, but it does make me reach for the mayo (and a lot of mayo). And you don't always want it cold. This is a real treat for four (or use just one crab and have it as a special meal for two). You can buy already cooked crab for it, but I prefer to cook it myself and deal with warm crabs. To dispatch the crabs humanely, have a look at how the redoubtable Mitch Tonks does it (www.mitchtonks.co.uk/recipes/south-devon-crab). Serve it with a green salad and some good sourdough bread.

SERVES 4

2 medium live crabs

sea salt and black pepper

2 tablespoons extra virgin olive oil (fruity instead of grassy), plus a splash more to serve

1–2 red chiles, seeded and chopped, depending on how hot you want it

2 garlic cloves, finely chopped

1 lemon, plus lemon wedges to serve

leaves from 15 sprigs of flat-leaf parsley, coarsely chopped

Fill a saucepan large enough to take both crabs with water. Bring to a boil and add 1 tablespoon of salt. Put the crabs in, return to a boil, and cook for 15 minutes, then lift them out.

When the crabs are cool enough to handle, put them on their backs on a cutting board and pull the legs and claws off. Remove and discard the triangular- or wedge-shaped tail flap and ease the top and bottom of the shell apart (you might need to insert a knife and twist it to help you). Remove and discard the stomach sac (you'll find it behind the mouth) and the translucent white/pale green, pointed gills ("deadman's fingers"). Scoop the brown meat out of the upper shell and place in a bowl. Split the body in half by giving it a good whack with something heavy. Carefully remove all the white meat (you will need a proper crab pick or skewer to get all the meat out of the internal tunnels). Give the claws one blow each to crack them enough for the chile and garlic flavors to penetrate (the back of a cleaver is good for this).

Heat the extra virgin oil in a large skillet or sauté pan, then add the chiles and garlic. Cook gently for a few minutes, then add the brown crab meat, the claws, and the legs. Heat through, then add the white meat, seasoning, a good squeeze of lemon juice, and the parsley. Add another good splash of the extra virgin oil. Serve immediately with lemon wedges. You'll need something heavy at the table for people to crack the legs with. Supply plenty of paper napkins, too—it's messy eating.

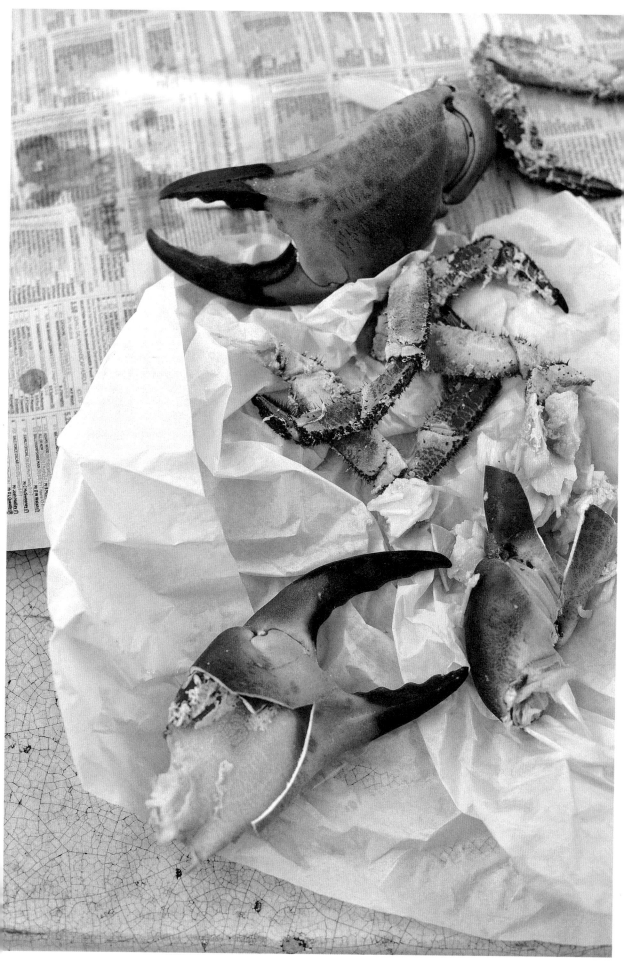

salmon tartare with pickled cucumber and rye crackers

Fresh Scandinavian fare. If you don't want to make rye crackers, serve rye bread or a spelt salad tossed with watercress (see page 224 for how to cook spelt). This recipe makes more rye crackers than you need, but there's no point not making a decent-size batch. When I'm cooking for myself, I eat the salmon tartare on its own with just rye crackers or salad, but if I'm doing it for friends, I add the dilled yogurt, too.

SERVES 4

FOR THE RYE CRACKERS

2½ cups rye flour, plus extra to dust

1 teaspoon salt

1 teaspoon packed light brown sugar

½ teaspoon baking powder

2 tablespoons cold butter, cut into cubes

⅔ cup whole milk

FOR THE SWEET-AND-SOUR CUCUMBER

1 cucumber

1 tablespoon sea salt flakes

2 tablespoons rice vinegar

2 tablespoons superfine sugar

1 tablespoon chopped dill leaves

FOR THE SALMON AND DILLED YOGURT

8 oz salmon fillet, skinned

1 tablespoon capers, rinsed, patted dry, and finely chopped

1 small shallot, finely chopped

2 tablespoons finely chopped flat-leaf parsley leaves

1 tablespoon lemon juice

2 tablespoons extra virgin olive oil

freshly ground black pepper

⅓ cup Greek yogurt

1 teaspoon chopped dill leaves

For the rye crackers, preheat the oven to 400°F. Lightly flour a large—or two medium—nonstick baking sheets.

Put the flour, salt, sugar, baking powder, and butter into a bowl and rub the butter in with your fingertips. Using a butter knife, mix in the milk, then use your hands to pull everything together into a soft dough. It will be sticky but don't panic; it will get easier to work with, so resist adding more flour.

Lightly dust a work surface with flour, then roll chunks of the dough into thin, irregular rounds. These need to be thinner than any pastry you have ever made, basically thinner than you can measure. As you form each cracker, transfer it to the prepared baking sheet(s). Prick a few holes in each of the circles with the tines of a fork. Bake for 10 minutes; keep an eye on them because they burn very easily. Transfer the crackers to a wire rack as soon as they are cool enough to handle and let stand until cold.

For the sweet-and-sour cucumber, cut the ends off the cucumber and peel it. Halve it lengthwise and scoop out the seeds with a teaspoon (discard them). Cut the flesh into very fine—almost transparent—slices, either across the cucumber or lengthwise so that you end up with ribbons. Layer in a colander with the salt, place a plate on top, and set over a bowl so the juices can run out. Let stand for two hours. Rinse the cucumber and carefully pat dry. Mix the cucumber with the rest of the ingredients and keep, covered, in the refrigerator until you are ready to serve.

To make the salmon tartare, cut the salmon flesh into small dice, about ¼ inch square. Put them in a bowl with the capers, shallot, parsley, lemon juice, oil, and black pepper. Mix and taste; you will probably find you don't need salt because of the lemon and capers. Cover and chill in the refrigerator. Mix the yogurt with the dill.

Serve the salmon tartare with the dilled yogurt, cucumber salad, and rye crackers.

white fish, saffron, and dill couscous pilaf

This recipe really is a boon. It is made in the time it takes couscous to plump up in hot stock (15 minutes), so it's a wonderful dinner after a long day, or an unusual midweek dish for friends. When they're in season, fava beans (slip the skins off after cooking), are a wonderful addition to the dish, although they make it more labor intensive.

SERVES 4

1 tablespoon olive oil

1 onion, finely chopped

2 garlic cloves, finely chopped

4 cardamom pods, crushed

1 cup whole-wheat couscous

1¼ cups fish stock

⅛ teaspoon saffron stamens

1 lb white fish fillet (cod, haddock, red snapper, Alaskan pollock), skinned

salt and black pepper

juice of ½ lemon

¼ cup chopped dill leaves

1½ tablespoons chopped pistachios

a few golden rose petals, torn

Heat the olive oil in a saucepan and sauté the onion until it is soft but not browned. Add the garlic and cook for two minutes, then add the cardamom pods and cook for another minute. Add the couscous and stir it around in the oil. Remove from the heat.

In another saucepan, bring the fish stock to a boil and add the saffron, stirring. Reduce the heat to a gentle simmer and add the fish. Poach gently for about four minutes (it will cook more when it is mixed with the couscous). Lift the fish out with a slotted spoon and break it up into big chunks.

Return the stock to a boil, then pour it onto the couscous, season, and fork through. Place the fish on top, cover with aluminum foil and a lid. Let stand for 15 minutes.

Carefully fork through the lemon juice, dill, and pistachios. Put it into a warm serving dish and sprinkle the rose petals on top. Serve immediately.

plenty more fish ... You don't have to make this with only white fish. You can change its character and make it with mackerel instead—it's oilier and richer—and use cilantro and toasted hazelnuts instead of dill and pistachios. Omit the roses in colder weather and instead add some dried barberries or a handful of chopped dried apricots or raisins. Some shreds of preserved lemon zest would be great in this, too.

you can go everywhere on an egg

As a child I used to have eggs, shelled and mashed with a pat of butter that melted into them, in a tea cup. They were my ultimate comfort food. Then, suddenly, we were forbidden eggs because their yolks contain cholesterol. A wilderness of uncertainty set in; most of us didn't know whether we should eat eggs or not. Now it's increasingly accepted that eating cholesterol doesn't lead to heart disease and eggs are back (mine mashed in a tea cup). Some still think you shouldn't eat them with abandon, but you wouldn't want to as they're so filling (a wonderful source of protein, the macronutrient that best satisfies hunger). When I'm sick of up-market food, an egg (and a pink grapefruit) is what I want. A pleasing lunch is a warm boiled egg broken up with a fork, seasoned, drizzled with olive oil, with tomatoes or baby broccoli alongside. Or chop warm hard-boiled eggs and stir into a vinaigrette with herbs and capers; good with greens and fish. And there are a million more ways to eat them ... they're great with spices and smoked salt, earthy with beans, an endless provider of easy meals. And, of course, they are excellent for going to work on.

good son-in-law eggs

In authentic son-in-law eggs, hard-boiled eggs are fried before being sauced. It contributes to the texture, but I'll forego that to eat something that hasn't been fried and yet offers wonderful contrasts. These are eggs you would give a good son-in-law (because you want him to be healthy).

SERVES 8

8 eggs

2 tablespoons peanut oil

6 shallots, finely sliced

2 tablespoons tamarind paste

2 tablespoons Thai fish sauce

2 tablespoons packed light brown sugar

3 tablespoons chopped cilantro leaves

2 red chiles, seeded and finely chopped

Hard boil the eggs for seven minutes, drain, and let sit in the warm saucepan with a lid on.

Meanwhile, heat the oil and cook the shallots over medium heat until golden brown and slightly crispy. Set half aside. To the other half, add the tamarind, fish sauce, sugar, and ½ cup of water. Bring to a boil and cook for about three minutes; the sauce will reduce and become slightly syrupy.

Shell the eggs and put them in bowls. Spoon some sauce over them and sprinkle with the remaining shallots, the cilantro, and chiles.

You are supposed to serve these with jasmine rice (and they are fabulous) but they're also good with brown rice. I love to top the rice with stir-fried greens or baby spinach or watercress (the leaves wilt in the heat of the sauce) to make a more complete meal.

japanese lessons

For me, discovering Japanese food was like being a reasonably good painter who suddenly finds a whole school of artists whose work is breathtaking. I had never looked beyond sushi when I won a haiku competition, the prize for which was a meal in a Michelin-starred Japanese restaurant in London. Going to Umu was like unlocking a secret. First, I literally couldn't find the way in. There didn't appear to be a door, although I knew I had the right address. I had to stand on the other side of the street and watch to see how other diners entered. One eventually came along, waved his hand over a sunken panel and the door opened. It was prophetic.

Umu is expensive but not glitzy. It is serene. The Japanese food experts I was with did the ordering … and it was a revelation. Each dish, served on plates and bowls of various textures, had a kind of quiet perfection, a completeness. There were expensive "wow" dishes such as wagyu beef (which redefines the term "melting") and a trembling custard of crab and ginger, but the dish I adored was the most simple: dashi, Japanese stock, with tofu that the chef made himself. The tofu was like silk; the dashi like a liquid that had washed over seashells. As this meal went on, I became more and more happy. The best thing I get from my time in the kitchen is a gentle joy that things work, that dishes balance, come out harmoniously. But my cooking has big flavors and bright colors. Here was food that was quiet, that you approached in a micro-eating style—you homed in on each texture, each color—the tingle of a shiso leaf, the heat of a dab of wasabi. Appropriately, it was like eating a series of haiku.

You might think this was because I was in a Michelin-starred restaurant but, some months later, I dined with—and took cooking instruction from—a Japanese food photographer called Yuki Sugiura. It was a drab day, filled with pewter-colored drizzle. Yuki is not quiet and Zen-like—she is warm and excitable—yet her apartment had the same peace as the restaurant. There was a big jug of rosehips on the table and the place was uncluttered. I sat down to another meal where texture, color, taste, and balance were key. There was freshly made dashi, an octopus salad with rice vinegar, carrots with a black sesame paste that Yuki had energetically pounded in a *suribachi* (a Japanese mortar), crunchy sweet-pickled lotus root, a wooden drum of warm rice. The incredible thing, however, was the cooked chrysanthemums. They are a much-loved seasonal treat in Japan, so I sat on a rainy day in south London at a table redolent with the flavors, textures, and colors of a Japanese fall.

There are only a few Japanese dishes in this book—and they have been changed to suit my kitchen—but I urge you to try more. In its use of vegetables and fish, it's a healthy cuisine. And there is something in Japanese cooking that you can apply in your kitchen no matter what you're making; it's a particular psychological approach to food. There is an intense appreciation of detail. One of the tenets of Japanese cooking is to try to have balance across a meal. The ideal is to have five colors within one meal. Texture is vital and that doesn't just come from the foods themselves, but from the way they are cooked. Again, the Japanese ideal is to include five different cooking methods in one meal, so you might have grilled, poached, steamed, braised, and fried food all at once. I'm not suggesting you specifically do this, of course, but that you think about the various components of a meal, bearing in mind a contrasting variety of colors and textures.

There are also considerations of setting and attitude. I read about these in *Washoku*, a fascinating cookbook by Elizabeth Andoh, an American who went to live in Japan. Two rather elevated phrases, coined by Sen no Rikyū, the sixteenth-century philosopher credited with refining the world of tea and the food served at the tea ceremony, sounded worth considering in all cooking. The first is *ichi go, ichi é* ("one moment, one meeting"), which is about creating pleasure at one particular meal, a fleeting but special experience of shared cooking and eating. The other, which rings even truer to me, is *wabi sabi* ("charm of the ordinary"), which is about the wonder of turning humble foodstuffs into simple but lovely meals (something that makes me happy on a daily basis).

All this is the antithesis of the worst Western eating where, starving and mindless, you sink your teeth hungrily into a fast-food burger. I'm not saying we should all become Zen about food or try to apply Japanese culinary principles, but once you start cooking with more vegetables, leaves, and grains, there is a spirit in Japanese cooking—the attention to color and texture—that makes you produce better food, and makes you eat it in a more mindful way. Eating is not just about sating appetite but about appreciating, with all your senses, what is put before you, and honoring the ingredients with which it is made. I know this sounds a little bit Californian for us no-nonsense and rather cynical Brits, but there is more to cooking and eating than ingredients and skill; there is an attitude that can make everything you serve, and everything you put in your mouth, taste better. And when you approach food this way, you eat less of it and you appreciate it more.

Now, if I could tap a little Japanese gong near your ear and give you a plateful of fall chrysanthemums, I would.

teriyaki salmon with pickled vegetables and sesame seeds

I could live on this. It's so easy and yet utterly beautiful looking, I always feel better after eating it. The pickled vegetables are a great thing to know about. Make extra and keep them in the refrigerator for eating at lunch. You can make this dish with mackerel and chicken breasts, too (chicken needs to be cooked for 20 minutes).

SERVES 4

FOR THE SALMON

¼ cup soy sauce

1 tablespoon sugar

2 tablespoons mirin

1 tablespoon dry sherry

4 (4½oz) salmon fillets

2 teaspoons black sesame seeds

FOR THE VEGETABLES

½ cup rice vinegar

1 tablespoon superfine sugar

½ cucumber, halved and seeded

2 small carrots, peeled

4 radishes, trimmed and cut into wafer-thin slices

⅓ daikon radish, peeled

½ teaspoon salt

1 tablespoon pickled ginger (plus whatever liquid clings to it)

¼ cup microgreens

For the salmon, mix the soy sauce, sugar, mirin, and sherry and stir to dissolve the sugar. Put the fish in the marinade, turn to coat, cover, and put in the refrigerator to marinate for 30 minutes.

To make the vegetables, heat the vinegar and stir in the sugar until it dissolves. Set aside to cool. (Or, if you are in a hurry, you can just whisk together the vinegar and sugar in a bowl until the sugar has dissolved.) Keeping them separate, cut the cucumber, carrots, radishes, and mooli into matchsticks, each about 2 inches long. Sprinkle the salt on the cucumber and put it into a colander for 10 minutes, Rinse and pat dry, then add all the vegetables to the vinegar mixture and toss to combine.

When you're ready to cook the fish, preheat the oven to 350°F. Bake the salmon, in its marinade, for 12 minutes; it will remain moist and only just cooked in the middle. Sprinkle with the black sesame seeds. Add the pickled ginger and microgreens to the vegetables, toss, and serve with the salmon. Offer rice on the side.

japanese ginger and garlic chicken with smashed cucumber

This dish has a great interplay of temperatures. The chicken is hot and spicy, the cucumber like eating shards of ice (make sure you serve it direct from the refrigerator). The cucumber recipe is adapted from a recipe in a wonderful American book called *Japanese Farm Food* by Nancy Singleton Hachisu. You can also make the chicken with boneless thighs and grill them.

SERVES 4

FOR THE CHICKEN

3½ tablespoons soy sauce

3 tablespoons sake or dry sherry

3 tablespoons packed dark brown sugar

½ tablespoons brown miso

⅔ cup peeled and finely grated ginger root

4 garlic cloves, finely grated

1 teaspoon togarashi seasoning, or ½ teaspoon chili powder

8 good-size skinless, bone-in chicken thighs, or other bone-in chicken pieces

FOR THE CUCUMBER

1½ cucumbers

2 garlic cloves, coarsely chopped

2 teaspoons sea salt

2 tablespoons pink pickled ginger, finely shredded

small handful of shiso leaves, if available, or mint leaves, torn (optional)

Mix everything for the chicken (except the chicken itself) to make a marinade. Pierce the chicken on the fleshy sides with a knife, put the pieces into a shallow dish, and pour the marinade over the meat. Massage it in well, turning the pieces over. Cover and put in the refrigerator for 30–60 minutes.

When you're ready to cook, preheat the oven to 350°F. Take the pieces out of the marinade and put them in a shallow ovenproof dish in which they can sit snugly in a single layer. Pour over half the marinade. Roast in the oven for 40 minutes, basting every so often with the juices and leftover marinade (don't add any leftover marinade after 20 minutes; it needs to cook properly because it had raw chicken in it). Check for doneness: The juices that run out of the chicken when you pierce the flesh with a knife should be clear and not at all pink.

When the chicken is halfway through cooking, peel and halve the cucumber and scoop out the seeds. Set on a board and bang the pieces gently with a pestle or rolling pin. This should break them up a little. Now break them into chunks with your hands.

Crush the garlic with a pinch of the salt and massage it—and the rest of the salt—into the cucumber. Put in a small plastic bag, squeeze out the air, and put in the refrigerator for 10 minutes. When you're ready to eat, transfer the cucumber to a strainer so the juices can drain away. Add the shredded ginger. You can add shiso leaves if you can find them (I can't, I have no Japanese store nearby). Nothing else really tastes like it, but I sometimes add mint. Serve the chicken with brown rice or rice vermicelli (the rice vermicelli is good served cold) and the cucumber.

try this with ... **edamame and sugar snap salad** Mix 2 tablespoons white miso paste, 1 tablespoon rice vinegar, 2 tablespoons peanut oil, 2 tablespoons water, 1 teaspoon honey, and ¾ inch piece of peeled, grated ginger root. Toss with ⅔ cup cooked edamame beans, 1½ cups raw sugar snap peas, sliced lengthwise, 8 sliced radishes, and a handful of mizuna. Serves 4.

smoky cornish game hens with red pepper puree and bitter leaves

This dish depends on contrast: hot Cornish game hens, cold yogurt, sweet bell pepper, bitter leaves. So try to use the right kind of salad greens. You can also make this with eight chicken thighs instead of Cornish game hens; just cook them on a hot ridged grill pan until golden and cooked through.

SERVES 4

FOR THE CHICKEN

4 Cornish game hens

2 teaspoon cayenne pepper

3 teaspoon smoked paprika

juice of 1 lemon

½ cup olive oil

leaves from 4 sprigs of thyme

4 garlic cloves, crushed

1 cup Greek yogurt

1 tablespoon extra virgin olive oil

FOR THE RED PEPPER PUREE

2 red bell peppers

olive oil

salt and black pepper

1 red chile, seeded and chopped

juice of ½ lemon

1½ teaspoons sherry vinegar

1 garlic clove

¼ cup extra virgin olive oil, plus extra to serve

FOR THE SALAD

3 tablespoons extra virgin olive oil

1 tablespoon lemon juice

3 cups bitter salad greens, such as frisée (use the lighter, less coarse parts from the middle), endive, dandelions, whatever you can get

Put the Cornish game hens in an ovenproof, nonreactive dish. Mix the spices, lemon juice, regular olive oil, thyme, and three of the crushed garlic cloves, pour the marinade over the hens, and turn to coat. Cover and put in the refrigerator for at least an hour.

To make the red pepper puree, preheat the oven to 375°F. Cut the bell peppers in half and take out the seeds. Put into a roasting pan and drizzle with a little regular olive oil. Season. Roast in the oven for 40 minutes, or until completely soft and charred in places. Remove from the oven. Reduce the oven temperature to 350°F. Lift the hens out of the marinade, shaking off excess, then roast for 45–50 minutes, until cooked through (check by inserting a knife tip between leg and breast; the juices that emerge should run clear with no trace of pink).

Put the roasted bell peppers into a food processor with their cooking juices, adding the chile, lemon juice, sherry vinegar, garlic, extra virgin oil, salt, and black pepper. Blend to a thick, coarse puree, then taste and check for seasoning. Put into a serving bowl.

Put the yogurt into a serving bowl and add the remaining crushed garlic clove, 2 tablespoons of water, and the 1 tablespoon of extra virgin oil.

For the salad, mix together the extra virgin oil, lemon juic,e and salt and black pepper and toss with the leaves. Serve the hens with the salad, yogurt, and roasted pepper puree.

Eat with whole-wheat flatbread or whole grains (try kamut for a change, see page 224 for more about it and how to cook it), with chopped cilantro or flat-leaf parsley leaves stirred in, dressed with extra virgin oil and lemon juice.

try adding ... saffron Heat ¼ teaspoon saffron stamens in the oil and lemon and mix in the other marinade ingredients. Smoked paprika and saffron are great together.

spring menu english spring, reconsidered

shaved vegetables with lemon and olive oil | salmon with baby leeks | blueberry and gin gelatins

When spring comes, our eating definitely changes. We want food that feels pure and clean, such as this, a pared-back meal built around what is perhaps the quintessential British spring and summer ingredient: salmon. But salmon is often served with mayo or hollandaise, accompaniments so rich they can actually upstage it and detract from its pureness. So here is salmon, reconsidered.

shaved vegetables with lemon and olive oil

This bewilders people. They eat it and say "What's in this?" When I say vegetables, olive oil, and lemon they don't believe me. You see, when you keep things simple you can taste some foods as if for the first time.

SERVES 8

FOR THE DRESSING

salt and black pepper

pinch of superfine sugar

1 tablespoon white wine vinegar

1 garlic clove, crushed

¼ cup extra virgin olive oil

½ tablespoons finely chopped chives

FOR THE VEGETABLES

6 carrots, peeled (leave the green tuft at the top if it is very fresh)

4 oz small mild radishes, washed and trimmed

2 small fennel bulbs

juice of 1 lemon

1 just-ripe avocado

1 small raw beet, peeled

To make the dressing, put the salt, black pepper, sugar, vinegar, and garlic into a small bowl and, using a fork, whisk in the extra virgin oil in a steady stream. Stir in the chives. Halve the carrots lengthwise and cut into fine slices, either using a sharp knife or a mandoline slicer. There will be a little wastage because you have to choose your best slices to present; the first and last slices aren't usable. Trim the top from each radish and cut off the bottom. Slice them finely lengthwise so you have thin, teardrop-shape slices.

Halve the fennel and trim off the tops (discard the slightly dried-out tips, but set aside any little leaves). Using a sharp knife or mandoline slicer, cut the fennel into wafer-thin slices. Squeeze on some lemon juice to keep the fennel from discoloring. Cut the avocado in half and remove the pit. Cut the flesh into thin slices, then carefully peel off the skin from each piece. Squeeze lemon juice on the avocado as well.

Cut the beet using a mandoline slicer—the slices need to be very thin—and arrange the vegetables prettily on eight plates, adding any fennel leaves. Drizzle some vinaigrette over each serving. Because the beet will start to bleed its crimson color, you need to be careful when assembling and serve immediately.

warm salad of salmon, baby leeks, parsley, and capers

We are pretty wedded to serving potatoes with salmon, but you can replace them with barley or spelt (see pages 223–224 for how to cook those). Just dress the grain while warm with some extra virgin olive oil and lemon, salt, and black pepper, then toss with chopped parsley leaves.

SERVES 8

FOR THE DRESSING

⅓ cup extra virgin olive oil

smidgen of Dijon mustard

1 small garlic clove, crushed

salt and black pepper

juice of ¼–½ lemon

FOR THE SALMON

1¾ lb baby leeks

1¼ lb baby new potatoes

2 tablespoons peanut oil

5 (7 oz) salmon fillets

8 eggs

¼ cup extra virgin olive oil

juice of ½ lemon

3 tablespoons capers, rinsed and patted dry

2 tablespoons coarsely chopped flat-leaf parsley leaves

To make the dressing, just whisk everything together with a fork, adding the smaller amount of lemon juice to start off with. Check the seasoning and add more lemon juice to taste.

If you want to serve the salad warm, you have to cook everything at the same time. Preheat the oven to 400°. Trim the leeks at the bottom and the top (be careful not to cut so much off the bottom that they won't hold together). Cook the potatoes in boiling salted water until tender, drain, and keep in the pot with the lid on to keep them warm.

Brush a baking sheet with the peanut oil. Put the fish fillets on it—not too close together—and cook for 12 minutes.

Meanwhile, boil the eggs for seven minutes and cook the leeks in boiling, lightly salted water for three or four minutes or until just tender. When the leeks are done, drain them really well, rinse immediately in cold water, and pat dry. Put into a shallow bowl. Season well and immediately drizzle with some extra virgin oil and lemon juice (I know you have dressing on the side, but these look and taste better if you dress and season them a little now).

Add enough extra virgin oil and lemon to the potatoes to give them a little gloss, then season. When the eggs are cool enough to handle, shell them and cut in half.

Break the salmon fillets up, leaving them chunky, and discard the skin. Now, lay all the elements on a plate, sprinkle with the capers and parsley, and drizzle the dressing (only as much as much as you need to dress it lightly) on top. Serve immediately.

blueberry and gin gelatins

Okay, it is boozy (sugar), but this is a "treat" dish. You will probably think there's a lot of gelatin in the recipe, but alcohol inhibits the setting properties so you need more. The Angostura bitters isn't absolutely necessary but it makes the gelatin a beautiful pale pink color and foxes diners … they can never guess the secret ingredient.

SERVES 8

1¾ cups tonic water

1 cup gin

finely grated zest and juice of 2 lemons (zest removed with a zester)

¾ cup granulated sugar

9 small gelatin sheets (about a generous ½ oz)

1 tablespoon Angostura bitters

1¾ cups blueberries

Put the tonic water, gin, lemon zest and juice, and sugar in a saucepan with ⅔ cup of water and bring to just below a boil, stirring occasionally to help the sugar dissolve. Reduce the heat to low and simmer for about five minutes.

Put the gelatin into a dish and cover with cold water. Let soak for about three minutes; it will soften but won't disintegrate.

Strain the boozy mixture into a clear container and add the Angostura bitters; you should end up with a nice pale pink color. Taste; you should get a little of the Angostura but it shouldn't overwhelm. Remove the softened gelatin, shaking off any excess liquid, and add it to the warm liquid, stirring to help it dissolve. (The liquid needs to be warm to help the gelatin melt, but you shouldn't put gelatin into boiling or hot liquid.)

Divide one-third of the liquid among eight glasses and add one-third of the blueberries. Let cool. Refrigerate the gelatins to help them set and reserve the rest of the geltain mixture.

Once the gelatins have a firmish surface, divide another one-third of the blueberries among the glasses and gently reheat half the remaining gelatin mixture, if necessary, to render it liquid once again (you should always be able to put your finger into it; if the liquid gets too hot, it will destroy the gelatin's setting qualities). Let cool a little and top off the glasses evenly with it. Put in the refrigerator to set. Repeat to use up the remaining berries and gelatin, then let sit for six hours to set firm before serving, just to be on the safe side.

madrid-style baked porgy

Porgy, also known as sea bream, is a great fish. One makes a good-size portion, it has gorgeous sweet flesh, and they look good, too, especially when treated very simply.

SERVES 4

4 (10½oz) porgies, scaled, trimmed, and cleaned

⅓ cup olive oil

juice of 1 lemon, plus lemon wedges to serve

salt and black pepper

4 garlic cloves, crushed

1 cup fresh bread crumbs

small handful of flat-leaf parsley leaves, finely chopped

extra virgin olive oil, to serve

Preheat the oven to 375°F.

Brush the fish inside and out with the regular olive oil, squeeze on some lemon juice, and season well. Lay the fish—in a single layer but close together—in an ovenproof dish. Toss the garlic and bread crumbs together and season. Sprinkle this all over the fish, then drizzle on the rest of the regular olive oil and lemon juice.

Bake in the hot oven for 20 minutes, throwing on the parsley after 15 minutes. The fish is cooked when the flesh near the bone is white and opaque. Drizzle with extra virgin oil and serve with lemon wedges.

another iberian idea ... **porgy with spanish salsa verde**

Cook the porgy as above, but omit the bread crumbs. To make the salsa, blend a small bunch of flat-leaf parsley leaves, the leaves from 10 sprigs of mint, 1 garlic clove, 1½ tablespoons capers, rinsed, 1 green chile, seeded, the juice of ½ lemon, salt, and black pepper in a food processor. With the motor running, add 1 cup extra virgin olive oil in a steady stream. Check for seasoning. (Sometimes I add a little chili sauce, so consider doing that if you like heat.) Put into a bowl, cover, and keep in the refrigerator, but return to room temperature before serving. Serves 4.

farareej mashri (egyptian grilled chicken)

This Egyptian chicken is so good—herbed and smoky with charring—that when I make it, I wonder why I bother to cook anything more complicated. Eat the yogurt bread (see below) on the side, or the Persian spice bread on page 115, or just buy some whole-wheat flatbread.

SERVES 4

12 garlic cloves, peeled and grated or crushed

sea salt and black pepper

juice of 2 lemons, plus extra if needed

⅓ cup olive oil, plus extra if needed

2 tablespoons finely chopped flat-leaf parsley leaves

8 boneless chicken thighs

extra virgin olive oil, to serve

Mix together all the ingredients except the chicken and extra virgin oil and pour the marinade over the chicken in a shallow, nonreactive dish. Turn to coat, cover, and put in the refrigerator for at least two hours.

Preheat the broiler to its highest setting. Take the chicken out of the marinade (if you find you don't have a lot, then mix in more oil and lemon and season again). Put the chicken on the broiler rack—skin side down first if you've left the skin on—and cook for about six minutes on each side, or until the chicken is cooked through. Baste every so often with the marinade and reduce the heat if it is charring too much before the meat is cooked through.

Sprinkle with a little sea salt, drizzle with good extra virgin oil (a punchy one), and serve with salad, flatbread, and Greek yogurt.

middle eastern yogurt bread

This is tangy—it's the yogurt—and simple to make. You can incorporate chopped olives, chile, crumbled feta, or sun-dried tomatoes (not very Middle Eastern but still good) into the dough. Just work it in when you punch down the bread before you shape it.

MAKES 1 MEDIUM ROUND LOAF

1⅓ cups whole-wheat flour

1 cup plus 3 tablespoons white bread flour, plus extra to dust

½ teaspoon salt

1 teaspoon dried active yeast

¾ teaspoon sugar

⅔ cup plain yogurt

3 tablespoons olive oil, plus extra for the top and for oiling

sesame seeds, cumin seeds, nigella seeds, or rosemary leaves, to finish

Mix the flours with the salt. Stir the yeast in a bowl with the sugar and 3½ tablespoons of warm water. Let rest for 15 minutes. Make a well in the flours and pour in the yeast mixture, then the yogurt and oil. Mix everything to a soft, but wet, dough.

Knead for 10 minutes on a work top dusted with flour until smooth and shiny, then oil the dough, put in a clean bowl, and cover with lightly oiled plastic wrap. Let rest for two hours; it should double in volume.

Punch down the dough, shape into a 9–10 inch loaf, and put on a baking sheet. Cover with the plastic wrap and let rest for 45 minutes. Preheat the oven to 400°F. Drizzle with oil, top with seeds or rosemary, and bake for 35 minutes.

chicken and fennel with honey, mustard, and orange

An easy midweek dish. Toss it all in the oven and let the heat do its work.

SERVES 4

⅓ cup orange juice, plus finely grated zest of ½ orange

¼ cup honey

2 tablespoons whole-grain mustard

2 tablespoons olive oil

8 chicken thighs, skin removed or not, as you prefer

sea salt and black pepper

6 sprigs of thyme

3 fennel bulbs

Preheat the oven to 400°F. Mix the orange juice, zest, honey, mustard, and oil. Put the chicken in a shallow ovenproof dish in which both chicken and fennel can lie together in a single layer. Pour two-thirds of the orange mixture overk the chicken, sprinkle with salt, and sprinkle with the thyme. Bake for 15 minutes.

Trim the tips of the fennel bulbs, retaining any feathery leaves, and remove the tough outer leaves. Quarter the bulbs and remove the core (don't take away too much, or the wedges will fall apart).

Take the chicken out of the oven, baste it with its juices, then tuck in the fennel and spoon the rest of the orange mixture over. Season, return to the oven, and cook for 30 minutes, basting every so often. The chicken should be dark gold and cooked through and the fennel tender and glazed. Serve with the pilaf below.

black-and-white pilaf

I'll be honest: This is black and beige, really … but that doesn't sound as good. The watercress tastes great with the orange in the chicken recipe above. Use these basic quantities (¾ cup brown rice and 1¼ cups liquid) for any brown rice-base pilaf and create your own changes.

SERVES 6

½ cup wild rice

1 tablespoon olive oil

1 onion, finely sliced

2 garlic cloves, finely chopped

4 cardamom pods, bashed (but leave the pods intact)

¾ cup brown rice

1¼ cups chicken stock or vegetable stock

salt and black pepper

1 cup watercress leaves

juice of ½ lemon

Put the wild rice in a saucepan and cover with water. Bring to a boil, reduce the heat to a simmer, and cook for about 45 minutes. Wild rice never softens completely, but becomes a little tender.

Heat the oil in a saucepan and sauté the onion over medium-high heat until golden brown. Add the garlic and cardamom and cook for a minute. Add the brown rice and stir for a couple of minutes, then the stock and black pepper. Bring to a boil, reduce the heat to low, and cover. Cook for 25–30 minutes; the stock will be absorbed. Make sure the rice doesn't boil dry, but don't add too much liquid.

Drain the wild rice, toss with the brown rice, and taste. When you cook grains in stock, they become pretty well seasoned anyway, but you might need a little more. Fork through the watercress and add as much lemon as you think you need. It just lifts the dish.

vietnamese beef with rice vermicelli and crispy vegetables

This is where meat plays a role, but isn't any more important than the vegetables. You don't actually need much (I've served this successfully with just 10 oz of meat). Limiting the meat keeps the dish fresh. Texture is very important here and the crunch is great. The vegeables and noodles with the sauce make a great healthy lunch on their own (no meat required).

SERVES 4

FOR THE MARINADE

1 shallot, chopped

4 garlic cloves, chopped

2 lemon grass stalks, chopped

1 tablespoon fish sauce

1 teaspoon packed light brown sugar

black pepper

FOR THE REST

1 lb tenderloin steak

4 oz rice vermicelli

½ cucumber, cut into fine batons

½ cup bean sprouts

2 cups shredded iceberg lettuce

1 carrot, peeled and cut into julienne

⅓ cup cilantro leaves

leaves from 12 sprigs of mint

1 tablespoon roasted peanuts, chopped

FOR THE DIPPING SAUCE

1 red chile, chopped, or to taste

1 garlic clove, chopped

2 tablespoons lime juice, or to taste

¼ cup Thai fish sauce

5 teaspoons superfine sugar, or to taste

Make the marinade by pounding the shallot, garlic, and lemon grass together in a mortar, then gradually adding the fish sauce, brown sugar, and black pepper. Rub it all over the steak, put in a bowl, cover with plastic wrap, and put in the refrigerator for an hour.

To make the dipping sauce, pound together the chile and garlic and gradually add the lime juice, fish sauce, and sugar. Taste for heat and sweet-sour balance, adjusting the levels of chile, sugar, and lime juice until it is as you prefer it. Add 1 tablespoon of water, or as much as you want; the sauce should be strong. Set aside.

Heat a ridged grill pan over high heat until really hot and cook the steak for 1½ minutes each side. The meat should be rare for this dish. Cover with aluminum foil to let the steak rest briefly.

Prepare the noodles according to package directions. Help to separate the strands using chopsticks, then drain, run cold water through them, and shake out as much water as you can.

Put the noodles into a large, shallow bowl and put the vegetables and herbs on top, each one in separate little piles. (You can toss it all together but I like the vegetables arranged separately.) Cut the beef into strips and serve it on a plate alongside, with the dipping sauce in a bowl. Sprinkle the peanuts over the beef or the salad, whichever you prefer, then serve.

butterflied leg of lamb with sekenjabin

This might seem like a short cooking time (especially if you want to eat the lamb pink), but that is the wonder of butterflied lamb. The meat is so spread out that the heat doesn't have far to penetrate. I leave the fat on to get a good flavor; those who don't want to eat it can cut it off.

Sekenjabin is a Persian mint syrup, but this version is less sweet and thick than they would normally have it. I like it better, to be honest; it's lighter and cuts through the meat better. In Iran, sekenjabin is taken on picnics and lettuce leaves are dipped in it. Pairing it with lamb seems like a wonderful Anglo-Persian mix.

Serve with whole-wheat flatbread (such as Cumin flatbread, see page 108) or a whole grain side dish (such as Spring couscous, see page 20). Fava beans are also perfect on the side, if you want another vegetable. This makes a wonderful celebratory spring or summer meal.

SERVES 8

FOR THE SEKENJABIN

¾ cup granulated sugar

⅔ cup white wine vinegar

½ cup mint leaves

FOR THE LAMB

1 (5 lb) leg of lamb, boned and butterflied

6 garlic cloves, chopped

½ cup mint leaves

salt and black pepper

3 tablespoons olive oil, plus extra to rub the meat

2 heads Romaine lettuce, leaves separated, washed, and patted dry

Make the sekanjabin the day before (just to get it out of the way). Put 1¼ cups of water into a saucepan with the sugar and bring gently to a boil, stirring to help the sugar dissolve. Add the vinegar, reduce the heat, and simmer for 15 minutes. You should end up with a syrup (it will thicken as it cools, although even then this is not a thick syrup). Take off the heat and add one-third of the mint leaves. Let stand until cold, strain to remove the mint, and refrigerate the syrup until you want to serve it.

When you are ready to cook the lamb, preheat the oven to 425°F. Pierce the lamb all over with a small, sharp knife to make little slits. Put the garlic, mint, salt, and black pepper into a mortar and grind it, adding the oil. You should end up with a coarse paste. (A mini food processor will do just as well as a mortar.) Push this paste into all the slits in the lamb. Now rub some oil over it and season well. Spread it out in a roasting pan, fatty side up. Put it into the oven and cook for 15 minutes. Reduce the oven temperature to 375°F and cook for another 15 minutes. The lamb will be pink. (If you want it more well done, then increase the cooking time by five minutes.) Cover with aluminum foil, insulate, and let rest for 15–20 minutes.

Chop the rest of the mint for the sekenjabin and add to the syrup.

Put the lettuce leaves into a wide, shallow bowl and serve them with the lamb, along with a smaller bowl containing the sekenjabin. Guests should dip the lettuce leaves in the sekanjabin and add them to their lamb. Serve the lamb's cooking juices, skimmed of excess fat, in a warm pitcher on the side.

chocolate and rosemary sorbet

This is a bitter, grown-up ice. I like it with slightly sweetened Greek yogurt and fresh raspberries. It's a clean combination, somewhat austere, but good.

SERVES 6

⅔ cup granulated sugar

1⅓ cups unsweetened cocoa powder

small sprig of rosemary

Put the sugar, cocoa powder, and 2 cups of water in a saucepan and heat, stirring gently to help the sugar and cocoa dissolve. Add the rosemary and bring to a boil. Boil for one minute. Take the pan off the heat and let cool with the rosemary still in the chocolate syrup.

Remove the rosemary and churn the liquid in an ice cream machine. If you don't have one, freeze the mixture in a shallow freezer-proof container, blending it in a food processor three or four times during the process in order to break up the crystals.

grapefruit and mint sorbet

Another fairly adult sorbet. Grapefruit are now much sweeter than they used to be—they're bred that way, especially pink and red ones—so try and get some good, tart, regular fruits. You want this to be mouth-puckering.

SERVES 6

¾ cup granulated sugar

finely grated zest of 1 white grapefruit (removed with a zester), plus the juice of 3

finely grated zest of 1 lemon (removed with a zester)

1½ cups mint leaves

Put the sugar and 1¼ cups of water into a small saucepan with both the zests. Place over medium heat and gradually bring to a boil, stirring from time to time to help the sugar dissolve.

Boil for eight minutes, then take the pan off the heat and add the mint leaves. Cover and let cool completely.

Strain the syrup through a strainer into a bowl and mix it with the grapefruit juice.

Churn the liquid in an ice cream machine. If you don't have one, freeze the mixture in a shallow freezer-proof container, blending it in a food processor three or four times during the process in order to break up the crystals.

pistachio and lemon cake

A perfect cake for spring. Take the cake out of the pan before pouring the syrup, or it sticks.

SERVES 8

1 cup olive oil, plus extra for the pan

1 cup unsalted, shelled pistachio nuts

1 cup stale bread crumbs

1¼ cups superfine sugar

2½ teaspoons baking powder

finely grated zest of 1 lemon, plus the juice of 2

4 eggs, lightly beaten

Oil an 8–9 inch cake pan and line the bottom with parchment paper. Put ¾ cup of the pistachios in a spice grinder or coffee blender and grind to a powder. (You can use a food processor but it won't do it as finely.) Mix with the bread crumbs, 1 cup of the sugar, baking powder, and lemon zest. Mix together the oil and eggs, beating lightly with a fork, then stir this into the dry ingredients. Scrape into the prepared pan and place in a cold oven. Set the oven to 350°F and bake for 50–55 minutes. It should be coming away from the sides of the pan.

Meanwhile, put the lemon juice and remaining ¼ cup sugar in a saucepan with ½ cup of water and stir over medium heat until the sugar dissolves. Bring to a boil, then reduce the heat and simmer for about seven minutes.

Turn the cake out of the pan, peel off the paper, and place on a plate, baked side up. While it is still warm, pierce it all over with a toothpick. Slowly pour in the syrup and leat it cool and sink in.

Just before serving, chop the remaining pistachios so some are fine- and others coarse. Sprinkle them over the cake.

beet and poppy seed loaf cake

You don't have to make the candied beet (it does mean you increase the sugar content), but the slices are absolutely beautiful. However, just icing and a sprinkling of poppy seeds is good, too.

SERVES 8

FOR THE CAKE

butter, for greasing

3 extra-large eggs

1 cup firmly packed light brown sugar

½ cup hazelnut oil

1 cup olive oil

½ teaspoon vanilla extract

1¼ cup regular whole-wheat flour

½ cup whole-wheat spelt flour

good pinch of salt

¾ teaspoon baking powder

¾ teaspoon baking soda

finely grated zest of 1 orange

2 tablespoons poppy seeds, plus 1 teaspoon to serve (optional)

2 tablespoons chopped toasted hazelnuts

8 oz raw beets (about 3 medium), peeled and coarsely grated

FOR THE CANDIED BEETS (OPTIONAL)

1⅓ cups granulated sugar

½ small "candy stripe" beet, finely sliced horizontally

½ small crimson beet, finely sliced horizontally

FOR THE ICING

½ egg white

1¼ cups confectioners' sugar, sifted

squeeze of lemon juice

Preheat the oven to 350°F. Butter a 9 x 5 x 3 inch loaf pan and line the bottom with parchment paper.

Beat the eggs with the sugar, using an electric mixer, until pale and light. Stir in the oils and vanilla, then, with the mixer on its lowest speed, mix in the flours, salt, baking power, baking soda, and orange zest. Stir in the 2 tablespoons of poppy seeds, hazelnuts, and beet. Scrape into the prepared pan.

Bake for 40 minutes, then reduce the heat to 340°F and cook for 20 minutes, or until a toothpick inserted into the center comes out clean. Let cool in the pan for 10 minutes, then turn out onto a wire rack and let cool completely.

Meanwhile, make the candied beets. Put the sugar in a saucepan with 1 cup of water and bring gradually to a boil, stirring a little to help the sugar dissolve. Boil for five minutes, then reduce the heat and cook the "candy stripe" beet slices for 15 minutes. Scoop them out, shake off the excess syrup, and set them on wax paper to dry a little (they will still be sticky but they'll dry out enough to use in about 30 minutes). Repeat with the crimson slices.

To make the icing, lightly beat the egg white, then gradually mix in the confectioners' sugar, beating until smooth. Add a squeeze of lemon juice. Spoon over the top of the cake, letting the icing drip down the sides. Put the prettiest slices of beet on top or sprinkle over the 1 teaspoon of poppy seeds, if you prefer. Let set before serving (although the icing will stay quite soft).

summer

eating in summer

The summer appetite is fickle. Sometimes it seems completely absent. It can be so hot that all you want is for your thirst to be quenched, then suddenly you can't resist the sweetness of fruit—you want the juice of a peach to run down your arm—or the smokiness of grilled chicken. It's certainly the easiest season in which to eat "healthily," and there doesn't have to be much cooking done at all if you don't feel like it. Tomatoes with olive oil, anchovies and parsley, fava beans with feta and mint, they're simple assembly jobs. Fruit and vegetables are abundant and varied, but it's also a good time to eat fish—it goes down easily—and the lighter grains. Whole-wheat couscous and bulgur wheat make perfect summer eating (and are quick to prepare, too).

Don't miss out on one of the key joys in cooking. Edible flowers and petals aren't girly or old-fashioned—they really enable you to be a painter in the kitchen—and summer herbs, such as tarragon, chervil, and basil, also help this scented quality to come to the fore.

early summer

arugula
asparagus
beet
carrot
cucumber
eggplant
fava beans
globe artichoke
green beans
peas
radish
sweet pepper
spinach
scallion
watercress
zucchini

apricot
blueberries
boysenberries
cherries
gooseberries
lime
mango
passionfruit
pineapple
rhubarb
strawberries
watermelon

duck
lamb

midsummer

scallion
sweetcorn
tomato

blackberries
figs
nectarine
peach
plum
raspberries

late summer

cantaloupe
grapes
melon

nectarine, tomato and basil salad with torn mozzarella

One of the best salads in the book, this shows just how perfumed basil is. You can omit the mozzarella if you are watching your fat intake (although first consider the discussion on fats on pages 284–285), or if you're not, use burrata, if you can get it, instead of mozzarella (it's even better).

This is a simple dish, so you do need to buy good-quality ingredie

SERVES 6 AS AN APPETIZER,
4 AS A MAIN COURSE

3 nectarines

10 oz tomatoes of mixed sizes
and colors

8 oz buffalo mozzarella, drained
of whey

leaves from 1 large bunch of basil

salt and black pepper

1½ tablespoons white balsamic
vinegar

3 tablespoons extra virgin olive oil

Halve and pit the nectarines and cut each half into four equal wedges. Halve smaller plum tomatoes or quarter larger ones, and slice the large tomato. Tear the mozzarella coarsely into pieces.

Get a wide, shallow bowl and layer the salad components, seasoning and sprinkling with white balsamic and extra virgin oil as you work. Serve immediately.

tons of tomatoes … tomato, melon, and cucumber salad

Put 1½ tablespoons white wine vinegar, 2 tablespoons peanut oil, ¼ cup olive oil, 18 mint leaves, ½ teaspoon Dijon mustard, salt, black pepper, and 1 teaspoon sugar into a blender and process. Check the seasoning; this is a sweet-sour dressing, so you need to get the balance of vinegar and sugar right. Halve 2½ cups cherry tomatoes (get mixed colors if you can) and seed 1 small melon (honeydew or cantaloupe). Cut the melon flesh into cubes. Peel sections from 1 small cucumber lengthwise so it ends up stripy, halve along its length, scoop out the seeds with a spoon, and slice the flesh. Toss the tomatoes, melon, and cucumber with the dressing and season. Serve the salad quickly, because the components turn flaccid if left for longer than 45 minutes. Serves 6–8 as a side dish, although it can make more of a main course salad if you add chunks of feta. (If you do this, add more torn mint leaves to the finished dish.)

chilled tomato soup with cumin and avocado

The flavor of the tomatoes is everything here, because little happens to them except for chopping and pureeing. The key thing is to get good ingredients and taste all the time to get the right balance of flavors (the seasoning, oil, and vinegar are all important) and textures.

SERVES 6–8

9 well-flavored tomatoes (about 2¼ lb)

1 cucumber, peeled

1 red bell pepper

4 scallions, trimmed

2 fat garlic cloves

2 teaspoons ground cumin, plus extra if needed

⅔ cup extra virgin olive oil, plus extra to serve

2 tablespoons sherry vinegar

2 teaspoons superfine sugar

salt and black pepper

2 avocados

juice of 2 limes

¼ cup chopped cilantro leaves

Chop the tomatoes, cucumber, bell pepper, scallions, and garlic coarsely (discard the seeds, pithy ribs, and stem of the bell pepper) and put into a blender—in batches—with the cumin, extra virgin oil, vinegar, sugar, and seasoning. Blend to a puree.

Push the pureed mixture through a nylon strainer into a large bowl. Before you blend the last batch, taste the puree to see whether you are getting the cumin flavor through. It should be subtle but clear; add a little more if you need it. When it's all been pushed through the strainer, taste for seasoning, cover, and chill.

To serve, halve and pit the avocados. Peel and cut the flesh into slivers or cubes (depending on the size of the bowls you are going to serve the soup in). Squeeze the lime over them and season well. Serve the soup cold, with a drizzle of extra virgin oil, the avocado, and cilantro.

burmese melon and ginger salad

Fresh and thirst-quenching, make sure you serve this really cold. I sometimes add cubed, seeded cucumber as well (it's great with melon). Some recipes include shredded cabbage, or try romaine lettuce instead. This is great with fish or pork, or as part of a mixture of salads. (Try it with Burmese-style chicken salad, see page 216.) You don't have to add coconut, but if you happen to have a fresh coconut, it will add flavor.

SERVES 4

3 cups peeled, seeded, and cubed melon, such as honeydew, cantaloupe, or watermelon

2 tablespoons peanut oil

2 shallots, finely sliced

1¼ inch of ginger root, peeled and cut into julienne

3 garlic cloves, very finely sliced

1 tablespoon Thai fish sauce

½ tablespoon superfine sugar

juice of 2 limes

2 tablespoons torn mint leaves

2 tablespoons chopped cilantro leaves

2 tablespoons torn basil leaves

1 tablespoon toasted sesame seeds

2 tablespoons fresh coconut shavings (optional)

1 tablespoon roasted peanuts, chopped

Put the melon into a serving bowl. Heat the oil in a skillet and sauté the shallots gently until they are beginning to soften. Add the ginger and cook for a minute, then the garlic and cook for another minute. Let cool.

Mix together the fish sauce, sugar, and lime juice and pour it over the melon in the bowl. Gently toss in the shallot mixture, then chill briefly. If you let it stand for longer than about an hour, the melon gets too soft and the dish loses its freshness.

Gently mix in all the herbs, the sesame seeds, coconut (if using), and peanuts. Serve immediately.

and also … kachumber (indian cucumber salad)

This is ubiquitous in India, and deliciously cooling. It's great with spicy chicken, but I also eat it just with grains and other salads. (It's great with Crazy salad, see page 230, although they come from different parts of the world.)

Chop 6 really well-flavored plum tomatoes and ⅔ of a peeled, seeded cucumber into small chunks. Mix in 4 radishes, cut into matchsticks, ¼ red onion, finely chopped, the torn leaves from 8 sprigs of mint, ⅓ cup coarsely chopped cilantro leaves, 1½ tablespoons extra virgin olive oil, 2 tablespoons lemon or lime juice, and 1 small green chile, seeded and finely chopped. Season well. Put 1 teaspoon cumin seeds into a dry skillet and toast for about a minute, or until you can smell the cumin. Toss this into the salad, too. Mix everything together, taste for seasoning, and serve immediately. (I sometimes drizzle plain yogurt—the really sour stuff, not a Greek one—over the top as well.) Serves 4.

summer menu lunch in sicily

sicilian artichoke and fava bean salad with saffron dressing | espresso granita

A lunch that is light but full of contrasting flavors; perfect for hot weather.
If you want starch alongside the beans, try Barley tabbouleh (see page 135)
or Summer fregola (see page 142).

sicilian artichoke and fava bean salad with saffron dressing

You can add other classic Sicilian flavors, such as chopped anchovies or capers, and I sometimes
include peas, tomatoes, or roasted peppers as well. It might seem paltry to serve just this as a main
course, but Sicilian flavors are big and satisfying. If you wanted to extend the meal, however,
roasted red snapper, seared tuna, roasted red peppers, or tomatoes would be good. Slipping the
skins off the fava beans is a bit laborious, but it's worth it for the emerald green color.

Artichoke hearts in oil are expensive, so I often buy them canned. Once they have marinated in oil
for a while they're really great. In fact, it's good to do this and have them on hand in the refrigerator.

SERVES 4 AS A LIGHT LUNCH

¼ cup raisins

1½ tablespoons lemon juice

½ tablespoons white balsamic
vinegar

good pinch of saffron stamens

1 teaspoon honey

salt and black pepper

⅓ cup extra virgin olive oil

½ (14 oz) can artichoke hearts,
drained

3 cups shelled fava beans

1½ teaspoons olive oil

4 shallots, finely sliced

2 garlic cloves, finely chopped

¼–½ teaspoon dried red pepper
flakes, to taste

2 tablespoons pine nuts, toasted

leaves from 1 bunch of mint, torn

Put the raisins to soak in boiling water for 30 minutes, then drain.
Make the dressing by mixing the lemon juice, white balsamic
vinegar, and saffron in a small saucepan and gently heating; the
saffron will color and flavor the liquid as it heats. Let cool, then
whisk in the honey, salt and black pepper, and extra virgin oil.
Slice the artichoke hearts, put them in a serving dish, pour on the
dressing, and gently turn to coat. It really helps the artichokes if
they can sit in this for a while (an hour is great).

Put the fava beans in a saucepan with boiling water and cook until
they are tender (about three minutes). Drain, run them under cold
water, and then slip off the skins. Set aside.

Heat the regular olive oil and gently sauté the shallots until soft
and pale gold, then add the garlic and chile and sauté for another
minute. Scrape these into the dish with the artichokes. Add all the
other ingredients to the dish and gently toss together. Taste for
seasoning and sweet-savory balance, then serve.

espresso granita

Dark and bitter-sweet, this is one of the classic Italian granitas. In Sicily, it is eaten with thick cream—you can decide whether that's on the menu or not—but it really doesn't need it.

SERVES 4

¾ cup coffee beans

⅔ cup granulated sugar

2 strips of lemon zest and a squeeze of lemon juice

Grind the coffee beans and put them in a saucepan with 2¾ cups of water, the sugar, and lemon zest. Bring to a boil, stirring to help the sugar dissolve, then take off the heat and let stand until lukewarm. Strain through a paper coffee filter. Add the lemon juice and let cool, then chill in the refrigerator.

Pour the mixture into a shallow freezer-proof container and put in the freezer. Coarsely fork through the crystals to break them up three or four times during the freezing process, to get a mixture of glassy shards. Spoon the granita into glasses and serve.

an alternative … **lemon and basil granita** We don't know for sure whether ices were invented in Sicily, or even Naples, but the Arabs who invaded certainly introduced the habit of using snow from Etna to cool their fruit juices. From that it is only a small step to granitas, which Sicilians adore. Make this if you don't care for the espresso granita. Mix 1 cup granulated sugar and 1½ cups of water in a small saucepan and add the finely grated zest of 3 lemons (removed with a zester). Heat gently, stirring every so often to help the sugar dissolve. Bring to a boil and cook for four minutes. Take off the heat and add 6 good-size sprigs of basil. Let steep for about 45 minutes. Remove the basil, strain the syrup, and add 2 cups lemon juice (that's the juice of about 7 large juicy lemons). Stir and pour the mixture into a shallow freezer-proof container. Freeze, forking through the mixture coarsely three or four times during the freezing process. Serve in frosted glasses with a little sprig of basil on top. Serves 8 (but you can halve the quantities, if you want).

cucumber and yogurt soup with walnuts and rose petals

I always love the look—and the idea—of Middle Eastern cucumber soups, but have never tasted one that actually has enough depth of flavor (not for me, anyway). So this isn't purely Middle Eastern, because I've used some stock, which they wouldn't do, but it has the right spirit: light, healthy, and "green" tasting. I actually prefer it without the dried fruit garnish, but that is traditional.

SERVES 8

FOR THE SOUP

2 cucumbers, peeled and chopped, plus matchsticks of cucumber to serve

1 cup walnuts, plus extra chopped walnuts to serve

4 garlic cloves, chopped

6 scallions, chopped

3 tablespoons chopped mint leaves

3 tablespoons chopped dill leaves, plus extra to serve

pinch of dried red pepper flakes

leaves from 5 sprigs of tarragon

1¾ slices stale white country-style bread, crusts removed, torn

1 cup strong chicken stock

1 cup Turkish yogurt (or Greek, Turkish is thinner)

⅔ cup extra virgin olive oil, or to taste

juice of ½ lemon, or to taste

2 tablespoons white balsamic vinegar, or to taste

salt and black pepper

TO SERVE

handful of raisins (optional)

pink or red rose petals

If you will be serving the soup with raisins, put them in a small bowl and cover with just-boiled water. Let stand for 30 minutes to plump them up, then drain.

Put all the ingredients for the soup into a blender, in batches if necessary, and process. You will have to stop every so often and move the ingredients around so that all of them get to be near the blade. Taste for seasoning; this soup needs really careful adjusting. You may find you need a drop more lemon juice or white balsamic or extra virgin oil instead of salt or black pepper.

Chill well, then serve in small bowls, with the raisins (if using), chopped walnuts, cucumber matchsticks, dill, and rose petals.

try a heartier version Cucumber soup is wonderfully adaptable and can be dressed in all kinds of ways. Instead of rose petals and walnuts, top this with spoonfuls of Salmon tartare (see page 53) or flaked hot-smoked salmon, or even with chopped, still-warm hard-boiled egg and sautéed shrimp. You could also try replacing the dill in the recipe with basil, and the walnuts with almonds, to make a more Italian soup. Top with finely chopped tomatoes and torn basil leaves mixed into a vinaigrette, or Almond and basil gremolata (see page 98).

hot-smoked salmon, rye, beet, and radish salad

Scandi fare. If you've never tried rye grains before, this is a good introduction. It won't surprise your palate, as we are already used to the rye bread-smoked salmon combo.

SERVES 4 AS A MAIN COURSE

FOR THE SALAD

4 cups rye berries

4 small raw beets

a little olive oil

salt and black pepper

12 radishes, preferably French Breakfast variety or other small mild variety

⅓ cups extra virgin olive oil (fruity instead of grassy)

juice of 1 small lemon

1¾ cups salad greens (a mixture including crimson-veined leaves looks beautiful)

1½ lb hot-smoked salmon (fillets or slices)

FOR THE DRESSING

⅓ cup buttermilk

2 tablespoons extra virgin olive oil

½ garlic clove, crushed

2 tablespoons chopped dill leaves

Soak the rye berries overnight, then rinse well. Put in a saucepan with plenty of water to cover, then bring to a boil. Reduce the heat a little and cook for 50–60 minutes, until tender. Check during this time to make sure there's plenty of water in the pan, adding boiling water if you need to.

Preheat the oven to 375°F. Trim the beets but don't peel them. Set them on a large piece of aluminum foil in a baking dish. Drizzle with a little regular olive oil and season. Scrunch up the foil around the beets to make a package and roast them for 30–40 minutes. To check whether they are ready, open the package and pierce them with the tip of a knife; they should be tender. Let cool, then peel—the skins should just slip off—and cut them into matchsticks. Trim the radishes and cut them into thin slices lengthwise.

When the rye is cooked, it should be plump and tender but will remain chewy. Drain and rinse with boiling water. While it is still warm, dress it with ¼ cup of the extra virgin oil and the lemon juice and season.

When the grain is at room temperature, gently toss it with the beets, greens, radishes, and the remaining 1 tablespoon of extra virgin oil (or arrange them on a plate without tossing them together). Quickly mix the ingredients for the dressing. Put the salmon on top of the rye and beets. Drizzle on some buttermilk dressing and serve the rest in a pitcher.

warm salad of pink grapefruit, shrimp, and toasted coconut

Some supermarkets do little packages of fresh, shelled coconut flesh in small chunks so you don't need to go to through all the palaver of smashing coconuts on the front doorstep (my usual trick).

SERVES 4 AS A LIGHT MAIN COURSE

FOR THE DRESSING

2 tablespoons lime juice

2 tablespoons Thai fish sauce

1 tablespoon light brown sugar (or jaggery if you can get it)

1½ tablespoons peanut oil

FOR THE SALAD

2 pink grapefruits

1oz fresh coconut flesh (about ⅓ cup when shaved)

1 tablespoon peanut oil

1 lb raw jumbo shrimp, shelled and deveined (ideally organic)

2 red chiles, seeded and finely chopped

salt and black pepper

good squeeze of lime juice

2 small butterhead lettuce, leaves separated and torn

about 30 mint leaves, torn

2 tablespoons chopped roasted peanuts

1 tablespoon white sesame seeds

To make the dressing, just mix all the ingredients together.

To cut the grapefruits into segments, cut a slice off the bottom and top of each fruit so they have a flat bottom on which to sit. Using a sharp knife, cut the peel and pith off each grapefruit, working around the fruit and cutting the peel away in wide strips from top to bottom. Working over a bowl, slip a sharp fine-blade knife in between the membrane on either side of each segment and ease the segment out.

Either shave—it's only really possible to do this if you have a chunk of coconut—or cut the coconut into fine slices using a sharp knife. Toast it in a dry skillet until golden brown; be careful because this happens quickly. Transfer onto a plate.

Heat the oil in a skillet and quickly sauté the shrimp over medium heat, cooking them until they turn from gray to pink (it will take only about three minutes). When there's one minute to go, throw in the chiles. Season and add a squeeze of lime juice. Immediately toss the shrimp with the lettuce, grapefruit, mint, and dressing. Sprinkle with the peanuts, coconut, and sesame seeds and serve.

try a crab version Mix 1 chopped and seeded red chile, 1 tablespoon Thai fish sauce, 1 tablespoon light soy sauce, 3 tablespoons rice vinegar, 1 small shallot, finely chopped, 3 tablespoons warm water, and 1½ tablespoons superfine sugar, whisking to make sure the sugar dissolves. Segment 2 grapefruits (see above). Arrange 4 cups salad greens, ⅓ cup basil leaves, and ⅓ cup mint leaves on four plates, top with the grapefruit and 1 lb white crabmeat and spoon the dressing over the top. Serve immediately with lime wedges. Serves 4.

goat cheese and cherry salad with almond and basil gremolata

There's nothing new about the combination of goat cheese and cherries, but this takes it to a new level; the macerated cherries are a dream. The gremolata is also good made with mint instead of the basil used here.

SERVES 6

FOR THE CHERRIES

3 cups cherries

1 tablespoon brandy or grappa (optional)

2 teaspoons white balsamic vinegar

¼ cup extra virgin olive oil

1 tablespoon lemon juice

FOR THE GREMOLATA

⅓ cup blanched almonds

finely grated zest of 1 lemon

1 garlic clove, very finely chopped

about 12 basil leaves

FOR THE SALAD

5½ oz goat cheese, crumbled into chunks

4½ cups mâche, baby spinach, or arugula, or a mixture

1 tablespoon white balsamic vinegar

3 tablespoons extra virgin olive oil (fruity instead of grassy)

salt and black pepper

Prepare the cherries so that they can macerate. Pit them: I just pull them apart with my fingers because it produces beautiful shapes, but use a knife if you prefer. Put into a bowl with all the other ingredients for the cherries, stir, and let stand for 30 minutes to 2 hours.

To make the gremolata, toast the almonds in a dry skillet until they are golden brown (be careful because this happens quickly). Transfer to a cutting board and let cool. Add the zest, garlic, and basil and chop finely with a sharp knife.

For the salad, toss the goat cheese with the greens, white balsamic vinegar, extra virgin oil, and seasoning. Arrange on a large plate or divide among smaller plates. Sprinkle the cherries with their macerating juices over the top, then the gremolata. Serve immediately.

turkish spoon salad with haydari

Turkish pepper paste has a bright, front-of-the-mouth chile flavor (there is a recipe for it in my book *Salt Sugar Smoke*). If you can't find it, use another chili paste. This is a dish for a special occasion. It's delicious and healthy, but such fine chopping takes time.

**SERVES 8 AS AN APPETIZER,
4 AS A LIGHT LUNCH**

FOR THE HAYDARI

1¾ cups Greek yogurt

¼ teaspoon salt

2 garlic cloves, crushed

1 green chile, seeded and
finely chopped

⅓ cup chopped dill leaves

FOR THE SALAD

4 ripe, really well-flavored
plum tomatoes

2 Romano peppers, seeded and
finely chopped

2 red chiles, seeded and
finely chopped

2 small cucumbers, peeled,
seeded, and finely chopped

2 shallots, finely chopped

3 tablespoons finely chopped
flat-leaf parsley leaves

2 tablespoons finely chopped
mint leaves

2 teaspoons Turkish pepper paste
or harissa

1 tablespoon pomegranate
molasses

2 teaspoons white wine vinegar

½ cup extra virgin olive oil,
plus extra to serve

salt and black pepper

seeds from ½ pomegranate
(optional)

TO SERVE

paprika or sumac

warm flatbread

To make the haydari, put the yogurt into a piece of cheesecloth. Gather up the edges of the cloth into a bag and gently squeeze it into the sink to help some of the excess moisture to run out. Put it in a strainer over a bowl and place in the refrigerator for 24 hours. More moisture will run out during that time, producing a firm mixture. Tranfer it from the cloth to a bowl and mix in all the other ingredients for the haydari.

Plunge the tomatoes into boiling water for 10 seconds, remove, and immediately run cold water over them. Remove the skins. Halve and seed them (chuck away the seeds) and finely chop the flesh.

Put the tomato flesh into a bowl with the Romano peppers, red chiles, cucumbers, and shallots. Add the herbs, pepper paste, pomegranate molasses, wine vinegar, and 2 tablespoons of the extra virgin oil. Season and gently stir. Let stand for 30 minutes to let the flavors meld.

The mixture will be a little watery after 30 minutes, so gently drain some of this away by putting the mixture into a large nylon strainer. You don't want a dry mixture, but you don't want a watery one either. Put into a bowl and add the rest of the extra virgin oil. Taste for seasoning and sprinkle with the pomegranate seeds (if using).

Sprinkle the haydari with paprika or sumac and drizzle with some extra virgin oil. Serve with the spoon salad and warm flatbread.

you can never have too many salads

The salad, over the last twenty years, hasn't just grown up, it has become a complex dish, multifaceted and capable of surprising. Time was when "salad" was a collection of limp leaves, woolly tomatoes, hard-boiled eggs, and a creamy dressing (and sometimes the globe of bleeding—in both usages of the word—pickled beets). Or, when we were dieting, that hard-to-love combination of undressed leaves and cottage cheese. Then a few "foreign" salads crept in, namely *salade Niçoise* and *salade tiède*. But the dish that really changed our attitude toward salads was the (now much-belittled) goat cheese salad. Once we'd eaten well-dressed leaves with disks of grilled, tangy cheese, we became open to the idea of different temperatures and textures as part of a salad.

Eventually, the salad stopped being only an appetizer or a side dish and moved into pole position as the main course. It wasn't just ladies who lunched who embraced them either, we all succumbed. Now salads are infinitely variable: they can contain sesame-crusted chicken and sautéed shiitakes, warm smoked haddock and eggs, hot roasted tomatoes, cold yogurt and pomegranate seeds. They're no longer just gentle, they can also be peppery, minerally, assertive, bitingly spicy. They can encompass opposites; in fact, contrast is one of their chief joys—hot and cold, subtle and strong, crisp and soft—and they feel vital. Sometimes, as I carry a large plate of salad to the table, edges splashed with vinegar and oil, greens practically tumbling over the sides, it seems like an almost living thing: big, sprawling, and beautiful.

When my eating started to change (to become—inadvertently—more "healthy"), I realized that my idea of salads had widened even more. Salads now reflect the latest shifts in our eating habits and have become increasingly inventive. Our growing familiarity with "unusual" ingredients—preserved lemons, Japanese pickled plums, Thai fish sauce, unusual grains—means that salads can be inspired by the food of the Middle East, Asia, and beyond. A salad can be a plateful of crisp raw vegetables—carrots, radishes, mooli, cucumber—sitting in little piles alongside fistfuls of mint and basil leaves, waiting to be doused in a spicy Vietnamese dressing. Our growing love of vegetables has led to all kinds of roots and greens—from celeriac to pea shoots–turning up in them. And they're not just for summer, we can eat a salad every day of the year.

Of course, a salad doesn't have to be complicated. We can go back to basics: eat a bowl of dressed watercress at every meal and we're giving our bodies the best food there is. Eat salad with your main course—cool leaves wilting in the heat of warm chicken is not going to make you feel deprived—or have it, as the French do, after the main course. It's a good—and delicious—habit to get into.

Why am I telling you all this? Think of what salads, predominantly, are: vegetables. There can be grains and meat, too, but there's always vegetables, which are the only thing nutritionists and experts don't argue about; they are universally agreed to be good for you (see pages 252–253 for more about this). Eating more salads—even just adding a having dressed green salad with every meal—means eating more vegetables. And that's a no-brainer.

dressing it up

These will dress about four servings … but it depends whether you are dressing greens, which need less dressing, or starches, which need more. There are loads of other dressings throughout the book.

FOR ASIAN HOT, SOUR, SALTY, AND SWEET

3½ teaspoons superfine sugar, or to taste

juice of ½ lime

1 small garlic clove, grated

½ teaspoon grated ginger root

¾ tablespoon Thai fish sauce, or to taste

1 red chile, seeded and finely chopped

¼ cup peanut oil

asian hot, sour, salty, and sweet

One of the most useful and versatile dressings I make. Toss it with simple batons of carrot and daikon radish (add basil, mint, or cilantro leaves, too), or use it for Eastern salads of duck breast, green beans, and greens, or seared tuna, herbs, and cellophane noodles. Use half the chile if you don't want the heat.

Whisk the sugar with the lime juice to help the sugar dissolve. Add the garlic, ginger, Thai fish sauce, and chile, then whisk in the oil. Taste for sweet-salty balance, adding sugar or fish sauce if you want.

FOR ROSE AND RASPBERRY

1 tablespoon raspberry vinegar (one containing raspberry pulp)

pinch of superfine sugar

salt and black pepper

3½ tablespoons extra virgin olive oil (fruity instead of grassy)

1¼ teaspoons rose water, or to taste

rose and raspberry

Fragrant and summery. Use it on a salad of grilled chicken (that you've marinated in pomegranate molasses and spices), or on a salad of chicken, cherries, watercress or arugula, and almonds. It's a great dressing for leaves to serve with Moroccan or Persian food.

You need vinegar that contains raspberry pulp, or use 1 tablespoon of regular raspberry vinegar mixed with two crushed raspberries (pushed through a nylon strainer to get rid of the seeds).

Put the raspberry vinegar into a small bowl. Add the sugar and seasoning (only a pinch of salt), then whisk in the extra virgin oil. Add the rose water little by little; it varies in strength so taste as you work. You may even want a little more than suggested.

FOR ANCHOVY, OLIVE, AND CAPER

1½ tablespoons white wine vinegar

1 garlic clove, grated

salt and black pepper

¼ cup extra virgin olive oil

½ tablespoon finely chopped flat-leaf parsley leaves

½ tablespoon capers, rinsed and chopped

4 anchovies, drained or rinsed and chopped

5 ripe black olives, pitted and finely chopped

anchovy, olive, and caper

This is a chunky dressing. It's good on tomatoes, sliced radishes, warm new potatoes (with green beans or chopped shallots), white beans, roasted red peppers, and warm hard-boiled eggs.

Simply mix everything together, then taste. Adjust the seasoning according to what you are going to dress; hard-boiled eggs and potatoes can take a well-seasoned dressing (you may even want to add a squeeze of lemon). If you are using this to dress tomatoes, it shouldn't be quite as sharp, so use less vinegar.

sweet saffron roasted tomatoes with labneh

Saffron and hot spices, sweet tomato flesh, clean acidic yogurt, there is an irresistible interplay of flavors here. Try to make sure you get some of the saffron juices to smear the labneh; the golden streaks on creamy white yogurt look beautiful.

Make this a complete main course by serving couscous on the side, or try kamut flavored with preserved lemons (see page 307). You can sprinkle either pistachios or almonds on top.

SERVES 8

FOR THE LABNEH

1¾ cups Greek yogurt

2 garlic cloves, crushed

3 tablespoons finely chopped cilantro, mint, or parsley leaves

pinch of salt

black pepper

FOR THE TOMATOES

18 plum tomatoes

¼ cup olive oil

2 teaspoons harissa

good pinch of saffron stamens, plus extra to serve

½ tablespoon sugar (unless you have great sweet tomatoes)

TO SERVE

Arab flatbread

1½ cups slivered almonds, lightly toasted

juice of ½ lemon

¼ cup extra virgin olive oil

2 tablespoons chopped cilantro leaves

Make the labneh the day before you want to serve the dish. Line a strainer with a piece of cheesecloth and set it over a bowl. Mix the yogurt with the garlic, herbs, salt, and black pepper. Transfer to the cloth, tie it up, and refrigerate. The yogurt will lose moisture over the next 24 hours, producing a firmer, "cheeselike" substance. Help it along by giving it a squeeze every so often.

Preheat the oven to 375°F. Halve the tomatoes and lay them in a single layer in a large roasting pan (or two small pans). Mix the regular olive oil, harissa, and saffron and pour the dressing over the tomatoes. Turn the tomatoes over in the oil to make sure they are well coated, ending with them cut side up. Sprinkle with the sugar and season. Roast in the oven for about 45 minutes, or until caramelized and slightly shrunken. Let cool a little.

Take the labneh out of its cloth.

Carefully move the tomatoes (they will be fragile and can fall apart easily) to a serving plate, dotting nuggets of the labneh among them as you work. You can also toast the flatbread, break it up, and arrange it among the tomatoes as well (or serve it on the side). Pour on any cooking juices that have collected in the tomato roasting pan, being sure to douse the flatbread if you have included it within the dish.

Sprinkle the almonds over the top, then heat another good pinch of saffron stamens with the lemon juice in a small saucepan. Add the extra virgin oil and mix with a spoon. Spoon the mixture over the dish; the golden dressing looks beautiful against the white labneh. Sprinkle with the cilantro and serve warm, or at room temperature.

bulgurian grilled zucchini and eggplants with tarator

Tarator—a nut-base sauce—appears in different guises in Bulguria, Turkey, and Greece. It can be made with hazelnuts, walnuts, almonds, or pine nuts and is just as good with a salad of raw cucumber, greens, herbs, and tomatoes as it is with cooked vegetables. It also keeps well in the refrigerator for a day or so; just take it out and let it come to room temperature before serving, otherwise it gets a bit solid.

FOR THE TARATOR

1 slice of country-style bread

2 garlic cloves

1 cup walnuts, plus extra to serve

½ cup extra virgin olive oil, plus extra to serve

juice of ½ lemon

salt and black pepper

⅔ cup Greek yogurt

2 tablespoons chopped dill leaves, plus extra to serve

FOR THE GRILLED VEGETABLES

5 large mixed green and yellow zucchini

2 large eggplants

olive oil

Tear the bread into pieces and put it into a food processor with the garlic and walnuts. Puree while adding the extra virgin oil and lemon juice. Add the seasoning and the yogurt with ¼ cup of water and puree again. Stir in the dill, taste, and adjust the seasoning. Put into a bowl and set aside until you're ready to serve (or cover and put in the refrigerator).

Trim each end from the zucchini and slice lengthwise about ⅛ inch thick. Remove the stems from the eggplants and cut them widthwise into slices of the same thickness as the zucchini. Brush all the sliced vegetables on both sides with regular olive oil.

Heat a ridged grill pan and cook the slices of zucchini on both sides until golden brown and soft. You will need to do this in batches. Do the same with the eggplants, making sure they get a good color on each side, then reduce the heat until the slices are soft and cooked through. Season the vegetables as you cook them.

Put the vegetables onto a serving plate, drizzling with a little extra virgin oil. Spoon some of the tarator over them (offer the rest in a bowl) and sprinkle with more walnuts and dill.

macedonian grilled vegetable salad

This is not like an Italian roasted vegetable salad, instead it is so soft it's almost a puree. It has a great smoky flavor that you can only achieve by grilling the vegetables until they are scorched, so do it. It is not possible to make this if you don't have a naked flame on which to cook the eggplants (a gas stove or a barbecue). The smoky flavor just isn't there otherwise, roasting or broiling don't come anywhere near. If you can't cook the eggplants over a flame, I'd make something else instead.

SERVES 8 AS AN APPETIZER (WITH OTHER MEZZE) OR AS A SIDE DISH

4 bell peppers, all red, or a mixture of red and yellow

olive oil

4 plum tomatoes, halved

salt and black pepper

2 eggplants

4 garlic cloves, crushed

¼ teaspoon dried red pepper flakes

2 tablespoons extra virgin olive oil (preferably a gutsy Greek one), or to taste

juice of ½ lemon

1½ tablespoons red wine vinegar

Preheat the broiler to its highest setting.

Halve, core, and seed the bell peppers and brush all over with regular olive oil. Line the broiler pan with aluminum foil (it helps collect the cooking juices and saves on cleaning up later) and set the peppers on it, cut side down. Add the tomatoes, cut side up, and drizzle them with oil. Season. Put under the hot broiler and cook until the skins of the bell peppers are soft and both vegetables are scorched in places. Reduce the heat—or move the broiler rack away from the heat source—and cook until both the bell peppers and the tomatoes are completely tender. You will need to remove the tomatoes before the bell peppers.

Pierce the eggplants all over so they won't burst, then hold each one over a naked flame on a gas stove (you can do two at a time if you are careful and have a couple of long forks or tongs). Cook all over. The skins should be scorched and the eggplants completely tender. It takes a while, and you do have to keep adjusting the flame, but be patient. Let cool a little, then remove the skin. Cut the flesh into small cubes.

Peel the skins from the roasted peppers—this should be easy if they got well scorched—and chop or slice the flesh. Chop the tomatoes. Mix all the vegetables together in a bowl and add all the other ingredients. Check to see whether you need more oil or seasoning. You can serve this warm or at room temperature. It tends to improve in flavor as it sits and is often even more delicious the following day.

fava bean puree with feta relish and cumin flatbread

One of those bits-and-pieces dishes that can be a good appetizer, or a complete main course with kebabs (try it with the lamb kebabs on page 141). Of course, you don't have to make the bread. You can just buy Arab flatbread and warm it up instead. Peppery French Breakfast radishes look– and taste—beautiful alongside. Add hard-boiled eggs (hen or quail) for a great lunch dish.

SERVES 6 AS AN APPETIZER, OR
MORE WITH OTHER MEZZE

FOR THE BREAD

¾ cup whole-wheat flour

⅔ cup all-purpose flour

¼ teaspoon salt

½ teaspoon active dried yeast

¼ teaspoon superfiine sugar

⅔ cup warm water

1 tablespoon olive oil,
plus extra to oil

½ tablespoon extra virgin olive oil

4 shallots, finely sliced

2 red chiles, seeded and
finely sliced

1 teaspoon black cumin seeds

FOR THE FAVA BEAN PUREE

3 cups shelled fava beans

½ tablespoon olive oil

1 small onion, finely chopped

3 garlic cloves, finely chopped

¼ teaspoon dried red pepper flakes

juice of 1 lemon, or to taste

¼ cup extra virgin olive oil

2 tablespoons light chicken stock
or water

FOR THE FETA RELISH

½ cup feta

¾ cup pitted and coarsely
chopped ripe black olives

2½ tablespoons extra virgin olive oil

½ garlic clove, finely chopped

1 tablespoon chopped dill or
parsley leaves or torn mint leaves

To make the bread, put the flours and salt into a bowl. Mix the yeast in another bowl with the sugar and half the water. Let stand somewhere warm for 15 minutes. Pour the yeast mixture into a well made in the flours, then mix in. Add the oil, then use enough of the remaining water to make a dough. Knead for 10 minutes, until soft, shiny, and elastic. Oil lightly, then put into a bowl, cover with plastic wrap, and let rest for two hours. It should double in size.

For the puree, cook the beans for three minutes in boiling water. Drain and rinse in cold water. Slip the skin off each bean. It's a pain at first, but quite soothing when you get into the rhythm.

Heat the regular olive oil in a large skillet and sauté the onion until it is soft but not browned. Add the garlic and chile and cook for another three minutes. Add the beans to help them meld with the other flavors and warm through for three minutes. Season.

Transfer the contents of the pan to a food processor and add the lemon juice, extra virgin oil, and stock or water. Pulse-blend to a coarse puree. Taste for seasoning; you may also want to add more oil or lemon. Scrape into a wide, shallow dish.

Crumble the feta into a small bowl and toss in the olives. Pour in the extra virgin oil; sprinkle with the garlic and herbs. Grind on some black pepper, mix gently, and sprinkle it over the puree.

Meanwhile, set your oven to its highest setting and put a large pizza stone into it. Punch down the bread, then divide it into six. Put on to a lightly floured tray, cover lightly with plastic wrap, and let stand for 10 minutes. Roll each piece into a circle about 6 inches across. Heat the extra virgin oil in a saucepan and cook the shallots until golden brown, then add the chile and cook for two minutes. Set this aside until the breads are cooked.

Slap the breads onto the pizza stone, in batches, and cook for two to three minutes, or until puffed up and blistered in patches. Wrap in a dish towel to keep warm. Spread the shallot and chile mixture over each and sprinkle with cumin seeds. Serve with the puree.

salad of smoked anchovies, green beans, and egg

I've eaten a lot of salade Niçoise in my time, usually when "on a diet" (and while trying to convince myself that the potatoes in it were okay). Here is something a little different, but—I think—better. And not a potato in sight.

SERVES 4 AS AN APPETIZER

FOR THE DRESSING

¾ tablespoon white balsamic vinegar

½ teaspoon Dijon mustard

¼ cup extra virgin olive oil (fruity French or Sicilian instead of bitter, grassy Tuscan)

juice of ¼ lemon, or to taste

salt and black pepper

FOR THE SALAD

2 cups green beans (the tops trimmed but not the ends)

small bunch of mild sweet radishes (preferably French Breakfast radishes), leaves removed and trimmed

4 extra-large eggs

2 shallots, very finely sliced

20 sprigs of watercress, coarse stems removed

10 cherry tomatoes or baby plum tomatoes, halved

handful of flat-leaf parsley leaves

5½ oz smoked anchovies, drained of oil

Make the dressing by whisking all the ingredients together. Check for seasoning.

Steam or boil the green beans until only just tender, then run cold water through them to set the color and cool them. Cut the radishes lengthwise into thin slices.

Boil the eggs for seven minutes. They should be hard-boiled but with a yolk that is still a little soft right in the center.

Toss all the vegetables and herbs together with most of the dressing and divide among plates or put into a wide, shallow bowl. Shell the eggs, carefully halve, and put these on the salad, then dot the smoked anchovies among the leaves. Grind some black pepper on top and drizzle on the rest of the dressing. Serve immediately.

fava bean, leek, tomato and dill pilaf

This is based on a Persian dish, where it is served with a fried egg on top—that makes a good dinner—but it would be equally good with Butterflied leg of lamb with sekenjabin (see page 76) or with roasted fish.

SERVES 4 AS A MAIN COURSE
(WITH EMBELLISHMENTS),
OR 8 AS A SIDE DISH

2 leeks

2 tablespoons olive oil

2 garlic cloves, finely chopped

3 plum tomatoes, peeled, seeded, and chopped (see page 101)

¾ teaspoon ground cumin

1¼ cups brown rice

½ cinnamon stick

2 cups vegetable stock, light chicken stock, or water

2⅔ cups shelled fava beans

juice of ½ lemon

¼ cup chopped dill leaves

1½ tablespoons extra virgin olive oil

salt and black pepper

Remove the tough outer leaves from the leeks and trim the tops. Cut into thin circles and wash thoroughly in running water.

Heat the regular olive oil in a heavy saucepan and sauté the leeks over medium heat for about six minutes, until they are beginning to soften but still hold their shape. Add the garlic and tomatoes and cook for another two minutes, then add the cumin and cook for another 30 seconds. Add the rice, cinnamon, and stock. Bring to a boil and boil fiercely until the surface of the rice looks pitted (as if there are little holes in the top). Reduce the heat to as low as possible, cover, and let cook for about 25 minutes. The liquid should be absorbed as the rice cooks, but take a peek to make sure the dish hasn't boiled dry before the rice is ready (it should be tender, but each grain will retain a nutty bite).

Meanwhile, boil the fava beans for about three minutes, until tender. Rinse with cold water, then slip the skins off (laborious but worth it for the color of the beans). Reheat by running boiling water through them, then carefully fork into the rice with the lemon juice, dill, and extra virgin oil. Taste for seasoning.

serve with any of the following

a fried egg on top

a good dollop of Greek yogurt, crumbled feta, and a drizzle of extra virgin olive oil

a bowl of yogurt and Hot pepper puree (see page 64)

omit the tomato in the pilaf and serve with Roasted tomatoes (see page 104)

Feta relish (see page 108)

summer menu unexpected flavors

white beans with roast peppers, eggs and hilbeh | persian spice bread | berry and hibiscus sorbet

It's good to throw a curve ball when you're thinking about meals for friends. They'll like it and will look at some ingredients in a completely new way, while it's a thrill for the cook to put unusual flavors together, especially in summer when the same dishes crop up again and again. This menu is not what anyone would expect.

white beans with roasted peppers, eggs, and hilbeh

A sprawling feast, but easy to put together. I actually got the idea from the Egyptian breakfast of beans, eggs, onion, preserved lemons, and flatbread; it has always seemed such a wonderful meal to me. This has elements you don't need to cook at all. Add other simple things, such as roasted or raw tomatoes, cucumbers with a minty dressing, pickled chiles, or feta cheese. Hilbeh is the red version of zhoug, a Yemeni relish. You'll need to soak the fenugreek seeds overnight.

SERVES 6

FOR THE HILBEH

2 tablespoons fenugreek seeds

1½ tablespoons olive oil

1 onion, chopped

4 garlic cloves, chopped

4 red chiles, seeded
and chopped

2 large tomatoes, seeded
and chopped

1½ teaspoons tomato paste

juice of 1 lemon

½ teaspoon ground cumin

½ teaspoon ground coriander

leaves from 1 small bunch
of cilantro

salt and black pepper

FOR THE REST

3 red bell peppers, halved

3 tablespoons olive oil

6 eggs

2 (15 oz) cans cannellini or navy
beans, drained and rinsed

1 small red onion, peeled and
finely sliced (the slices should
be almost transparent)

The night before, put the fenugreek seeds in cold water to cover.

Next day, when ready to cook, drain the fenugreek and preheat the oven to 375°F.

To make the hilbeh, heat the olive oil in a skillet and sauté the onion for about seven minutes, until it is soft and pale gold. Add the garlic, chiles, and drained fenugreek and cook for another two minutes, then add the tomatoes and cook for another minute, followed by the tomato paste and lemon juice. Put the mixture into the bowl of a food processor.

Toast the cumin and coriander in a dry skillet and add them to the food processor, too, with the cilantro leaves and some salt. Pulse-blend for about 30 seconds—it should be like a relish, not like a puree—then scrape into a bowl. It can be served warm or at room temperature.

For the rest, brush the bell peppers with some of the olive oil and put into a small roasting pan. Season. Roast in the oven for 40 minutes, or until completely tender and slightly charred. Cut them into strips about ¼ inch in width.

Cook the eggs in boiling water for seven minutes. The yolk should still be a little soft right in the middle.

Put the beans into a skillet with 1 tablespoon of olive oil and sauté and toss until they are warmed through. Put them into a bowl with the strips of roasted pepper and some of the finely sliced onion on top (provide the rest on the side). Serve with the eggs—letting each person peel their egg and put it on top of their beans—the hilbeh, and bread; try the Persian spice bread (see right).

persian spice bread

This is unusual; you don't think of turmeric flavoring bread. You can use any dried fruit: dates, figs, and cherries are all good. It is based on a recipe in *Malouf*, Greg Malouf's inspiring book on modern Middle Eastern food. You could also serve homemade or store-bought whole-wheat Arab flatbread with this menu, if you prefer.

MAKES 8 ROLLS

1¼ teaspoons active dried yeast

1½ tablespoons packed light brown sugar

¾ cup warm water

1 egg, lightly beaten, plus 1 egg yolk, to glaze

1 tablespoon olive oil, plus extra to oil

1⅓ cups all-purpose flour, plus extra to dust

1⅓ cups whole-wheat flour

½ teaspoon salt

½ teaspoon turmeric

⅓ cup chopped pitted dates

2½ tablespoons butter, cut into 8 pats

1½ teaspoon cumin seeds, lightly crushed

Put the yeast into a bowl with ¼ teaspoon of the sugar and 3½ tablespoons of the water and let stand in a warm place to froth (it will take about 15 minutes). Mix half the beaten egg (retain the other half) with the 1 tablespoon of olive oil.

Mix together the flours, salt, remaining sugar, and the turmeric in a bowl. Make a well in the center and pour in the frothy yeast followed by the egg and oil mixture. Add the remaining water. Gradually bring the dry ingredients into the middle, using a blunt knife, then start working the mixture with your hands.

Knead for 10 minutes, or until the dough is shiny and feels elastic. Very lightly oil the ball of dough with your hands, then put it into a bowl and cover with lightly oiled plastic wrap. Let stand in a warm place to rise for an hour (it should double in size). Punch down the dough, then return it to the bowl and let stand, covered with the plastic wrap, for another hour.

Divide the dough into eight equal balls. Roll each out on a lightly floured surface into a circle about 5 inches across. Divide the dates among these, putting them in the center, and put a little pat of butter on top of the dates. Pull the dough up over the dates and butter, pinch it, then smooth it over and turn what is now a ball of dough over so that the seam is underneath. Set these on a nonstick baking sheet, cover loosely with lightly oiled plastic wrap, and let stand for 15 minutes. Meanwhile, preheat the oven to 400°F.

Mix the reserved half egg with the egg yolk. Brush the tops of each roll with it and sprinkle with the cumin seeds. Bake in the oven for 15 minutes, by which time the rolls should be golden brown and cooked through. Let rest for about 10 minutes before serving.

berry and hibiscus sorbet

Hibiscus flowers are very citrussy, so they add an extra mouth-puckering element to the sorbet. (Dried hibiscus flowers are easily available from online stores.)

¼ cup dried hibiscus flowers

1 cup plus 2 tablespoons granulated sugar

3–3½ cups mixed berries (blackberries, raspberries, hulled and halved or quarter strawberries, loganberries, bosenberries)

Put 1 cup of water and the hibiscus flowers in a saucepan and bring to a boil. Remove the pan from the heat and let stand for about 30 minutes so the flowers can flavor the water. Strain. The liquid should taste citrussy. Return the liquid to the saucepan.

Add the sugar and heat gradually to help the sugar dissolve. Add the berries and poach gently for about three minutes. Let get completely cool.

Blend the mixture in a food processor—not a blender, which would break down the seeds and make the sorbet bitter. Push the pureed fruit and syrup through a nylon strainer.

Churn the mixture in an ice cream machine following the manufacturer's instructions. If you don't have a machine, pour into a wide, shallow, freezer-proof container and put into the freezer. Take the mixture out of the freezer three or four times during the freezing process and blend in the food processor. This breaks down the ice crystals and incorporates air to produce a smooth sorbet.

scandi salmon burger with dill and tomato sauce

I've been very taken with salmon burgers while traveling in Scandinavia. For some reason, I always feel too full and as if I've eaten poorly when I have a hamburger (however "good" it is). This has a different effect. If you can't find rye bread, use a good whole-wheat bread instead. Or, of course, eat it without bread.

SERVES 4

FOR THE BURGERS

1 lb skinless salmon fillet

2 tablespoons butter

½ onion, finely chopped

2 tablespoons finely chopped chives

2 tablespoons mayonnaise

1 tablespoon crème fraîche or Greek yogurt

salt and black pepper

peanut oil

FOR THE SAUCE

⅔ cup Greek yogurt

1 tablespoon mayonnaise

1 tablespoon finely chopped dill leaves, plus sprigs of dill to serve

½ small garlic clove, crushed

1 small well-flavored tomato

TO SERVE

4 slices of rye bread

baby salad greens

sliced cucumber

Chop the salmon flesh into fine dice—about ⅛ inch square—but you don't have to be pedantic about the shape. Melt the butter in a skillet or sauté pan and sauté the onion over gentle heat until soft but not brown. Add the salmon with the chives, mayonnaise, crème fraîche, salt, and black pepper. Mix, cover, and put into the refrigerator for 30 minutes. Form the salmon into four patty shapes. Set these on a tray or plate, cover, and refrigerate for another 30 minutes.

For the sauce, stir the yogurt with the mayonnaise and add the dill and garlic. Cover and put in the refrigerator so the flavors can meld.

About 30 minutes before you want to serve the dish, seed the tomatoes and chop them finely (no need to skin them). Set aside, ready to add to the mayonnaise at the last minute. (Even without the seeds, the tomatoes make the sauce sloppy if they're in it too long, and the flesh of the tomatoes softens, too.)

Preheat the broiler to its highest setting and place the oven shelf 2 inches below the heat. Brush a piece of aluminum foil with a little oil and set the salmon patties on top. Broil them for about two minutes, then reduce the heat to medium (or move the burgers farther away from it, if you can't reduce the heat) for about another two minutes, until cooked through. You don't need to turn them over—they are pretty fragile—because they will cook through anyway.

Add the tomatoes to the yogurt mixture and spread some on each slice of rye bread (toasted or not, as you prefer). Add the greens and cucumber and put a salmon burger on each slice of bread. Top with more of the sauce, a sprig of dill, and serve.

salmon on the plate

This is clean tasting but rich at the same time. I love the utter plainness of it. However, you need good salmon for something this simple. It's surprising what you can do with raw salmon, especially for those of us brought up in a culture that always serves it cooked. Apart from these two recipes and the one on the next page, you can use it for a Japanese rice bowl; Sashimi; or an Avocado, raw salmon, and brown rice salad (see pages 43, 210, and 306).

SERVES 8 AS AN APPETIZER

1½ lb skinless salmon fillet (wild or organically farmed)

½ cup light, fruity extra virgin olive oil

flaked sea salt and freshly ground black pepper

2 tablespoons coarsely chopped dill leaves

juice of ½ large lemon

With a sharp knife, slice the salmon finely, as if you were slicing smoked salmon. Arrange the slices on individual plates in such a way that they are not overlapping.

Brush with the extra virgin oil, then sprinkle with salt, black pepper, and dill. Squeeze lemon juice over the salmon slices and serve immediately.

eastern salmon carpaccio

This packs a punch and is satisfying. To stretch it and make it less intense, serve it on lightly dressed greens with thinly sliced avocado. You could treat tuna or mackerel in the same way. When I need a healthy, quick lunch, I eat the fish on grated carrot and daikon tossed with herbs and watercress, with the sauce spooned on top. (Keep a jar of it in the refrigerator.) Filling and sinus-clearing.

SERVES 6 AS AN APPETIZER

1¼ lb spanking-fresh skinless salmon fillet

¼ cup cilantro leaves

6 basil leaves

about 12 mint leaves

1 cup Japanese carrot and daikon salad (see page 273), finely chopped

½ small red onion, finely sliced (almost shaved)

3 tablespoons Vietnamese dipping sauce (see page 75)

lime wedges, to serve

Using a sharp knife, slice the salmon finely, as if you were slicing smoked salmon. Put it onto a serving plate or individual plates.

Tear and sprinkle the herb leaves over the top. Spoon the carrot and daikon salad on top and sprinkle with red onion.

Spoon the dipping sauce on top and serve with lime wedges.

citrus-marinated salmon with fennel and apple salad

This is the kind of dish I could eat at every meal: clean tasting, with bright flavors. If you want bread with this, rye is the obvious choice. Or try Rye crackers (see page 53).

SERVES 6

FOR THE SALAD

¼ cup superfine sugar

⅓ cup rice vinegar

1 teaspoon whole-grain mustard

1 fennel bulb

juice of ½ lemon

½ red onion, finely sliced

1 large, tart green apple
(such as Granny Smith)

1 small beet, cooked, skin slipped
off (see page 36)

2 tablespoons coarsely
chopped dill leaves

FOR THE SALMON

1lb very fresh salmon fillet
(tail end is good for this)

¼ cup light, fruity extra virgin
olive oil

sea salt flakes

freshly ground black pepper

juice of 1 lemon

Make the dressing for the salad by mixing the sugar with the vinegar and stirring until dissolved. Whisk in the mustard until well combined.

Don't make the salad too far in advance because it becomes flaccid if it sits around. Try to prepare it no more than 30 minutes before serving.

Quarter the fennel, trim the tops, and remove any coarse outer leaves. Core each quarter. Using a sharp knife or a mandoline slicer, cut the fennel into wafer-thin slices. Put the fennel into a bowl and toss with the lemon juice. Add the onion. Halve and core the apple and cut the flesh into matchsticks. Add the apple to the fennel and lemon with the dressing. Toss. Cut the beet into matchsticks or thin slices and set aside; the beet needs to be added at the last minute or it will stain everything.

Using a sharp knife, slice the salmon finely, as if you were slicing smoked salmon (leave the skin behind). Arrange the slices on individual plates (or a serving plate), not overlapping. Brush the slices with the extra virgin oil, then sprinkle on salt and black pepper. Squeeze lemon juice over the salad and let stand for two or three minutes before serving. Add the beet and dill to the salad and serve with the salmon.

another rare bite ... **japanese seared tuna and radish salad** Sprinkle freshly ground black pepper all over 14 oz tuna loin. Heat 1 tablespoon peanut oil in a skillet until hot. Add the tuna and cook briefly on all sides, just until the tuna turns white. Set aside and pour 1 tablespoon rice vinegar over it. Make a dressing by whisking together ½ tablespoons whole-grain mustard, 2 teaspoons juices from a jar of pickled ginger, 2 teaspoons grated ginger root, 1 tablespoon soy sauce, 1 tablespoon rice vinegar, salt, black pepper, 2 tablespoons peanut oil, and 2 tablespoons light, fruity extra virgin olive oil. Cut the tuna into thin slices (about the thickness of smoked salmon slices) and divide between four plates. Arrange 2 cups mizuna, 12 radishes, cut into matchsticks, and ¼ finely sliced small red onion alongside. Spoon the dressing over both salad and fish and serve. Serves 4.

salmon grilled in newspaper with dill and cucumber sauce

This recipe seems strange, I know, and it's only for the summer months when a barbecue is an option … but it is a great way to cook salmon. The results are so moist. It's also a bit of "event" cooking (mainly because nobody believes it will work). Once the salmon is cooked, it is well behaved and can be left—wrapped in the paper—for a good half hour before you serve it.

Directions to use a broadsheet newspaper are because of size, not the content of the newspaper. (*USA Today* is a national newspaper that is the right size.)

SERVES 10

FOR THE SALMON

4 lb whole salmon, scaled and cleaned

olive oil

salt and black pepper

4 handfuls of soft herbs (cilantro, chervil, parsley)

bunch of scallions (about 8), trimmed and coarsely chopped

2 lemons, sliced

8 layers of broadsheet newspaper

FOR THE SAUCE

2 tablespoons extra virgin olive oil

3 shallots, finely chopped

1 cucumber, peeled, halved, seeded, and finely chopped

2 tablespoons chopped dill leaves

1½ tablespoons drained, rinsed, and chopped capers

1½ tablespoons drained chopped pickles

1¼ cups Greek yogurt

squeeze of lemon juice

Heat the barbecue to a good hot smolder.

Rub the salmon all over with olive oil, including the inside. Season all over, too, and in the cavity. Stuff with half the herbs, half the scallions, and some of the lemon slices.

Open out the newspaper—you should be faced with double pages—and put your salmon in the middle. Put the rest of the herbs, scallions, and lemon slices on top and underneath the fish. Wrap the paper around the salmon—use all the paper—and tie it up with kitchen string. Put the package under running tap water and soak it thoroughly, then lay it on the barbecue.

Cook for 20 minutes on each side (depending on the heat of your coals). Your fire should be warm, but not so hot that the newspaper catches alight. You can unwrap the fish and check it carefully for doneness, rewrapping in a couple of layers of aluminum foil and cooking for a little longer if it needs it, but there is something great about presenting it in the newspaper.

Meanwhile, make the sauce by mixing all the ingredients for it together with a fork. Taste for seasoning. Cover and keep in the refrigerator until you want to serve it.

You can either take the salmon to the table in its newspaper or unwrap it behind the scenes and present it on a serving plate— but why bother with the latter? As you unwrap the newspaper, it will bring most of the salmon skin with it. Serve pieces of the warm salmon with the sauce.

roasted sea bass with spiced eggplant, lemon, and honey relish

A very special dish. This looks and feels impressive and luxurious and, to be honest, it isn't cheap to make, but you don't cook this kind of thing every day.

SERVES 8

FOR THE RELISH

2 eggplants

3 tablespoons olive oil, plus extra if needed

1 large or 2 small onions, chopped

2 plum tomatoes, finely chopped

2 garlic cloves, finely chopped

1 red chile, seeded and chopped

2 teaspoons ground cumin

2 teaspoons cayenne pepper

salt and black pepper

2 tablespoons juice from the preserved lemon jar

2 tablespoons honey, or to taste

1 small preserved lemon (if store-bought, or ½ homemade one)

¼ cup chopped cilantro leaves

FOR THE FISH

⅓ cup olive oil, plus extra to oil

1 (5½ lb) sea bass, scaled and cleaned

2 dried chiles, crumbled

2 heads garlic, cloves separated but not peeled

⅓ cup dry white wine

Slice the stems from the eggplants, then cut the flesh into chunks. Heat 2 tablespoons of the oil and sauté the eggplants, in batches in a heavy saucepan over medium heat until golden brown. As the eggplants are ready, set them aside. (You may have to use more oil.) Now add another 1 tablespoon of oil to the pan and cook the onions for about 10 minutes, until soft and golden brown. Add the tomatoes and cook for another five minutes. Add the garlic, chile, cumin, and cayenne and cook for another two minutes, then return the eggplants. Pour in ½ cup of water, season, then add the preserved lemon juice and the honey and bring to a boil. Immediately reduce the heat and simmer gently for 10 minutes. The mixture should have the consistency of a thick sauce.

Shred the zest of the preserved lemon—discard the insides—and add half of it to the relish. Taste and see whether you would like to add the rest or not; the relish should be quite assertive. You also need to judge the seasoning and the sweet-tart balance. Now stir in the cilantro. Let cool to room temperature (you can keep it in the refrigerator but return to room temperature before serving).

For the fish, preheat the oven to 400°F. Lay a large piece of aluminum foil in a roasting pan or on a baking sheet (it should be big enough to come up in a "tent" around the fish) and lightly oil the center. Put the sea bass on top and season it inside and out. Sprinkle the chiles over the fish. Throw the garlic cloves around it and drizzle the olive oil over the top. Pull the foil up around the fish and pour in the wine. Pull the sides of the foil together and scrunch the edges together to make a tent around the fish (the fish needs space to steam, so it must not be tightly wrapped in the foil). Cook in the hot oven for 30 minutes. Check for doneness after 25 minutes; the flesh near the bone in the thickest part of the fish should be completely white, not glassy, and coming away from the bone. Either serve the fish in the foil in which it was cooked, or carefully lift it onto a serving plate. Serve with the eggplant relish. Couscous, bulgur wheat, or brown rice is good on the side.

smoked paprika sardines with white beans and roasted tomatoes

Make the roasted tomatoes in advance (I often have a load of them, and there are a few in this book, because they're so useful and good for you) and you can put this dish together quickly. The oily sardines and the smoky paprika are gorgeous against the earthy beans. You don't need any additional starch. Substitute the white beans with chickpeas if you prefer, or serve the fish and tomatoes with lentils instead of beans (use the recipe on page 164, omitting the cilnatro). This is just as good with mackerel, serve one per person and broil for three to five minutes on each side.

SERVES 6

FOR THE ROASTED TOMATOES

9 large plum tomatoes

3 tablespoons olive oil

¾ tablespoon balsamic vinegar

2 teaspoons harissa (optional)

½ teaspoon sugar (if your tomatoes aren't sweet)

salt and black pepper

FOR THE SARDINES AND BEANS

3 tablespoons olive oil

1 red onion, very finely sliced

2 garlic cloves, finely chopped

2 (15 oz) cans cannellini beans

2 good squeezes of lemon juice, plus lemon wedges to serve

1 tablespoon finely chopped flat-leaf parsley leaves

12–18 sardines (depending on size), scaled and cleaned

1 teaspoon smoked paprika

2 fistfuls—literally—of baby spinach leaves or arugula

extra virgin olive oil, to serve

Start by roasting the tomatoes. Preheat the oven to 375°F. Halve the tomatoes and lay them in a single layer in a small roasting pan or ovenproof dish. Mix the regular olive oil, balsamic, and harissa (if using) together and pour the mixture over the tomatoes. Turn the tomatoes over in the oil to make sure they are well coated, ending with them cut side up. Sprinkle with the sugar (if using) and season. Roast in the hot oven for 45 minutes, or until the tomatoes are caramelized and slightly shrunken.

Heat 1 tablespoon of the regular olive oil in a large skillet and sauté the onion gently until soft but not browned. Add the garlic and cook for another two minutes. Add the beans and another 1 tablespoon of the oil. Season and let them heat through and become imbued with the cooking juices. Add a good squeeze of lemon juice and the parsley. Taste; beans need plenty of seasoning.

For the sardines, preheat the broiler to its highest setting. If the sardines haven't been scaled, use your fingers to remove the scales under a cold running tap water. Make sure to remove any traces of blood from the inside, too. Dry. If your sardines are medium-large in size, cut two slashes in the flesh on each side (without cutting right down to the bone). These will help the heat to penetrate.

Mix the smoked paprika and the last 1 tablespoon of oil together. Line a broiler pan with aluminum foil and lay the sardines on this. Brush the fish with the paprika oil and season on both sides. Place under the hot broiler and cook for two or three minutes each side, or until completely cooked through.

Meanwhile, quickly reheat the beans—tossing them in the pan instead of stirring, so you don't crush them—and toss in the spinach or arugula. It will wilt slightly. Add some more lemon juice and check the seasoning. Drizzle with extra virgin oil. Serve the sardines with the beans, roasted tomatoes, and lemon wedges.

squid with couscous, chile, mint, and lemon

It's hard not to love food like this: big flavors, easy preparation. The couscous doesn't have to be hot, so you can get it ready in advance; just add the herbs and cook and add the green beans at the last minute (it's never a good idea to have green beans waiting around, because they become limp). The only thing you might have to adjust if you make the couscous in advance is its seasoning and the amount of olive oil, because it does soak up dressing as it sits. Then cook the squid—it takes just over a minute—and you're all set.

SERVES 4–6

FOR THE SQUID

1¾ lb squid, cleaned

3 tablespoons olive oil

juice of ½ lemon

FOR THE COUSCOUS

1½ cups whole-wheat couscous

⅓ cup extra virgin olive oil

salt and black pepper

1½ cups green beans (tops trimmed but not the bottoms)

2 tablespoons olive oil

6 shallots, sliced

3 garlic cloves, finely sliced

2 red chiles, seeded and finely chopped

6 scallions, trimmed and sliced on the diagonal

leaves from 12 sprigs of mint, torn

1 tablespoon flat-leaf parsley

1½ tablespoons capers, rinsed

finely grated zest and juice of 1 lemon (zest removed with a zester)

Cut the little wings from the main body of the squid. If the squid are big, slice these wings into three or four strips. Slice the whole body into rings, about ½ inch thick. Wash the squid, making sure that you have removed any remaining whitish gunge from inside the bodies. Drain, cover, and keep in the refrigerator until needed.

Put the couscous into a bowl and add 2 tablespoons of the extra virgin oil, 2 cups of boiling water and seasoning. Cover with plastic wrap and let plump up for 15 minutes.

Steam the green beans until they are tender but still al dente, then run cold water through them and drain.

Heat the 2 tablespoons of regular olive oil in a skillet and sauté the shallots until they are just soft and still pale, then add the garlic, chiles, and scallions and cook for another two minutes or so.

Fork through the warm couscous to fluff it up, then add the green beans, all the stuff in the skillet, the herbs, capers, lemon zest and juice, and, finally, the remaining extra virgin oil. Taste; you might want to add a little more seasoning. Put into a wide, shallow bowl.

Pat the squid dry with paper towels. (If the squid is damp, it won't cook well.) Heat the 3 tablespoons of regular olive oil in a large skillet or wok until really hot. Stir-fry the squid for 40 seconds, then reduce the heat and cook for 30 seconds. Squeeze in the lemon and season. Spread the squid on top of the couscous and serve immediately.

summer menu let's start with white peaches

broiled summer herb mackerel | poached white peaches with rosé wine gelatin

It's good to plan a menu around a specific ingredient, or a particular feel. I began here with the dessert. White peaches are so elegant, so beautiful, that you don't need to embellish them. From there, I worked backward to greenery and silver scales. Nothing here is difficult to cook, yet it's probably the loveliest menu in the book.

broiled summer herb mackerel, mushrooms, and green veg

This is one of those dishes that doesn't actually require much skill, just some juggling, but is wonderful to pull off. (Make life easier for yourself by making the puree in advance and then reheating it.) It's the mixture that's so impressive and satisfying, the layers of flavors and textures. Rich contrasts with fresh, sweet with savory. You don't really need anything starchy with it, but you could offer bulgur wheat dressed with a little olive oil and lemon zest and juice.

SERVES 6

FOR THE VEGETABLES

4 cups peas, fresh or frozen

⅓ cup strong chicken stock

3 tablespoons lemon juice

1½ tablespoons extra virgin olive oil

sea salt and black pepper

1½ cups shelled fava beans

1½ tablespoons olive oil

6 oz wild or shiitake mushrooms

12 asparagus spears, trimmed

FOR THE MACKEREL

6 whole mackerel, scaled, trimmed, and cleaned

leaves from a bunch of mint, torn

bunch of dill, coarsely chopped, plus extra leaves to serve

olive oil

First make the pea puree. Cook the peas in boiling water until tender, then drain. Put in a blender with the stock, lemon juice, extra virgin oil, and seasoning. Puree until smooth. Cook the beans in boiling water for three minutes. Drain, then slip off the skins.

Now for the mackerel. Wash the fish and remove any blood inside (it can be bitter). Dry with paper towels, then make three deep slashes in both sides of each. Stuff the herbs inside each cavity. Rub the fish with oil and lay on a broiler pan lined with aluminum foil. Pat sea salt all over the fish, including in the slashes.

You need to track back the time of the cooking so all the vegetables and fish are ready together. Preheat a broiler to its highest setting. Heat the regular olive oil in a skillet and quickly sauté the mushrooms until browned. Season and toss in the fava beans to heat them through. Gently warm the pea puree. Steam the asparagus for about four minutes, or until only just tender.

Broil the mackerel for three to five minutes on each side, depending on size, until crisp and charred. Serve with the puree and the beans, asparagus, and mushrooms, sprinkled with dill.

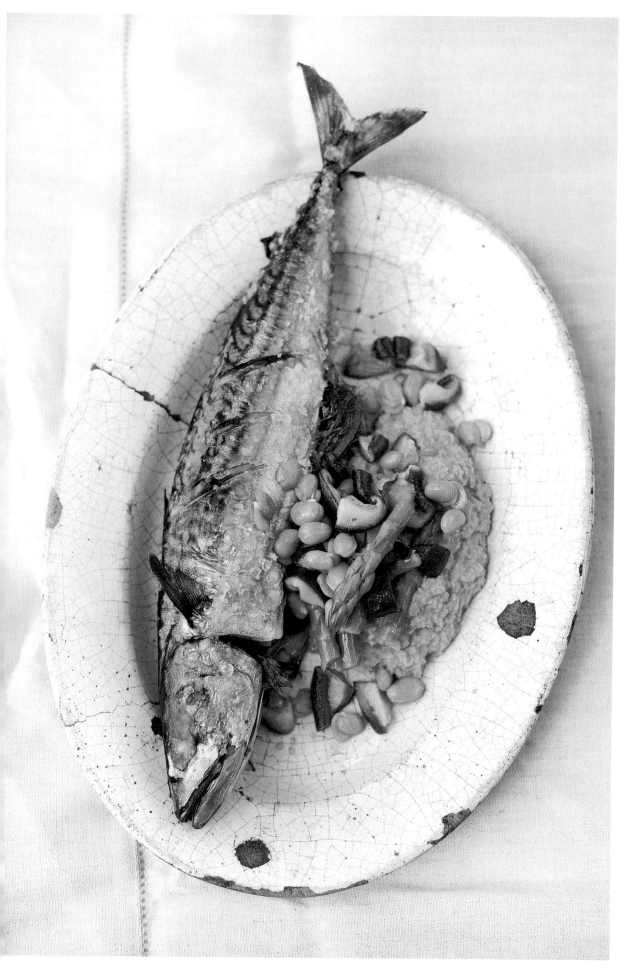

poached white peaches with rosé wine gelatin

A beautiful dessert. If you find perfectly ripe white peaches, you can dispense with a formal dessert entirely for this menu. Just serve the peaches as they are (although the gelatin does accentuate what is good about them: their color).

SERVES 6

FOR THE GELATIN

peanut or other flavorless oil, for the molds

9 small sheets gelatin (about a generous ½ oz)

¾ cup granulated sugar

2 cups rosé wine

FOR THE PEACHES

1 (750 ml) bottle of white wine

¾ cup granulated sugar

2 strips of lemon zest, plus juice of ½ lemon

6 white peaches

Lightly oil six ⅔-cup dessert molds.

Cover the gelatin with some cold water and let soak until completely soft. Gently heat the sugar in 1 cup of water until it has dissolved and remove from the heat. Wait until the syrup is lukewarm, then lift the gelatin out of its water and squeeze out the excess liquid. Add to the syrup mixture and stir until the gelatin has completely melted, then pour in the rosé wine. Divide the gelatin among the molds, cover, and refrigerate until set.

For the peaches, put the white wine, sugar, and lemon zest and juice in a saucepan wide enough to hold the peaches in a single layer. Bring gently to a boil, stirring to help the sugar dissolve.

If the peaches are ripe and not too big, poach them whole, otherwise halve them. Add them to the wine and poach gently, turning every so often, until just tender. Remove the peaches and boil the poaching liquid until reduced and slightly syrupy. Let cool—the liquid will thicken—then remove the zest. While the peaches are still warm, gently slip off their skins.

To unmold the gelatins, dip the molds briefly—for only about four seconds—in hot water. Invert each onto a plate and give it a good shake; the gelatin should slide out.

Gently place a whole peach, or two peach halves (with a little syrup) beside each gelatin and serve.

seared tuna with chile and peanut dressing

This is, like all seared tuna dishes, really quick to cook. You can serve it with the rice vermicelli and vegetables that form part of the Vietnamese beef recipe (see page 75), or simply with brown rice.

SERVES 4

FOR THE DRESSING

2½ tablespoons peanut oil

4 shallots, finely chopped

3 red chiles, seeded and finely chopped

2 garlic cloves, finely chopped or grated

1 inch ginger root, peeled and grated

4 teaspoons packed light brown sugar, or to taste

1 tablespoon Thai fish sauce, or to taste

juice of 2 limes, or to taste

⅓ cup raw peanuts

2 tablespoons chopped cilantro leaves

FOR THE TUNA

2 tablespoons peanut oil

½ cup soy sauce

1 tablespoon packed light brown sugar

4 (6 oz) tuna steaks

salt and black pepper

juice of 1 lime

For the dressing, heat 1 tablespoon of the peanut oil in a skillet and cook the shallots over medium-high heat until golden brown. Add the chiles, garlic, and ginger and cook for another two minutes, then add the sugar. Cook until the sugar slightly caramelizes, then add the fish sauce and lime juice.

Toast the peanuts in a dry skillet, then coarsely chop them. Stir them into the mixture in the skillet with the rest of the oil, the cilantro leaves, and 1½ tablespoons of water. Taste for a balance of sweet, sour, and salty flavors and add more sugar, lime, or fish sauce as needed. Set aside while you cook the tuna.

For the tuna, place a ridged grill pan over high heat, or get a barbecue up to cooking temperature. Mix the oil with the soy sauce and sugar, then put the tuna in the marinade, turning the steaks over so they get well coated, and season well. Cook the tuna on the preheated barbecue or ridged grill pan for about 1½ minutes on each side (this gives you a moist, slightly raw interior), basting with the marinade. Squeeze some lime juice over each steak and serve with the peanut dressing. A salad of baby spinach and sugar snap peas sprinkled with sesame seeds is wonderful on the side.

baked stuffed red snapper

I often make this with red mullet, a fish that lifts my spirits—its lightness immediately makes you think of olive groves and blue sea. However, you'll have to substite another white firm fish, and red snapper has to be one of the best choices.

You can also use other whole white fish, such as porgy, rockfish, grouper, sea trout, or orange roughy—whichever fish you choose, just make sure it is scaled, trimmed, and gutted and cleaned.

SERVES 4

salt and black pepper

2 (1–1½ lb) red snappers or other white fish, scaled, trimmed, and gutted cleaned

olive oil

½ onion, finely chopped

2 tomatoes, finely chopped

3 garlic cloves, finely chopped

leaves from 3 sprigs of thyme, plus sprigs of thyme to cook

1 (6 oz) package spinach, coarse stems removed

1½ cups fresh whole-wheat bread crumbs

juice of 1 lemon

Preheat the oven to 375°F.

Season the fish inside and out and rub olive oil all over them.

Heat 1 tablespoon olive oil in a skillet and sauté the onion over medium heat until soft and pale golden brown. Add the tomatoes and garlic and cook until the tomatoes are really soft. Sprinkle in the leaves from the three sprigs of thyme, season, and cook for another few minutes. Chop the spinach, add it to the pan, and let it wilt, stirring a little to help incorporate it into the tomatoes. It will release some water, but that's okay as will be adding bread. Mix in the bread crumbs and add a little more oil if you don't now have a moist stuffing. Check for seasoning, too.

Divide the stuffing between each fish cavity, then put them in an ovenproof dish where they can lie in a single layer. Sprinkle thyme sprigs over and around the fish and drizzle with olive oil. Bake in the hot oven for about 25 minutes, then check for doneness. The flesh should be white, not glassy, and coming away from the bone. Squeeze the lemon juice on top and serve.

also try ... **a sweet-sour sicilian-inspired stuffing**. Sauté 2 chopped shallots and 1 chopped garlic clove in 1 tablespoon olive oil until soft (but still pale). Add 2 tablespoons pitted and chopped ripe black or green olives, ⅓ cup toasted pine nuts, 2 tablespoons raisins or dried currants, the juice and finely grated zest of 1 lemon, 2 tablespoons chopped flat-leaf parsley or torn mint leaves, and 1 tablepoon rinsed capers. Heat through so the flavors meld. Chuck in 1½ cups bread crumbs, season and mix. Stuff the fish as above and cook in the same way.

whole roasted fish with tahini dressing and barley tabbouleh

I've used red mullet, which is popular in the UK, but use any white, round whole fish, such as red snapper, porgy, rockfish, grouper, sea trout, mackerel, or orange roughy. You can use another grain instead of barley (farro or wheat berries would be good, see pages 223–224 for how to cook them). In winter, you can make tabbouleh such as this using pomegranates, green olives, and chopped walnuts in place of the tomatoes and olives.

SERVES 4

FOR THE TABBOULEH

¾ cup pearl barley

3 tablespoons extra virgin olive oil, or to taste

1 tablespoon lemon juice, or to taste

1 tablespoon white balsamic vinegar

salt and black pepper

1 tablespoon olive oil

1 small red onion, inely chopped

2 garlic cloves, finely chopped

2 teaspoons ground cumin

1 red chile, seeded and finely shredded

big handful of mint leaves, torn

⅓ cup finely chopped flat-leaf parsley leaves

5 well-flavored plum tomatoes, peeled, seeded, and finely chopped (see page 101)

1 cucumber, peeled, seeded, and finely choppedr

FOR THE TAHINI DRESSING

2 tablespoons tahini

juice of ½ lemon, or to taste

2 tablespoons extra virgin olive oil

1 garlic clove, crushed

FOR THE FISH

4 (8 oz) whole white fish, scaled, gutted, and cleaned

¼ cup olive oil

juice of 1 lemon

a little sumac

Put the barley into a saucepan and cover with plenty of cold water. Bring to a boil, then reduce the heat and cook for 30 minutes, or until tender. Drain, rinse with boiling water, shake dry, and immediately mix with the extra virgin oil, lemon juice, vinegar, and seasoning. Let cool to room temperature.

Heat the regular olive oil in a saucepan and sauté the onion until it is soft but not browned. Add the garlic, cumin, and chile and cook for another couple of minutes. Let cool. Stir the onion mixture into the barley along with the herbs, tomatoes, and cucumber. Check for seasoning. You may also want to add a little more extra virgin oil or lemon juice.

To make the tahini dressing, beat the tahini (just use a fork), then add ⅓ cup of water, the lemon juice, extra virgin oil, and garlic. (Make sure you add the water before the lemon juice, or the tahini suddenly thickens.) Taste and season. You may also want to add a little more water or lemon juice; different brands of tahini have varying consistencies, so add water and seasonings accordingly. Your finished mixture should have the consistency of heavy cream.

When ready to cook the fish, preheat the oven to 350°F. Season the fish in their cavities and put them in an ovenproof dish where they can lie in a single layer. Mix the regular olive oil with the lemon juice and pour all over the fish. Season the outside. Bake for 15 minutes. Drizzle the fish with some of the tahini dressing (serve the rest on the side) and sprinkle both dressing and fish with sumac. Serve with the barley tabbouleh.

israeli chicken with moghrabieh, harissa-grilled peaches and mint

The chicken here is based on a recipe in Paula Wolfert's excellent book *Mediterranean Cooking*. (If you don't own anything by Paula Wolfert, seek her out. Her books are full of dishes that are "accidentally" healthy.)

Moghrabieh (Middle Eastern giant couscous), or Lebanese couscous, is difficult to find, but Amazon sells it. You could also use Israeli couscous, sometimes called pearl couscous, or matfoul, a bulgur wheat product, and cook it in the same way. Either can be used as a salad base.

SERVES 4

FOR THE CHICKEN AND
MOGHRABIEH

⅓ cup hot mustard (I use
English mustard)

8 skinless bone-in chicken thighs
(or other chicken joints)

3 tablespoons packed dark
brown sugar

salt and black pepper

3 tablespoons olive oil

⅓ cup orange juice

1 cup whole-wheat moghrabieh
(Lebanese couscous)

1 tablespoon extra virgin olive oil

good squeeze of lemon juice

FOR THE PEACHES

3 just-ripe peaches, halved
and pitted

2 tablespoons olive oil

3 tablespoons harissa, or to taste
(reduce the amount if you want it
less hot)

juice of ½ lemon

leaves from 1 small bunch of
mint, torn

Preheat the oven to 375°F.

Spread the mustard on both sides of the chicken thighs and put them into a small roasting pan or gratin dish in which they will fit snugly. Sprinkle with half the sugar and season. Drizzle with 2 tablespoons of the regular olive oil and all the orange juice. Roast in the oven for 20 minutes. Take the pan out, turn the chicken over, baste it, and sprinkle with the rest of the sugar. Season and return to the oven for another 15 minutes. The chicken should be dark gold.

When the chicken has about 15 minutes of cooking time left, turn to the moghrabieh. Heat the final 1 tablespoon of regular oil in a saucepan, add the moghrabieh, and stir over medium heat until golden brown; after about four minutes, you should be able to smell it getting toasted. Cover with boiling water, season, and simmer gently for about 10 minutes, until the moghrabieh is tender. Drain, toss with the extra virgin oil and the lemon, and season.

Meanwhile, cut the peach halves into wedges and toss in a bowl with the 2 tablespoons of regular olive oil and the harissa. Heat a ridged grill pan until it is really hot. Lift the peach slices out of the harissa mixture, shaking off the excess, and cook on both sides until tender. Remove from the pan and squeeze lemon juice on top. Once the moghrabieh is ready, toss it with the peaches and mint. Serve with the chicken.

skewered chicken with lime, chile, and mint salad and radish sprouts

A child-friendly dish (my kids love it and they're pretty fussy). The salad is fabulous (hot and fresh) and goes with any spicy grilled or roasted meat dish. Radish sprouts are beautiful but hard to find. It is easy to grow them, honestly. (You can buy seeds from www.mountainroseherbs.com.)

SERVES 6

FOR THE CHICKEN

12 skinless boneless chicken thighs

1½ tablespoons peanut oil

juice of 1 lime, plus lime wedges

FOR THE MARINADE

finely grated zest of 4 limes and juice of 6

2 red chiles, seeded and shredded

3 tablespoons soy sauce

½ tablespoon Thai fish sauce

6 garlic cloves, crushed

2 tablespoons chopped mint leaves

freshly ground black pepper

FOR THE DRESSING

2 tablespoons rice vinegar

1 tablespoon superfine sugar

½ tablespoon Thai fish sauce

juice of 1 lime

2 teaspoon ginger syrup

1 tablespoon chopped peanuts (optional)

2 tablespoons peanut oil

salt and black pepper

FOR THE SALAD

10 radishes, cut into matchsticks

5 napa cabbage leaves, shredded

1 carrot, cut into matchsticks

½ cup torn cilantro leaves

leaves from 4 sprigs of mint, torn

2½ cups mizuna or arugula

1 cup radish sprouts

Soak six bamboo skewers in water for 30 minutes; this stops them from burning when the chicken is cooking.

Cut the chicken into cubes. Mix all the ingredients for the marinade together. Put the chicken into the marinade, turning it to make sure it is all coated, cover with plastic wrap, and put in the refrigerator. Let chill for one to four hours.

To make the dressing, whisk all the ingredients, except the oil, together. The sugar should dissolve in the lime juice. Now whisk in the oil and taste for seasoning.

Have everything for the salad prepared and ready to mix.

Thread the chicken onto the skewers and heat the oil in a large skillet (it needs to be big enough to accommodate the length of the skewers and let the chicken touch the bottom of the pan). You can also grill the chicken in a ridged grill pan, in which case brush each of the skewers with oil instead of putting the oil in the pan. Shake the marinade off the chicken.

Cook on all sides, starting on a high heat to get a good color all over, then reducing the heat so the chicken can cook all the way through. The whole process takes about 10 minutes. Add salt and black pepper and squeeze lime juice over them.

Toss all the salad ingredients with the dressing and serve the skewers on the salad. Serve extra wedges of lime on the side and offer brown rice.

pollo alla diavola with green beans and sicilian bread crumbs

This chile-hot Italian chicken is usually cooked on the barbecue or broiled, but roasting works well, too, and requires much less attention. Go as hot with the chile as you dare.

The Sicilian bread crumbs are good with other vegetables, too, and feel free to improvise with them, adding chile, capers, or grated lemon zest when serving them with other vegetable dishes.

When choosing Cornish game hens, look for small ones in the 1¼ lb range to for individual servings. Particulary large game hens may be okay to serve two people with small appetites. You can either cut the amount you cook (if you know your diners), or expect some leftovers.

If you prefer to make this with chicken thighs (skin on or off, as you prefer), use only ⅓ cup of olive oil in the marinade and cook the pieces for 40–45 minutes at 350°F.

SERVES 8

FOR THE CORNISH GAME HENS

leaves from 4 sprigs of rosemary, chopped

2 tablespoons dried oregano

½ cup olive oil

freshly ground black pepper

juice of 1 large lemon

1–1½ tablespoons dried red pepper flakes (use your discretion, it depends how hot you prefer it)

8 Cornish game hens

flaked sea salt

FOR THE BEANS WITH CRUMBS

3 tablespoons olive oil

4½ slices country-style bread, crusts removed, torn into small pieces

¼ cup raisins

¼ cup pine nuts

4 garlic cloves, finely sliced

4 cured anchovies, drained of oil and finely chopped

1½ lb green beans, tops trimmed but not the bottoms

juice of ½ lemon

about 2 tablespoons extra virgin olive oil

black pepper

leaves from about 8 sprigs of mint, torn

For the game hens, mix together the herbs, olive oil, black pepper, lemon, and red pepper flakes. Pour this all over the hens in a nonreactive dish or dishes and use your hands to rub it in, inside and out. Cover with plastic wrap and let stand in the refrigerator to marinate. A couple of hours is all they need, but turn them over every so often. When ready to cook, preheat the oven to 375°F and lift the hens out of the marinade. Season the birds with sea salt and roast for 50 minutes. Check that they are completely cooked; if you pierce a thigh, the juices that run out should be clear with no trace of pink. Cover with aluminum foil, insulate with towels (reserved for this purpose), and let rest for 15 minutes.

For the beans, heat 2 tablespoons of the olive oil a skillet and sauté the bread until it is golden brown on all sides. Add another 1 tablespoon of oil and add the raisins, pine nuts, garlic, and anchovies. Let the pine nuts get toasted (this happens pretty quickly so beware) and press the anchovies with a wooden spoon to break them up. Take off the heat and keep warm while you are cooking the beans.

Cook the beans in boiling salted water until tender (but al dente). Drain them, toss in a serving bowl with the lemon juice, extra virgin oil, and seasoning, and stir in the bread crumbs and mint.

Serve the Cornish game hens with the beans. You don't need starch (though Summer fregola is good, see page 142), but roasted red peppers (which you can make in advance) are good on the side.

lamb kebabs with georgian adzhika

This sauce is hot, although my version is actually less spicy than it would be eaten in Georgia. Because chiles vary, I would add half the amount suggested here, taste, then add more if you want.

MAKES 6

FOR THE KEBABS

1¼ lb cubed leg of lamb

¼ cup olive oil

1½ teaspoons ground cinnamon

1 teaspoon ground allspice

2 teaspoons cayenne pepper

2 garlic cloves, crushed

FOR THE ADZHIKA

4 garlic cloves, coarsely chopped

1 celery stick, coarsely chopped

4 red chiles, chopped

1 red bell pepper, chopped

½ cup dill leaves

½ cup cilantro leaves

3½ tablespoons red wine vinegar

¼ cup extra virgin olive oil

Trim the lamb of any fat or sinew. Mix all the other ingredients for the kebabs in a bowl and put the lamb in it. Turn the meat over in the marinade, cover with plastic wrap ,and put in the refrigerator to marinate for 2 to 24 hours. Turn the meat over every so often. Soak six bamboo skewers in water for at least 30 minutes so they won't burn on the barbecue or ridged grill pan.

To make the adzhika, put the garlic in a food processor and blend. Add the celery, chiles (seeded if you prefer), and bell pepper and pulse-blend to a salsalike mixture. Add the herbs and pulse about three times; you don't want a puree, just a rough, lumpy mix. Scrape into a bowl and add salt, the vinegar, and extra virgin oil.

Thread the lamb cubes onto the skewers and season with salt. Cook on a hot ridged grill pan, or a barbecue, until golden brown all over, turning them regularly. It's best if they are still rare in the middle, so these only need about seven minutes in total. Serve with the adzhika, or either of the sauces below.

more sauces … **raisin, chile, and pine nut salsa** Hot, sweet, and with a streak of minty freshness, this is Sicilian in influence. Put 2 small garlic cloves in a mortar and crush with a little sea salt. Add ½ cup pine nuts and crush coarsely. Now add 2 tablespoons raisins, 1 red and 1 green chile, seeded and finely chopped, the torn leaves from about 12 sprigs of mint, 2 finely chopped scallions, 2 tablespoons white balsamic vinegar, the juice of ½ lemon, black pepper, and ½ cup extra virgin oil. Give a brief bash to start to bring the flavors out. Taste, adjust the seasoning, and serve. Serves 6.

mint and almond pesto Put ⅓ cup toasted almonds in a food processor with 4 garlic cloves, 1⅔ cups mint leaves, ⅔ cup flat-leaf parsley leaves, 1 tablespoon honey, the juice of 1 lemon, and salt and black pepper. Puree while adding 1¼ cups extra virgin oil in a steady stream. Taste for seasoning. Pour a layer of olive oil on top to protect it and cover with plastic wrap until ready to serve. Serves 6.

lamb scottadito with summer fregola

Literally, lamb that "burns your fingers," this is a great casual dinner or weekend lunch dish. It does need to be cooked at the last minute, but it's easy. It's best to cook it with the fat on; if you or your guests don't want to eat it, just cut it off.

Fregola is really a type of large couscous from Sardinia. If you can't get it, use a grain such as farro or spelt (see page 223 for how to cook that).

SERVES 6

FOR THE LAMB

18 best end lamb cutlets, well scraped (get your butcher to do it)

3 tablespoons olive oil

juice of 1 lemon, plus lemon wedges to serve

1½ tablespoons chopped oregano leaves

3½ tablespoons dried red pepper flakes (or even more for extra heat)

FOR THE FREGOLA

1¾ cups fregola or Israeli couscous

¼ cup extra virgin olive oil

1½ tablespoons lemon juice

salt and black pepper

1 tablespoon olive oil

4 shallots, finely chopped

6 oz cherry tomatoes, quartered or chopped

leaves from 1 small bunch of basil, torn, or 3 tablespoons coarsely chopped flat-leaf parsley leaves

Put the cutlets into a large, shallow, nonreactive bowl. Add the regular olive oil, lemon juice, oregano, and red pepper flakes. Turn everything over with your hands, cover, put in the refrigerator, and let marinate for a couple of hours. Turn the meat over every so often if you can.

Cook the fregola in boiling water for 10 minutes, then drain and immediately add the extra virgin oil, lemon juice, salt, and black pepper. Fork this through.

Meanwhile, heat the 1 tablespoon of regular olive oil in a small skillet and cook the shallots until they are soft but not golden brown. Add to the fregola with the tomatoes and herbs.

Heat a ridged grill pan over high heat. Lift the lamb out of the marinade, shaking off the excess liquid (there shouldn't be much). Season the meat well. When the pan is really hot, cook the chops on each side until well browned. Press the meaty part of the chops down on the ridges with the back of a wooden spoon as you are cooking. They should still be pink in the middle, so about 1½ minutes on each side is enough. Insert a sharp knife into one of them to see how well the meat is done, but make sure you serve the chop the other way up so people can't see the slit.

Put the cutlets on a plate with the lemon wedges and serve immediately with the fregola. Make sure you supply napkins. Your guests will almost certainly want to clean every last morsel of meat from the chops, so fingers will definitely be in use.

japanese beef with country-style ponzu and wasabi

Sometimes you want a burst of protein. I don't eat red meat that often, but I do sometimes get a craving for it (and so does my teenage son). This is an occasional—and expensive—treat, and I love its cleanness. It's filling, too. You can serve Japanese pickled vegetables alongside (see page 60) if you want to extend it.

The ponzu dressing is from an inspiring book, *Japanese Farm Food*, by Nancy Singleton Hachisu, and is much simpler to make than regular ponzu.

SERVES 6

FOR THE PONZU

½ cup Japanese soy sauce

½ cup bitter orange juice (such as from Seville oranges), or a mixture of lime and orange juice

1 tablespoon chopped chives

FOR THE BEEF

sea salt

1 lb top-quality filet mignon or tenderloin steak, all visible fat removed

wasabi (preferably fresh, then grated), to serve

shreds of zest from 2 lemons, plus lemon wedges to serve

2 small red chiles, seeded and finely sliced

To make the ponzu, just mix all the ingredients together. Cover and put in the refrigerator.

Sprinkle sea salt all over the beef. Sear it all over either on a very hot ridged grill pan, or on a barbecue. Immediately wrap in paper towels and put in the refrigerator for one hour to cool.

Cut into slices across the grain and lay them out, overlapping, on each serving plate. Give everyone a little wasabi on the side of the plate and sprinkle the beef with the lemon zest and chiles. Put a little dipping bowl of the ponzu on each plate. Offer wedges of lemon in a bowl as well.

tagliata

A quick Italian steak salad that is a real treat. Cherry tomatoes, dressed with some lemon juice and extra virgin olive oil, are wonderful alongside.

SERVES 8

4 (10 oz) tenderloin steaks, fat removed

4 garlic cloves, unpeeled

8 cups mixed watercress and arugula leaves

olive oil

salt and black pepper

½ cup extra virgin olive oil

4 sprigs of rosemary

2 strips of lemon zest, plus the juice of 1 lemon

1–1¾ oz Parmesan, shaved

You need to work fast for this recipe. Get your steaks to room temperature. Bash the garlic cloves with the side of a knife and put the salad greens in a wide, shallow bowl.

Heat a heavy skillet until really hot, add a thin film of regular olive oil, and heat until the oil is just beginning to smoke. Season the steaks all over and sauté them for 2½ minutes in total, turning every 20 seconds so they get cooked evenly. Put the steaks on a warm plate, cover with aluminum foil, and let rest.

There won't be much oil in the pan, but whatever there is, pour it out. Don't wipe the pan: there's flavor in it. Add the extra virgin oil to the pan and set it over medium heat. Throw in the garlic, rosemary, and lemon zest. Let the flavorings meld in the oil for three minutes, then add the lemon juice.

Cut the steaks into slices about ¼ inch thick. Strain half the dressing in the pan through a strainer onto the greens in the bowl. Spread the steak and Parmesan over the greens, too, then strain the rest of the dressing over the top. Sprinkle more salt over the whole dish along with a good grinding of black pepper and serve immediately.

how many diets can you fit into a life?

During my life I've followed the Mayo Clinic, Scarsdale, F-plan, Atkins, Cabbage Soup, Cambridge, Lighter Life, South Beach, and Dukan diets. I have spent so much energy angsting about them I could weep. Friends, especially women (many of them thin), have done the same thing. (If there is a more effective way to keep women down, insecure, and wasting time, I have yet to find it.)

Analysts Mintel found one in four adults in the UK are trying to lose weight "most of the time"—that's thirteen million people. In the United States, about forty-five million people are on a diet, according to the Boston Medical Center. Everyone has an opinion on the best or fastest way. You'll be told you're wasting your time, or that you should be on a different plan. Smug skinny people will say you lack willpower, or don't move enough.

If you're reading this page, you've probably dieted, too. If you've bought this book, you probably love food passionately and find it hard to diet. I'm in exactly the same position. Unfortunately, once you start dieting, it's difficult to stop, because you're on the whole deprivation <-> rebellion, eating too little <-> overindulging roller coaster.

I believe that, without our collective neurosis about appearance, we would each hit an acceptable weight that suited us (we might be rounded, we might be skinny, but it would be right). But we don't live in that kind of society. Further, we live in a culture that is so full of fattening food—refined carbs, especially sugar—that eating in a balanced way is harder than it was. My children want a "treat" (a sweet one) on the way home from school every day, because everyone else has one. When I was little, sweet treats were for the weekend. So we're judged more severely on how we look, yet there's more temptation to eat things that will make us unhealthy and put on weight. Not ideal for a sane, balanced approach to food.

I don't advocate being skinny; I gave up that option years ago. In my twenties, I managed to stay at one hundred and five pounds (I'm five feet four inches tall) by being extremely strict for five days and eating what I wanted at the weekend. It was a grim existence— although it "worked" for my appearance—and it certainly wasn't healthy. But it's not "healthy" to be overweight either and, while this book isn't about losing weight, we need to look at it. Dieting—even if it just means cutting down for a few days—is okay from time to time. (After Christmas or a week's vacation in Paris you're going to have put on a few pounds.) But constant dieting is not a good way to live. It's unhealthy and it's miserable.

Diets do work—some spectacularly—but only while you're on them. I can hear you groaning as I say this (as I've groaned when people have said it to me), but you need to get to a weight you're comfortable with *and then you need to change the way you eat.* I have spent years not listening to this. In fact, I could have punched people who said it to me. So I am not *instructing* you; it's your battle. But the food in this book (bar the cakes and sorbets, which are for weekends) and the information in it should help you stay at a decent weight without feeling deprived. I adore food. But I got sick of dieting. And this is the most satisfying food I have ever eaten.

ricotta with summer berries and honey

No cooking required. Just good, pure ingredients. Go to a deli and buy fresh ricotta instead of the stuff filled with preservative you find in supermarkets. There's a world of difference.

SERVES 4–6

1¼ cups fresh ricotta

a little confectioners' sugar (optional)

3 cups raspberries, blackberries, boysenberries, or red currants

lovely scented honey (orange blossom or thyme are good)

Line a strainer with cheesecloth. Set it over a bowl and add the ricotta to it. Pull the cloth around it and set a plate on top. Put into the refrigerator and let stand for a couple of hours.

Pull the cloth off and taste the ricotta. If you feel it needs to be sweeter, mash a little confectioners' sugar into it. Divide the ricotta among serving plates, or put it onto one large plate.

Sprinkle some berries alongside each serving and drizzle with the honey.

other fruity ways with ricotta... You can serve ricotta like this with other fruits. Good ripe figs are delicious (in which case, use a good lavender honey—it's perfect with figs) and white currants look wonderful (their almost pearlized skin is gorgeous against the creamy ricotta). Poached peaches or apricots are wonderful, too (see page 130, but add less sugar to their poaching liquid because you will be drizzling them with honey). If you're using golden stone fruits, such as nectarines, sprinkle them with pistachios before serving. Another idea is to slightly sweeten the ricotta with confectioners' sugar and serve it in a mound with fresh cherries sprinkled all round it.

gooseberry, almond, and spelt cake

Sweet-tart and moist. There's sugar in this, of course, making it an occasional treat. But it's made partly with whole-wheat spelt flour, which is both better for you than white flour and also brings a nutty tone. You can replace it with whole-wheat flour, if you prefer.

SERVES 8

1 stick unsalted butter, plus extra for greasing the pan

⅔ cup firmly packed light brown sugar

3 extra-large eggs, lightly beaten

½ cup spelt flour, sifted

3 tablespoons all-purpose flour, sifted

¾ cup ground almonds (preferably freshly ground; sometimes sold as almond meal)

¾ teaspoon baking powder

2⅓ cups fresh gooseberries, trimmed, or 1½ cups drained, canned gooseberries

¼ cup granulated sugar

⅓ cup slivered almonds

confectioners' sugar, to dust

Preheat the oven to 375°F. Butter an 8 inch springform cake pan.

Beat the butter and light brown sugar until light and fluffy. Add the eggs, a little at a time, beating well after each addition. If the mixture starts to curdle, add 1 tablespoon of the spelt flour. Fold in the rest of the flours, the almonds, and baking powder, using a large metal spoon, then scrape into the prepared pan.

Toss the gooseberries with the granulated sugar and spread them over the top of the cake. Bake for 20 minutes. Sprinkle with the slivered almonds and return to the oven for 10 minutes. The cake is ready when a toothpick inserted into the center comes out clean.

Let cool in the pan, then carefully remove the ring and bottom of the pan. Dust with confectioners' sugar before serving.

a cherry version ... This is just as good made with cherries. Just pit 1 lb (about 3⅔ cups) of them and throw them onto the cake just before it goes into the oven. They'll be soft in the time that it takes the cake batter to cook. This makes a wonderful squishy cake.

raspberries with basil and buttermilk sherbet

A sherbet is an unusual thing. It is made with milk and sugar syrup and feels, in the mouth, more like sorbet than ice cream. This buttermilk version is mouth-puckeringly refreshing.

In order to cut down on sugar, the syrup for the raspberries contains less than is normal. Once you get rid of the notion that fruits have to be in a thick syrup, it is liberating. They taste better. But you do need to adjust your expectations when it comes to texture.

SERVES 6

FOR THE SHERBET

⅔ cup granulated sugar

1 cup buttermilk

juice of 2 lemons

FOR THE RASPBERRIES

⅓ cup granulated sugar

3 strips of lemon zest, plus
the juice of 1 lemon

3 sprigs of basil, plus a few extra
small sprigs or leaves to serve
(optional)

2⅔ cups raspberries

For the sherbet, heat ⅓ cup of water and the sugar together until the sugar has completely dissolved, then let cool. Stir in the buttermilk and lemon juice and either churn in an ice cream machine according to the manufacturer's instructions, or freeze in a shallow, wide freezer-proof container, removing it three or four times during the freezing process and blending it in a food processor, or mashing it (vigorously) with a fork.

To prepare the raspberries, put the sugar and lemon zest into a saucepan with 1¼ cups of water and gently heat, stirring a little to help the sugar dissolve. Boil for two minutes, then remove from the heat, add the lemon juice and basil, and let cool. The basil will flavor the syrup. Put the raspberries into a serving bowl and strain the cold syrup over them. (The berries become flaccid if they are left too long in the syrup, so don't leave these for longer than 15 minutes before you want to serve them.)

Serve the raspberries, with a few basil leaves or sprigs (if using), along with the buttermilk sherbet.

figs and melon with ginger and star anise

Figs and melons are great "almost fall" fruits, so they're good at the end of summer. Melons are kind of musky, figs rich and sexy, while the warm spices anticipate the season to come.

SERVES 6

⅔ cup granulated sugar

¾ inch piece of ginger root, peeled and sliced

1 star anise

juice of 5 juicy limes, plus 2 wide strips of lime zest

6 large figs (not too ripe), stem trimmed, halved

1 honeydew melon or cantaloupe, peeled and seeded

Put the sugar into a saucepan—one large enough to hold the figs in a single layer—with 1¼ cups of water. Add the ginger, star anise, half the lime juice, and both strips of zest. Heat the pan, stirring to help the sugar dissolve. Bring to a boil and boil for four minutes. Reduce the heat.

Add the figs and poach them gently for three to four minutes; you just want them to be there long enough to flavor the syrup a little and also take in some of the flavorings in the pan. However, yu don't want them in there so long they fall apart. Lift the figs out with a slotted spoon and put them into a bowl.

Discard the zest and the star anise from the syrup. Reduce the poaching liquid by about one-quarter by boiling it, then add the rest of the lime juice and let cool. Add the melon to the figs and pour the cold syrup over the fruit.

Let the fruit macerate in the syrup for at least 30 minutes (but no more than three hours because the melon gets too soft). This is good with Greek yogurt and a drizzle of honey.

loving breakfast

The breakfast I ate as a teenager now horrifies me: a slice of white toast with Dairylea and a cup of sweet tea, or maybe a bowl of Frosties. No wonder I was nodding off in Spanish class by eleven o'clock. As an adult, I didn't fare much better. I like nothing better than a French breakfast. Baskets of brioche, croissants, tartines … my autobiography could be called "Viennoiserie were my downfall." I haven't banned these (I couldn't, so I leave them for the weekend) but they put weight on and, more importantly, leave you hungry. Breakfast is the most important meal we eat—it's when we "break the fast"—and as such needs to give us energy that will last. (Many experts are convinced that people who skip breakfast in order to lose weight eat more at the other meals during the day, and snack more, too.) Yet the most popular breakfast foods in Western culture are refined carbohydrates. Processed cereals, muffins, croissants, and white bread are just about the worst things you can eat (not just at breakfast but at any time of day). Even the glass of fruit juice we down is basically sugar; it may contain vitamins, but it's much better to eat whole fruit (you then get fiber as well) than drink the juice. No breakfast, or a breakfast that doesn't fill you up, means the hormone ghrelin, which sends you the signal telling you you're hungry, isn't suppressed and you'll overeat at lunch time (or hit the cookie jar midmorning). So breakfast is important.

I didn't start eating better breakfasts because somebody told me I should. It happened out of curiosity and a love of food. I grew more interested in it as a meal when I saw what people in other countries ate first thing. Breakfast in a guest house in Mexico was sliced avocado, salty fresh cheese, warm black beans, and mangoes with lime. There wasn't a box of cereal in sight. In Germany, I had "eggs in a glass" every morning: two soft-boiled eggs that are ingeniously shelled and put into a glass (which kind of makes them special), with the sort of bread that requires a lot of chewing (and luckily I love). In Greece, it's tomatoes, cucumber, feta cheese, olives, yogurt, and fruit. But it was the Scandinavian breakfast that really got me going. Breakfast in a hotel in Helsinki a few summers ago offered homemade muesli, oatmeal, fruit compote, cheeses, hard-boiled eggs, tomatoes, cucumber, and sliced bell peppers, cured herring, gravlax, ham, and five types of dense whole-grain bread. Every morning I approached breakfast as I do a good dinner.

I didn't eat everything offered, but getting protein first thing (fish, eggs, and cheese) really makes you feel full, while the complex carbs (oatmeal and solid whole-grain bread) kept me going, too. I breakfasted the Finnish way for two weeks—it was my favorite meal of the day—and was rarely hungry before three in the afternoon. Returning home I was terrified to get on the scale. I had, as the advice goes, breakfasted like a king. I knew this was supposed to be good for you, but I was sure I'd pay for it. However, my bathroom scale showed that I hadn't put on a single pound. And I'd had boundless energy every day.

We're all short of time in the morning. That is partly why cereal manufacturers convinced us that a bowl of processed grains is adequate (we wanted to believe it). For all the boring reasons you've ever heard—they have added sugar, added salt—they aren't good enough.

Make your own cereal with whole grains, nuts, and seeds or, if you want to buy muesli, check the sugar and salt content on the package. You'll find, however, that homemade muesli is cheaper as well as more delicious. And you know exactly what's in it, because you've made it.

I've given "best case scenario" recipes for some breakfasts (proper slow-cooked oatmeal, for example), but there's nothing wrong with the quick-cooking type; it certainly beats packaged cereal hands down. I love a bowl of oatmeal that has simmered—with the occasional stir—on the stove for five minutes while I've been trying to find my youngest's school shoes. We live in the real world. But you'll probably find, if you start to eat oatmeal regularly, that you'll look forward to it way more than you did the bowl of cold cereal you used to down. And you might make more time for it.

The main thing to be is open-minded. I like thinking about breakfast as a meal, like any other, with all the pleasures that entails, instead of something that you wolf down before leaving the house. Don't let one of your three meals a day be dictated by breakfast cereal manufacturers. Think savory, too. Think creatively. It might not be your bag, but cured herrings make a great breakfast (very filling), or try some smoked fish every so often. Or omelets—filled with shredded cheese, shredded spinach, or watercress—in fact, eggs done any way are great (they're full of protein and keep you going until lunch time). Then there's kedgeree (made with brown rice and lentils), or toasted sourdough with avocado or labneh and roasted tomatoes, or mushrooms sautéed and splashed with soy sauce ... Hungry yet?

A breakfast high in protein has proved the best for me. It keeps me full for longer and I find that even "good carbs," such as oatmeal—if I eat it every day—keep weight on. Your experience of your own body will tell you what will work best for you.

Nobody's going to deprive you of your glass of freshly squeezed, but try to eat fruit instead of drink it (or do both). Stewed apples—I try to add very little sugar—are cheap and help you to get the first of your five a day in at breakfast, and even out of season I make red fruit compote with big bags of frozen berries: add enough sugar to sweeten, throw in fresh blueberries, and eat with yogurt. (I go for whole-fat, which tastes better and keeps you feeling full for longer than low-fat versions. Many low-fat yogurts are high in sugar or sweeteners, so check the label. And read more about fats on pages 284–285.)

Breakfast—even midweek—can be as enjoyable as dinner. And if you're into food, that's another wonderful meal to think about. Breakfast can be varied, even exotic, filling enough to keep you away from hitting the cookies or doughnuts at 11 o'clock and—this is the real plus—delicious. Even when they're a croissant-free zone.

turkish poached eggs with spinach and yogurt

The Turks are good with eggs. You wouldn't think that poached eggs could become an exotic feast, but here they do. A lovely simple breakfast, lunch, or dinner for two.

SERVES 2

½ cup Greek yogurt

1 garlic clove, crushed

1–2 flatbreads

2–4 eggs

2 tablespoons butter

½ teaspoon cumin seeds

½ teaspoon dried red pepper flakes

3½ cups spinach leaves, tough stems removed, washed

1 tablespoon olive oil

salt and black pepper

Mix the yogurt with the crushed garlic. Warm or toast the flatbread and put a piece on each of two plates. Top each piece with some of the yogurt, spreading it out.

Meanwhile, poach the eggs, either one or two per person, depending on appetite. At the same time, heat the butter until it is foaming, then add the spices and cook for a minute. Put the spinach in a skillet with the olive oil and quickly heat it, allowing the spinach to wilt. Season. Try to have all these components ready at the same time.

Put some spinach on top of the yogurt, top with the eggs, and pour the warm spiced butter on top. Season and serve.

roopa's indian scrambled eggs

A Punjabi dish from my great friend Roopa Gulati. You can get rid of the seeds in the chiles if you want to (you lightweight …). This makes a great breakfast (especially at the weekend) or lunch. Never was Indian food on the table so quickly. Roopa recommends eating this with fresh carrot chutney. I'd suggest either of the carrot salads on pages 273 and 277.

SERVES 3–4

1 teaspoon cumin seeds

2 tablespoons sunflower oil

2 large red onions, finely chopped

2 green chiles, chopped (with their seeds)

½ teaspoon coarsely ground black peppercorns

3 tomatoes, finely chopped

6 eggs, lightly beaten and seasoned with salt

2 tablespoons chopped cilantro leaves

Heat the cumin seeds in a dry skillet for a minute or two, until you can smell their aroma. Put into a mortar and crush to a powder. Heat the oil in the skillet and cook the onions over medium heat until golden brown. Add the chiles and black pepper and continue cooking for another two minutes.

Stir in the tomatoes and cook until they get soft and any excess liquid has cooked off; it will take at least five minutes.

Reduce the heat slightly and add the eggs. Don't stir them for about two or three minutes, then gently lift and turn them over in the pan. Continue cooking until set. Just before serving, toss in the cumin and finish with the cilantro leaves.

shaken currants with yogurt and rye crumbs

A Scandinavian breakfast that is great in the summer when there are loads of berries around (you can make this with any kind of berry, however, it's not great with strawberries because they get too soft). The berries' tartness as they burst against the deep, almost coffee-flavored rye bread crumbs is a good morning wake-up call for the taste buds. Have some pickled herring alongside (read about it on page 155, you might be persuaded) and imagine you are starting the day in Helsinki...

SERVES 4

2 cups fresh currants, any color, or a mixture

⅓ cup granulated sugar

3½ oz dry dark rye bread

2 tablespoons packed dark brown sugar

plain yogurt, or Greek yogurt, to serve

Wash the currants but don't dry them. Spread them out on a large tray or roasting pan and sprinkle them with the granulated sugar. Let them rest there for a couple of hours, shaking from time to time, then transfer them to a jar and keep in the refrigerator.

For the crumbs, preheat the oven to 210°F. Break the bread up into little chunks with your hands (you don't want something as small as bread crumbs you produce in the food processor). Spread them out on a baking sheet (no need to grease it), put into the oven, and toast for 15 minutes. Leat cool, then mix them with the dark brown sugar.

Serve the currants with the yogurt and rye crumbs.

more fruity breakfasts ... I cook all kinds of fruit in the summer for breakfast, even using bags of frozen berries (they're cheaper than fresh, even at the height of the berry season). Just put them in a saucepan, heat gently, add enough sugar to sweeten slightly, and let cool. You can also bake apricots, nectarines, or peaches. Preheat the oven to 350°F. Use 16 apricots or 8 nectarines or peaches. Pit the fruits. Halve the apricots, or cut the nectarines or peaches into 8 wedges each. Lay them in a gratin dish. Add 1 cup of water, the juice of 1 orange, and 2 teaspoons vanilla extract, then sprinkle with ¼ cup packed light brown sugar. Bake for 20–25 minutes, or until the fruit is tender. Serves 4–6.

fall

eating in fall

Fall is the best season for the cook. It spans both warm and
cool months and the slide toward the latter is kindly, almost
imperceptible. After a summer of wavering appetite (it can
be too hot to cook, too hot to eat), I love the pull toward the
kitchen that cooler weather engenders. September is almost
embarrassingly fulsome as summer and fall merge, bringing
a collision of pumpkins and apples, plums and zucchini.
Many of the ingredients we used to see as summery have a
longer season now: late raspberries can appear in fall; mounds
of eggplants, grilled to meltingness, make perfect autumnal
eating; tomatoes go on and on (though once summer has
gone, they're better roasted). Then coolness really comes.
You need a sweater and you want to eat the sweet, starchy
flesh of pumpkin or squash.

Don't forget that some of the best autumnal eating can be
found at the back of your kitchen cupboard. I fall again
for lentils—green (I use Puy, a French variety), black, and
workaday brown—and am glad to get back to the heartier
grains, too.

early fall

arugula
beet
broccoli
carrot
cauliflower
celeriac
celery
chard
eggplant
fennel
green beans
horseradish
leek
parsnip
pumpkin
radish
scallion
sweetcorn
sweet pepper
sweet potato
tomatillo
tomato
watercress
wild mushrooms
winter squash
zucchini

apple
blackberries
cranberries
figs
grapes
lime
melon
nectarine
peach
pear
plum
raspberries

duck
lamb

mid fall

brussels sprout
jerusalem artichoke
kale
spinach
turnip

persimmon
pomegranates
quince
raspberries

duck
lamb
partridge
pheasant
rabbit
venison

late fall

chicory
turnip

pear
persimmon
tamarillo

roasted tomatoes and lentils with dukka-crumbed eggs

You will end up with more dukka than you need for this dish, but it seems silly to make a smaller amount. Put it into an airtight container and keep it for sprinkling on braised beans, bean purees, or for eating with hard-boiled eggs and radishes. You can use pumpkin seeds instead of sunflower seeds, if you prefer.

SERVES 6 FOR LUNCH OR A LIGHT MAIN COURSE

FOR THE DUKKA

½ cup hazelnuts (skins on)

⅓ cup sesame seeds

1 teaspoon nigella seeds

1 tablespoon sunflower seeds

3 tablespoons coriander seeds

1 tablespoon white peppercorns

1½ tablespoons cumin seeds

1 teaspoon ground paprika

½ tablespoons sea salt flakes

FOR THE TOMATOES AND EGGS

12 large plum tomatoes, halved

3 tablespoons olive oil

2 teaspoons harissa

½ tablespoons sugar

salt and black pepper

6 extra-large eggs

FOR THE LENTILS

1 tablespoon olive oil

½ onion, finely chopped

1 celery stick, finely chopped

1 garlic clove, finely chopped

1⅓ cups Puy or green lentils

1 sprig of thyme

1 bay leaf

juice of ½ lemon

1 tablespoon sherry vinegar

¼ cup extra virgin olive oil

2 tablespoons chopped cilantro leaves

To make the dukka, put the hazelnuts in a dry skillet and toast over high heat until they smell roasted. Be careful not to go too far, because they burn easily. Transfer to a plate to cool a little, then crush them in a mortar to a coarsely ground mixture.

Put the sesame seeds into a dry skillet with the nigella and toast until the sesame seeds are golden brown. Follow with the sunflower seeds. Coarsely crush all the toasted seeds and add to the nuts. Toast the coriander seeds until they smell toasted, then grind them coarsely. Do the same with the peppercorns, then the cumin seeds. Combine the nuts, seeds, and toasted spices with the paprika and salt. Store in an airtight container until you need it.

For the tomatoes, preheat the oven to 375°F. Lay the tomatoes in a single layer in a roasting pan. Mix the olive oil and harissa together and pour over the tomatoes. Turn to coat, ending cut side up, then sprinkle with sugar and season. Roast in the oven for 45 minutes, or until caramelized in parts and slightly shrunken.

Meanwhile, cook the lentils. Heat the oil in a saucepan and gently sauté the onion, celery, and garlic until soft but not browned. Add the lentils and turn them over in the oil. Chuck in the thyme and bay leaf. Pour in 3 cups of water, season lightly, bring to a boil, reduce the heat, and simmer, uncovered, until the lentils are just tender. This could take 15–25 minutes, depending on their age, so watch them; they can turn to mush quickly. When they are cooked, they should have absorbed all the liquid (simply drain them if they haven't). Remove the thyme and bay leaf. Add the lemon juice. Mix the vinegar and extra virgin oil together and stir it into the lentils with the cilantro. Taste for seasoning.

Cook the eggs in boiling water for six minutes. They should still be a little runny in the middle. Rinse them in cold water and, once cool enough to handle, quickly peel. Roll them lightly in the dukka and set each on top of a serving of lentils and tomatoes, or if you prefer to see the yolk, break the egg in half and sprinkle some dukka on top. Serve immediately.

eastern broth with shallots, lime, and cilantro

This is a basic recipe. You can add tofu, slices of shiitake mushrooms, bean sprouts, cooked chicken, or raw shrimp. It's wonderful, though—and totally head-clearing—just as it is. The sugar (it's only a small amount) is there to achieve that wonderful hot, sour, salty, sweet balance that is characteristic of Southeast Asian food, but omit it if you really want to stay away from sugar.

SERVES 4

12 shallots, peeled

4 cups well-flavored chicken stock

1½ inch piece of ginger root, peeled and sliced

2 lime leaves (if you have them)

1 red chile (or ½ chile, depending on how hot you want it), finely sliced

juice of 1 lime, or to taste

small bunch of cilantro, chopped or not, as you prefer

1½ teaspoons Thai fish sauce, or to taste

1 teaspoon superfine sugar, or to taste

2 scallions, cut into very fine julienne strips

Halve the shallots and cut them into slices lengthwise.

Put the stock into a saucepan and bring to a boil. Reduce the heat and add the ginger, lime leaves, and shallots. Simmer gently for about 15 minutes, then add the chile and simmer for another couple of minutes. Add all the other ingredients and taste for seasoning. Aim for a good balance of chile, lime, fish sauce, and sugar (hot, sour, salty, sweet).

You don't have to remove the ginger, but warn people it's there.

or in the japanese style ... **miso broth with greens** A good quick lunch if you have some stock in the refrigerator. You can add spinach instead of bok choy, if that's what you have. Bring 2 cups well-flavored chicken stock to a boil in a saucepan and stir in ¼ cup sweet white miso paste. Reduce the heat to a simmer. Put ½ green chile, chopped, 2 scallions, chopped, 2 tablespoons coarsely chopped cilantro or mint leaves, 1 garlic clove, chopped, and ½ inch piece of ginger root, peeled and chopped, into a mortar and pound to a paste. Stir the flavorings into the broth, then add the juice of ½ lime (or more to taste) and 3 oz baby bok choy, quartered lengthwise. Cook for a few minutes to wilt the greens, taste for seasoning, and serve. Serves 2.

miraculous broth

Despite all the food trends that come and go, some dishes never change. Like soup. Ancient recipes for soups and broths are similar to those in modern cookbooks—it's always a liquid, usually stock, plus vegetables or grains—and the way you turn to them when you feel under the weather shows sound survival instincts. Doctors were recommending chicken broth to combat colds as early as the twelfth century and, according to American food historian Ken Albala, this is because they are anti-inflammatory and easy to digest. They don't just appear to soothe you as you carefully sip another spoonful; they actually do you good. If you're in the habit of eating chicken soup when you're ill, you'll know that it's miraculously restorative.

There are a lot of soup recipes in this book—and they're great for increasing your vegetable intake—but I want to talk about broth, because you don't even need a recipe for that. "Broth" sounds like something your granny made, but I just mean a pot of stock—usually chicken in my house—that you can transform, depending on how you feel and what's in your veggie drawer. You do need to start with decent stock. I sometimes use store-bought stuff, but it's usually not strong enough. Make your own if you can.

Broths don't need to be pureed and they can be made in an ad hoc way. If you have a pot of stock, you're already halfway there. Want something chunky? Add chopped pumpkin, canned white beans, sliced garlic, and a tablespoon of tomato paste. Cook until the pumpkin is tender, add shredded spinach and herbs (basil or flat-leaf parsley leaves) and Parmesan shavings and you're ready to go. In the summer, use zucchini, green beans, and diced tomatoes. Fancy something from northern climes? Then cook some spelt or barley in the broth before adding salmon (fresh or hot-smoked) and dill and spoon some sour cream or buttermilk on top. If you need a jolt of spice, make an Eastern-style hot-and-sour soup by adding chile, slices of ginger, tamarind paste, or lime juice and maybe a dash of Thai fish sauce. Craving that sweet-sour thing? Throw in a little brown sugar, too. You can add chopped leftover chicken, shrimp, bok choy, bean sprouts, and sliced mushrooms. You just need to simmer your soup for as long as it takes to cook (or, if you're using leftovers, to warm through) the various components. Whether you're concerned about your intake of carbs or just keeping an eye on how many vegetables you're eating, a brothy soup is a great thing to eat, filling, and satisfying.

It's lunch time, it's raining, and my boiler has once again given up the ghost. Thank God there's a pot of stock in the refrigerator. By the time it boils, I'll have chopped some vegetables, decided how I want to flavor the soup (miso today, I think), and soon I'll be eating a bowlful of lip-smacking nourishment. You have to agree, it beats a take-out.

carrot and ginger soup with cucumber raita

Indian heat, intensely carrot flavor. If you don't want to use carrot juice—and this tastes best if you use some you've juiced yourself—then replace it with stock or water.

SERVES 4

FOR THE SOUP

2 tablespoons olive oil

1 onion, finely chopped

1 celery stick, finely chopped

10 carrots, finely chopped

2 garlic cloves, finely chopped

1 inch piece of ginger root, peeled and finely chopped

2 teaspoons ground cumin

2 cups chicken stock

2 cups carrot juice

salt and black pepper

FOR THE RAITA

¼ cucumber

½ cup plain yogurt

1 garlic clove, crushed

about 1 tablespoon torn mint leaves

Heat the oil in a saucepan. Cook the onion over medium heat with the celery and carrots, stirring them around and browning them a little. Now add the garlic, ginger, and cumin and cook for another couple of minutes. Add the chicken stock and carrot juice, season, and bring to a boil.

Reduce the heat to a simmer and cook for about 20 minutes, until the carrots are completely tender. Let cool a little while you make the raita.

Halve the cucumber lengthwise and use a teaspoon to scoop out the seeds. Chop the remaining flesh and mix it with the yogurt, garlic, and mint.

Puree the soup in a food processor or with a handheld immersion blender. Reheat, check for seasoning, and serve with some raita spooned on top of each bowl.

a caribbean version ... **I-tal carrot and sweet potato soup** Made for me by a friend who follows some Rastafarian dietary guidelines. They believe food should enhance your "levity" (life energy). I couldn't believe something that tasted this good could also be, well, so utterly simple. Put 4 cups of fresh carrot juice into a saucepan and add 2 chopped leeks, 2 peeled and chopped sweet potatoes, 3½ tablespoons coconut cream, 1 crushed garlic clove, 1 seeded and chopped red chile, a ¾ inch piece of ginger root, peeled and finely chopped, and the leaves from 2 sprigs of thyme. Season, bring to a simmer, and cook for 10 minutes or until the sweet potato is tender. Now leave it as it is or puree the soup. Return to the heat and add 2 cups baby spinach leaves and a drained 15 oz can of chickpeas (optional). Let the spinach wilt and add plenty of chopped cilantro. Serves 6.

grilled fish and saffron broth with corfu garlic sauce

This is rich, so it makes a main course instead of an appetizer. You can serve the broth without the garlic sauce; it's still very good. The sauce has many other uses, too; serve it with other meaty fish, or with lamb, pork, or chicken as well as with roast or raw vegetables.

SERVES 4

FOR THE FISH

8 red snapper fillets

juice of ½ orange

10 crushed black peppercorns

¼ cup extra virgin olive oil

2 tablespoons olive oil

FOR THE SAUCE

1 slice country-style bread, without crusts

½ cup walnuts

3 garlic cloves

¼ teaspoon salt, or more to taste

½ cup extra virgin olive oil

1–2 tablespoons red wine vinegar

black pepper

FOR THE BROTH

2 thin leeks

3 small fennel bulbs

8 new potatoes, peeled and halved

2 tablespoons olive oil

6 shallots, sliced

1 small dried chile, crumbled (optional)

generous pinch of saffron stamens

2½ cups well-flavored fish stock

Put the red snapper into a dish with the orange juice, peppercorns, and extra virgin oil. Turn the fish over and cover with plastic wrap. Put in the refrigerator and let marinate for three to four hours.

For the sauce, put the slice of bread in a bowl. Sprinkle with three to four tablespoons of water. Let soak until the bread feels softish. Cook the walnuts in a dry saucepan until they smell toasty, then remove from the pan. Put the garlic and salt into a mortar and crush the garlic. Squeeze the water from the bread and grind it in as well, then add the nuts and pulverize them. Add the extra virgin oil, pounding, then the vinegar to taste, adding more salt if you need it and some black pepper. You can do this in a food processor, but it doesn't produce such a good texture. If it seems too thick, mix in hot water until you have the texture you want, then adjust the seasoning. Set aside.

Trim the bottom and top of the leeks and remove the outer leaves. Cut into 1 inch lengths. Wash carefully, getting any grit out without breaking up the pieces. Trim off the fennel tips, reserving feathery leaves, and remove any tough outer leaves. Quarter the bulbs lengthwise and carefully trim the bottom of each, but don't cut too much off or the fennel will fall apart.

Cook the potatoes in boiling salted water for 12–15 minutes, or until tender, then drain. Meanwhile, heat the olive oil in a sauté pan and gently sauté the shallots, leeks, and fennel for five minutes, until slightly soft. Add the chile (if using), saffron, and stock and bring to a boil. Reduce to a simmer and cook, uncovered, for 15 minutes, adding the potatoes a few minutes before the end. The liquid should reduce a little. Add any reserved feathery fennel leaves.

Take the fish out of the marinade and place two skillets over medium heat. Heat 1 tablespoon of the regular oil in each and divide the fish skin side down between them, cooking for one minute; it's nice to get a slight gold color on the skin. Turn carefully, reduce the heat to low and cook for another minute.

Ladle the broth and vegetables into bowls and place two fish fillets on each. Serve with a dollop of sauce and offer the rest in a bowl.

beluga lentil, roasted grape, and red belgian endive salad

Whoever thought of calling black lentils "beluga" was a marketing genius. Of course, it's basically a gimmick—they don't taste any better than geen lentils—but the moniker makes them seem luxurious (yes, lentils now have that much cachet …) and their color is fantastic. It makes you think up all kinds of painterly platefuls on the black and crimson theme. You can add crumbled goat cheese or a blue cheese to the dish, and chopped toasted walnuts work well, too.

SERVES 4 AS A LIGHT MEAL

2 tablespoons olive oil

½ red onion, finely chopped

½ celery stick, finely chopped

1 garlic clove, finely chopped

1⅓ cups black lentils

¼ cup extra virgin olive oil, plus extra for the endive

1 tablespoon white balsamic vinegar

good squeeze of lemon juice, plus extra for the endive

salt and black pepper

2 tablespoons coarsely chopped flat-leaf parsley leaves

1 cup seedless red grapes, broken up into sprigs (not too small, because they shrink on cooking)

1½ teaspoons balsamic vinegar

2 small heads of red Belgian endives

Heat 1 tablespoon of the regular olive oil in a saucepan and add the onion and celery. Sauté until the vegetables are soft but not browned. Add the garlic and cook for another two minutes, then add the lentils and enough water to cover by about 2 inches. Bring to a boil, then reduce the heat and simmer until the lentils are tender (check after 15 minutes; lentils need different cooking times, depending on their age). Drain and add the extra virgin oil, white balsamic vinegar, lemon juice, salt and black pepper, and parsley. The lentils should be moist but not swimming in oil. Let cool to room temperature.

For the grapes, preheat the oven to 400°F. Put the grapes on a baking sheet and drizzle with the remaining 1 tablespoon of regular olive oil and the regular balsamic vinegar. Bake in the hot oven for 15–20 minutes.

Break the endives into leaves. Arrange them on plates, drizzle with extra virgin oil, and squeeze some lemon over them. Spoon the lentils on top and finish with grapes.

celeriac, radicchio, fennel, and apple salad with hazelnuts

This was inspired by rémoulade, but I didn't want to make it with just mayonnaise (I find that a bit cloying). It's good as a side salad, particularly with hot-smoked salmon or smoked mackerel (in which case, do use the horseradish; in fact, if it is to accompany smoked fish, you can use both dill and horseradish). It's good, too, to cut through the richness of both roasted pork and cheese.

SERVES 4 AS A SIDE DISH

FOR THE SALAD

juice of ½ lemon

¼ head of celeriac

1 small fennel bulb

2 small tart apples, preferably tawny- or red-skinned

¼ head of radicchio, shredded

1 tablespoon chopped dill leaves or freshly grated horseradish

½ cup toasted hazelnuts, coarsely chopped

2 teaspoons poppy seeds (optional)

FOR THE DRESSING

1½ tablespoons Greek yogurt

2 tablespoons mayonnaise

½ teaspoon Dijon mustard, or to taste

¼ tablespoon cider vinegar

2 tablespoons olive oil

¼ teaspoon honey

salt and black pepper

Put the lemon juice into a mixing bowl. Peel the celeriac and cut the flesh into matchsticks, tossing them into the bowl containing the lemon juice as you work to stop the celeriac from discoloring.

Quarter the fennel, trim the tops, and remove any coarse outer leaves. Core each quarter. Using a sharp knife or a mandoline slicer, cut the fennel into wafer-thin slices. Toss the fennel into the bowl with the celeriac.

Halve and core the apples and cut into matchsticks, immediately adding them to the bowl and tossing in the lemon.

To make the dressing, put the yogurt into a bowl and, using a fork, mix in the other ingredients with 1 tablespoon of water. At some stages, it might seem that the mixture won't come together into a smooth amalgam, but just keep whisking. Taste for seasoning and balance.

Add the dressing, radicchio, dill or horseradish, and hazelnuts to the celeriac bowl and stir everything together. Taste for seasoning, you may want a little more mustard as well as salt or black pepper. Transfer to a serving bowl and sprinkle with poppy seeds (if using).

carrot, cabbage, and apple salad with caraway

A big, sprawling, healthy salad with plenty of crunch and Scandi flavorings. If you have young kale, you can add it raw (just remove and discard the firm central ribs and shred the leaves). Add whatever seeds you fancy (pumpkin, sunflower, sesame, or flaxseed).

SERVES 6 AS A SIDE DISH

FOR THE DRESSING

1 teaspoon caraway seeds

1½ tablespoons honey

2 teaspoons whole-grain mustard

juice of 1 lemon

salt and black pepper

¼ cup canola oil

FOR THE SALAD

¼ red cabbage

¼ savoy cabbage

1 tart, firm apple

1 large carrot, peeled

10 radishes

To make the dressing, bruise the caraway seeds in a mortar and pestle to release their fragrance. Put the honey, mustard, and half the lemon juice into a small bowl. Add the salt, black pepper, and caraway. Now add the canola oil gradually, whisking with a fork as you do so. Taste for seasoning.

Remove the tough core from each cabbage quarter and discard. Pull off any slightly soft or discolored outer leaves, then shred the cabbages finely. Halve and core the apple (no need to peel it) and cut it into matchsticks. Immediately toss in the remaining lemon juice to stop the apple from discoloring. Trim the carrot and cut it into matchsticks, too. Trim the radishes and cut them finely (use a mandoline slicer if you have one).

Toss all the vegetables and the apple in a bowl with the dressing. Taste for seasoning, then serve.

another fruity salad ... farro, hazelnuts, grapes, and figs

Beautiful. And very autumnal. Add cheese to make a more substantial main course dish (goat cheese or a blue are good). Put 1 tablespoon white balsamic vinegar, ¼ cup hazelnut or walnut oil, 2 tablespoons fruity extra virgin olive oil, and ½ teaspoon honey into a small bowl, season, and whisk with a fork to make a dressing. Put 1 cup semi-pearl farro in a saucepan, cover with water, and bring to a boil. Reduce the heat to a simmer and cook for 20–25 minutes; it should be soft but still have a little bite. Drain, season, and add the juice of ½ lemon and 1 tablespoon olive oil. Let cool to room temperature. Taste for seasoning; farro can take quite a bit. Add the leaves from 1 head of red Belgian endive, 3 cups watercress or arugula, coarse stems removed, 8 ripe figs, stems snipped off, halved, ¼ cup halved seedless black grapes, and 1 tablespoon toasted hazelnuts, coarsely chopped. Gently toss with the vinaigrette. Serve immediately. Serves 4–6 as a side dish.

the question of lunch

Proper weekday lunches are a thing of the past. We are all, apparently, too busy. Sometimes I watch old French and Italian movies just to see what a civilized lunch culture was like. Antipasti *and* a main course? Wow, those were the days.

I'm guilty of demoting lunch myself. I eat it at my desk, but at least that also happens to be the kitchen table (however, the laptop remains open). This isn't a great way to live, but it's not my job to call for a change in modern working habits. I want to help you reclaim lunch, even if you eat it while surfing the net and barking orders (or taking them).

If you eat lunch at work, it needs to be portable; if you eat it at home, it needs to be quick. The easy thing—and what I, a carb lover, am always tempted to do—is to make a cheese sandwich. Okay, it's not a bag of Doritos and a bucket of Gatorade, but it's not ideal. There's no veg. It's built on carbs (bad for blood sugar spikes and laying down fat, but better if you are eating proper whole-grain bread). With a sandwich, I am usually hungry again by four o'clock. I tried to work out—apart from laziness—what made me choose it so often. I concluded that I didn't think I "should" have anything more elaborate. In our workaholic culture, it's hard to think we "deserve" to stop and eat a considered meal. But it's the second chance in every twenty-four hours for some food pleasure, and the meal that needs to keep us going until dinner. It's also a chance to eat food that is really *good* for you.

I had to work hard, but I've managed to change my lunch habits. If you aren't worried about carb intake, then a sandwich (on whole-grain bread) is fine, but look at incorporating vegetables. There are loads of things in this book that can work inside two slices of bread (houmous, carrot salads, Thai chicken salad, and roasted tomatoes and avocado for starters). If you are watching your carb intake, you can halve the bread quotient by having a tartine (use a slice of toasted sourdough) or smørrebrød (a slice of rye) instead. And for some reason—perhaps its visual nature—the open sandwich lends itself more to creativity.

If we journey beyond bread, there are masses of healthy dishes to make and keep in the refrigerator, or seal in a box and take to work. You can incorporate these into daily cooking, preparing extra to create a stash of good things. Grilled eggplants, raw vegetables with punchy Asian dressings, lentils, beans, and whole grains are perfect (and grains and beans really fill you up), and there are salads for every season in this book that you can make ahead. Keep dressings (there's plenty of options on page 103, and throughout the book) in jars in the refrigerator to anoint leaves (and get more greens under your belt) at the last minute.

Then there are things you don't even need a recipe for, but that will do you the world of good: watercress and orange salad; a salad of chicken, blueberries, and brown rice; avocado vinaigrette; sliced tomatoes with olive oil, garlic, and chopped anchovies. Some of the dishes I suggest for breakfast are worth considering, too. Stick a list of options on the refrigerator door. Life really is too short to eat a cheese sandwich every day. *Le déjeuner, il pranzo*—call it what you will—lunch can open the door to a world of possibilities. You may even become the subject of lunch box envy.

lunches for work or home

Goat curd and blueberry salad (add spelt)   17

Feta and orange salad with honeyed almonds   18

Spring couscous   20

Lentilles en salade   30

Radish and caper salad   30

Hot-smoked salmon, rye, and beet salad   96

Grilled zucchini and eggplants with tarator   106

Macedonian grilled vegetable salad   107

White beans and roasted peppers with hilbeh   114

Beluga lentil, roasted grape, and red Belgian endive salad   172

Celeriac, radicchio, and apple salad   174

Carrot, cabbage, and apple salad with caraway   175

Grilled eggplants with date and yogurt salad   187

Kisir   187

Burmese hot and sour cabbage salad   198

Smoked mackerel and beet relish   206

Thai-style chicken and mango salad   216

Burmese-style chicken salad   216

Crazy salad   230

Mustardy farro and roasted winter vegetable salad   269

Moroccan carrot salad   272

Spiced carrot, date, and sesame salad   273

Carrot and daikon salad with peanut dressing   274

Mandalay carrot salad   277

Fruited rye grains with gorgonzola   287

Avocado, raw salmon, and brown rice salad   306

more lunches for home

40   Rice paper rolls, filling only (eat it with brown rice)

43   Japanese rice bowl

48–49   Any of the broccoli dishes

53   Salmon tartare with cucumber and rye crackers

66   Shaved vegetables with lemon and olive oil

75   Vietnamese vermicelli and crispy veg (omit the beef)

157   Turkish poached eggs with spinach and yogurt

202   Roasted tomatoes, hummus, and spinach on toast

238   Roasted tomatoes and avocado on toast

244   Soy mushrooms with egg ribbons and sesame

259   Winter greens with onions, tahini, and sumac

282   Kale pesto with whole-wheat linguine

292   Cranberry beans and kale with anchovy sauce

295   Soba noodles with chile, broccoli, egg, and sesame

Any soup or broth

32   Silken tofu, shrimp, and chive soup

35   Peruvian chicken soup

88   Chilled tomato soup with cumin and avocado

94   Cucumber and yogurt soup with walnuts

167   Eastern broth with shallots, lime, and cilantro

169   Carrot and ginger soup with cucumber raita

226   Lentil and roasted tomato soup with saffron

258   Japanese family chicken, egg, and rice bowl

260   Spinach, pomegranate, and bulgur soup

261   Kale, salmon, and barley soup with buttermilk

fall menu the first meal with pumpkin

roasted veg with agresto | cavolo pilaf with figs | watercress salad | blackberry-apple rye galette

I love this kind of meal. There's no meat in sight yet it is rich, satisfying, and deep. And imagine what all these vegetables will do for you. The dessert isn't healthy—there's a lot of sugar in it—but the pastry is made of rye flour and, of course, there's plenty of fruit. I've suggested other options, if you do want to serve something sweet that is better for you.

roasted pumpkin and jerusalem artichokes with agresto

Full of autumnal flavors, sweet with roasted vegetables and nuts. Agresto is an Italian sauce, good with meaty fish and chicken as well as with vegetables. Don't omit the bitter red endive leaves; they are necessary to contrast with the sweet artichokes and pumpkin.

SERVES 6 AS A MAIN COURSE WITH ANOTHER DISH, OR 8 AS A SIDE

FOR THE VEGETABLES

2 lb Jerusalem artichokes

juice of 1½ lemons

3¼ lb pumpkin or winter squash

salt and black pepper

3 tablespoons olive oil

3 large or 4 small heads of red Belgian endive

1½ tablespoons extra virgin olive oil

FOR THE AGRESTO

3 garlic cloves

good pinch of sea salt flakes

1½ cups chopped walnuts

⅔ cup blanched hazelnuts, coarsely chopped

1 cup extra virgin olive oil

1 cup verjuice or white wine vinegar

leaves from 1 large bunch of flat-leaf parsley, chopped

Preheat the oven to 350°F. Scrub the Jerusalem artichokes thoroughly and cut off any tufty parts. You don't need to peel them (too much work, and besides their skins look wonderful and give texture). Halve them lengthwise and put them into a bowl of water mixed with the juice of 1 lemon to stop them from discoloring. Halve the pumpkin or squash and scoop out the seeds and fibers. Cut the flesh into wedges, about 1 inch thick at the thickest part. Peel each slice.

Drain the Jerusalem artichokes and put them and the pumpkin in a roasting pan in which they can lie in a single layer. Season and add the regular olive oil. Toss everything around, put into the oven, and cook for 40 minutes, until the vegetables are tender and the pumpkin slightly charred at the edges.

Meanwhile, put the garlic into a large mortar with the salt and grind to a paste. Add the nuts and pound these. Add the extra virgin oil gradually, pounding, then the verjuice. Stir in the parsley and pound; you want a coarse puree. Add black pepper and taste for salt.

Separate the leaves of the endive heads and put them in a serving bowl with the rest of the lemon juice and the extra virgin oil. Season and toss. Push the greens to the outside of the dish, spoon the roasted vegetables into the center, and serve with the agresto.

cavolo nero and bulgur pilaf with glazed figs

Bulgur is nutty but also soft, so it's one of the most usable grains. If you can't get cavolo nero, which is also known as Tuscan kale and black kale, use regular curly kale instead. Add chunks of labneh (see page 104), crumbled feta or goat cheese, and toasted hazelnuts to make the dish more substantial. Ideally, the figs should be ready at the same time as the bulgur, so track back the time for cooking (but they can wait at room temperature if you'd prefer to do them in advance).

SERVES 6

FOR THE PILAF

1 fennel bulb

1 red onion, cut into semicircle slices

1½ tablespoons olive oil

2 garlic cloves, crushed

pinch of dried red pepper flakes (optional)

5 juniper berries, crushed

1¼ cups bulgur wheat

1½ cups chicken stock or vegetable stock

2 strips of orange zest

salt and black pepper

1 lb cavolo nero or kale

1½ tablespoons extra virgin olive oil

good squeeze of orange juice

FOR THE GLAZED FIGS

8 plump, firm figs

3 tablespoons honey

2 tablespoons balsamic vinegar

Preheat the oven to 400°F.

Trim the tips from the fennel (reserve any feathery leaves), then quarter the bulbs and remove any tough or discolored outer leaves. Carefully cut out the core at the bottom of each (don't cut off so much that the fennel falls apart). Sauté the onion and fennel in the regular olive oil in a heavy saucepan. When the vegetables are tinged with gold in patches, add the garlic, chile (if using), and juniper and cook for another couple of minutes. Add the bulgur to the pan, pour in the stock, add the orange zest, and season. Bring to a boil, then reduce the heat to its lowest, cover, and cook for about 15 minutes. The stock will be absorbed. Remove the pan from the heat and let sit, still covered, for another 15 minutes.

Meanwhile, snip the stem from each fig, then halve the fruits lengthwise. Put them in a gratin dish where they can sit snugly in a single layer. (If there is too much space around, the moisture evaporates and they burn.) Drizzle the honey and vinegar over the figs and season. Roast in the oven for 20 minutes, spooning the juices over a couple of times during the cooking. The figs should be dark, rich looking, and tender, but should not have collapsed.

At the same time, remove and discard the tough central ribs from the cavolo nero. Wash the leaves and chop them (not too small). Put them into a saucepan of boiling water and cook for four minutes. Drain really well, season, and stir in the extra virgin oil.

Remove the orange zest from the bulgur and fork it through to fluff it up. Now fork the cavolo nero into the bulgur and check the seasoning. Put into a warm, wide, shallow serving bowl and put the figs on top, drizzling the cooking juices from the figs over as well. Squeeze the orange juice over the whole thing and serve with the roasted vegetables and agresto (see page 178).

watercress and carrot salad

I try to get watercress in at least once a day and it's not hard if you make a simple salad to eat after or with your main course (or make it the basis of a main course salad). Its health properties are simply undeniable (you can read more about it on page 253).

Watercress is slightly peppery, but not so assertive that you can't blend it with plenty of other ingredients. It goes with fresh-tasting foods—fennel, cucumber, dill, and mint—and contrasts well with sweet, rich, or meaty ingredients such as roasted bell peppers and pumpkins, apples and pears, cherries, and wild mushrooms. It's good tossed into warm dishes (such as pilafs), where it wilts a little, but not so much that it slumps.

It's available at different times of the year, depending on where you live (Wholefoods is a good place to look), although interestingly it was traditionally harvested when there was an "r" in the month, so it used to be a leafy green for the colder months of the year. You can use other types of cress, such as upland cress, curly cress, or land cress, or arugula instead.

SERVES 6–8

FOR THE SALAD

3–4 carrots

½ bunch of watercress, coarse stems removed

1½ teaspoons mixed seeds (optional)

2 teaspoons poppy seeds

FOR THE DRESSING

1½ teaspoons sherry vinegar

1 tablespoon orange juice

1 teaspoon Dijon mustard

1 teaspoon honey

salt and black pepper

¼ cup extra virgin olive oil

If you have thin carrots, you can cut them lengthwise into quarters. For bigger carrots, either cut them into matchsticks (time-consuming) or ribbons. To make ribbons (which is easier with bigger carrots), halve them lengthwise then, using a potato peeler, create ribbons by pushing the peeler along the carrot. You always end up with pieces that can't be used this way, so just keep them for soup (or eat them).

To make the dressing, put everything except the extra virgin oil into a small bowl and whisk with a fork. Now add the oil gradually, whisking as you work. Check for seasoning. This is a strong dressing, but you're dressing fairly robust ingredients. Toss with the carrots, watercress, and mixed seeds (if using). Sprinkle with the poppy seeds (they look great against the carrot) and serve.

blackberry and apple rye galette

This only just gets inclusion in a healthy book, I'm not going to pretend that pastry is actually "good" for you. But it does use rye flour and there's plenty of fruit here. You could serve a no-pastry fruity dessert instead: baked apples, or stewed apples and blackberries with yogurt and a little maple syrup would be wonderful. But this is the only pastry in the whole book and is so gorgeously autumnal—it's the nutty rye flour in it—that I couldn't resist.

SERVES 6

FOR THE PASTRY DOUGH

1 cup rye flour

1 cup all-purpose flour, plus extra to dust

pinch of salt

1¼ sticks cold butter, cut into cubes

2 tablespoons packed light brown sugar

1 egg yolk

FOR THE FILLING

2 sweet, crisp apples

juice of ½ lemon

finely grated zest of 1 orange

¼ cup firmly packed light brown sugar

1½ cups blackberries

⅔ cup hazelnuts

FOR THE GLAZE

1 egg, lightly beaten

¼ cup granulated sugar

Sift the flours together, then add the grains caught in the sifter back into the mixture. Add the salt and rub in the butter with your fingers until you have small pea-size lumps. Rub in the sugar, too, then add the egg yolk and 1½ teaspoons of very cold water, a little at a time, until you can bring the mixture together into a ball. Press it into a disk, wrap in plastic wrap, and chill for an hour.

Unwrap the dough and roll it out on a lightly floured surface to a circle of about 13 inches, trying to roll it evenly. Move it onto a baking sheet lined with parchment paper. Don't worry if the dough is crumbly; just patch it up. This is a forgiving type of tart because it is freeform.

Peel, core, and slice the apples, then put them in a bowl with the lemon juice, orange zest, and half the brown sugar. Add the blackberries and toss around with your hands.

Blend the hazelnuts coarsely in a food processor—you should end up with a mixture that is partly ground, partly chunky—and add the rest of the brown sugar.

Sprinkle the nut mixture on the dough, leaving a width of about 2 inches all the way round. Put the fruit on top of this, then carefully lift up the edges of the dough to enclose the fruit all the way around. Again, just patch the dough together if it breaks; nobody will ever know. Put the galette into the coldest part of the refrigerator for 30 minutes (or your freezer, if it's big enough, for 10 minutes or so). Preheat the oven to 340°F.

For the glaze, mix the egg with 2 tablespoons of the sugar and brush it over the dough. Sprinkle the remaining 2 tablespoons sugar over the whole tart. Bake in the hot oven for 50–60 minutes. The pastry should be golden brown and crusted with sugar, and the fruit should be tender.

persimmon, pomegranate, and red belgian endive salad with goat cheese and toasted hazelnuts

There are some combinations I can't get away from, and fruit with cheese and nuts is one of them. The loveliness of persimmons eludes some people, but it's often because they eat them when they are unripe. The fruits for this can't be too ripe—once persimmons are soft, it is hard to cut them without them falling apart—but leave those you've bought in a bowl in the kitchen and keep checking them (pushing the flesh gently) to gauge how ripe they are. You get to know, with experience, when it's the right time to eat them.

SERVES 4

½ teaspoon white balsamic vinegar

salt and black pepper

scant ¼ teaspoon Dijon mustard

1¼ tablespoons extra virgin olive oil (don't use anything too strong, and fruity instead of grassy is best)

1¼ tablespoons hazelnut oil

2 head of red Belgian endive

½ bunch of watercress

2 persimmons

1 pomegranate

3 tablespoons halved hazelnuts

5 oz creamy goat cheese, broken into chunks

Make the dressing so it's ready to go. Just put the white balsamic, seasoning, and Dijon mustard into a small bowl and whisk in the extra virgin and hazelnut oils with a fork. Check for seasoning.

Separate the leaves of the endives (don't use the bottoms) and remove and discard the coarse stems from the watercress. Put all the leaves into a wide, shallow bowl.

Remove the calyx from each persimmon and slice them as finely as you can; use either a thin knife, such as a fish filleting knife, or a mandoline slicer.

Halve the pomegranates and try to dislodge the seeds by hitting the fruit with a wooden spoon while holding it over a bowl, cut side down; if the fruit is ripe enough, the seeds should just fall out. If this doesn't work (it doesn't always), then gouge out the seeds with a spoon. You do have to go through the laborious task of removing the white membrane around the seeds.

Put the nuts into a dry skillet over medium heat and toast them; this can take as little as 30 seconds so keep watching or they will burn. Put the nuts into a bowl to cool.

Add the persimmons and nuts to the leaves with three-quarters of the dressing and toss. Now add the goat cheese and sprinkle the pomegranate seeds on top. Drizzle with the rest of the dressing and serve immediately.

grilled eggplants with date, walnut, and yogurt salad

A good midweek dinner. Dates are high in sugar, which is why they were eaten by desert nomads; it was said you could survive on dates and camel milk. You can use less sweet dried fruits (such as cranberries or dried sour cherries), but dates have a wonderful affinity with eggplants.

SERVES 4

½ cup Greek yogurt

½ cup pitted and coarsely chopped dates

½ cup toasted walnuts, coarsely chopped

⅓ cup olive oil

2 garlic cloves, crushed

4 eggplants

salt and black pepper

juice of 1 lemon

To make the salad, stir the yogurt to loosen it, then add the dates, walnuts, 1 tablespoon of the olive oil, and the garlic.

Remove the stems from the eggplants, then cut lengthwise into slices ½ inch thick. Brush both sides with some of the remaining oil, season them, and heat a ridged grill pan (or just use a skillet). Cook on both sides until slightly charred and soft. You'll need to do this in batches and keep adjusting the heat; first you need to brown the eggplants on each side, then reduce the heat to cook them through. When the slices are ready, squeeze lemon juice over them, season again, and layer up in a serving dish.

Serve the eggplants with the date salad and Kisir (see below).

kisir

An autumnal tabbouleh, best when the tomatoes are still good and the pomegranates are arriving.

SERVES 4

1 tablespoon olive oil

1 small red onion, finely chopped

2 garlic cloves, finely chopped

2½ teaspoons ground cumin

1 red chile, seeded, shredded

1½ tablespoons tomato paste

1½ cups bulgur wheat

4 well-flavored plum tomatoes, peeled, seeded, and chopped

handful of mint leaves, torn

1¼ cups finely chopped parsley

juice of 1 lemon, or to taste

⅓ cup extra virgin olive oil

1½ tablespoons pomegranate molasses

seeds from 1 pomegranate

Heat the regular oil in a saucepan and sauté the onion and garlic for two minutes. Add the cumin and chile and cook for a minute. Stir in the tomato paste and add ⅔ cup of boiling water. Mix in the bulgur, remove from the heat, cover, and let sit for 15 minutes. Fork through the grains gently to separate them. You will be worried the mixture seems dry and that some of the grains are "nutty"; don't worry. You are about to add wet ingredients that will make all the difference, so resist the temptation to add more water.

Fork in the tomatoes and herbs. Mix the lemon juice, extra virgin oil, and pomegranate molasses in a small bowl. The bulgur shouldn't be too dry but it shouldn't be soaked, so add three-quarters of the dressing, then judge to see whether you need more. (You can add more oil or lemon if you want to, but don't make it soggy.) Toss in the pomegranate seeds. Taste for seasoning; it needs a generous amount. The kisir will sit until you want to serve it. You can keep it in the refrigerator, covered, but return to room temperature to serve.

japanese eggplants with miso

The first time I tasted this dish I couldn't believe it: the salty-sweet miso topping soaks into the eggplant flesh, completely flavoring it. It makes the best of the eggplant's spongelike texture. I like it made with a mixture of sweet and salty miso, but you can use white miso alone (the sweet one), if you prefer. (It's white by name, but yellow in color, just to confuse things, available online.) Look for togarashi, a Japanese spice blend containing chile, orange peel, sesame seeds, and ginger, from Japanese food suppliers or gourmet food stores.

SERVES 4 AS A SIDE DISH

6 long, thin eggplants

2 tablespoons peanut oil

2 tablespoons white miso paste

2 tablespoons brown miso paste

2 teaspoons packed light brown sugar

3 tablespoons mirin (Japanese rice wine) or dry sherry

1 tablespoon sake or dry sherry

¼ teaspoon (or less, it's powerful) togarashi, or chili powder

1 tablespoon toasted white sesame seeds

Preheat the oven to 350°F.

Halve the eggplants and cut a lattice pattern on the flesh side without cutting right through to the skin. Brush with the oil and put into an ovenproof dish. Bake in the hot oven for 40 minutes, or until completely tender, covering with aluminum foil about halfway through.

Meanwhile, mix together the miso pastes, sugar, mirin, and sake in a small saucepan and heat gently. Remove from the heat and add the togarashi.

Spread the miso mixture on top of each eggplant and return to the oven. Cook for about another five minutes, until golden brown. The tops of the eggplant halves should be moist and shimmering, not at all dry. Sprinkle with the toasted sesame seeds and serve.

middle eastern-spiced squash and white beans with lemon and mint

I use cannellini beans here, but you can use navy, cranberry, or chickpeas (garbanzo beans), however, chickpeas produce a less thickly textured dish. If you prefer to cook dried beans from scratch, use ¾ cup. Soak them overnight, or for at least 5 hours, then rinse, cover with fresh water, and cook for about an hour, or until only just tender. Don't add any salt until they're cooked.

You don't have to use fresh mint, but do what they do in parts of the Middle East and sauté some dried mint in a couple of tablespoons of olive oil and pour it over the top. It might sound odd but it's good: slightly musty (in a good way). You can, of course, use chopped cilantro or flat-leaf parsley leaves instead of (or as well as) the mint.

SERVES 6

2 tablespoons olive oil

1 large onion, finely chopped

1 large carrot, finely chopped

4 garlic cloves, finely chopped

2 red chiles, seeded
and chopped

5 plum tomatoes, chopped

1 tablespoon ground cumin

1 tablespoon tomato paste

1 butternut or acorn squash
(about 2¼ lb) , peeled, seeded,
and cut into chunks

2 cups vegetable stock or water

salt and black pepper

15 oz can cannellini beans, drained
and rinsed

juice of ½ lemon, plus finely grated
zest of 1 lemon (removed with
a zester)

leaves from 6 sprigs of mint, torn

Heat half the olive oil in a heavy casserole or dutch oven and add the onion and carrot. Cook until the onion is slightly softened and lightly browned. Add the garlic, chiles, and tomatoes and cook for another five minutes or so. Now add the cumin, cook for a minute, then stir in the tomato paste.

Heat the rest of the olive oil in a large skillet and sauté the squash (you'll probably have to do this in batches) until golden brown all over and beginning to soften.

Add the squash to the onion with the stock or water and season. Bring to a boil, then reduce the heat, cover, and cook gently for 40 minutes. After 30 minutes, remove the lid and add the beans.

The dish is ready when the squash is completely tender and the texture is thick. Add the lemon juice and half the zest and check the seasoning. Sprinkle with the mint and the rest of the zest. Serve with bulgur wheat (or bulgur mixed with lentils is wonderful with this dish) and a green vegetable.

play with this ... To make it Italian, add 2 bay leaves and a sprig of rosemary to the squash. Chop 1 garlic clove, the finely grated zest of 1 lemon and 1 tablespoon of rosemary leaves and sprinkle on top. To go Moroccan, add 1 teaspoon ground ginger, ½ cinnamon stick, and ½ tablespoons harissa. Green olives are good, too. Finish off with preserved lemon shreds, cilantro leaves, and toasted slivered almonds. For a Spanish feel, add 2 teaspoon smoked paprika and finish with cilantro and parsley as well.

home-style punjabi lentils (tarka dal)

In a book full of big flavors, this is an oddity. It's muted, plain, some might even describe it as bland. But there are days when it's just what you want. We tend to dress lentils up; here they are cooked with spices, but still very much themselves. From time to time, I try different dals—sweet and sour recipes, chile-hot bowls—but I come back to this. It is kind of the Indian equivalent of our chicken soup. It's grounding and soothing. It's also the perfect central dish on which to hang other brighter flavors if that's what you want; a wonderful plain canvas. Try Kachumber (see page 89) or Ginger and mango relish (see page 220), or just enjoy its total plainness.

SERVES 4

FOR THE DAL

1 cup channa dal, or yellow split peas (chana dal keep their shape better)

½ teaspoon turmeric

1¼ inch ginger root, peeled

salt and black pepper

FOR THE TEMPERING

2 tablespoons sunflower oil

1½ teaspoons cumin seeds

1 teaspoon dried red pepper flakes

1 small red onion, finely sliced

1¼ inch piece of ginger root, peeled and finely chopped

2 garlic cloves, chopped

1 large plum tomato, chopped

½ teaspoon garam masala

2 tablespoons coarsely chopped cilantro leaves (optional)

Put the yellow lentils into a heavy saucepan. Add 2 cups of water, the turmeric, and the chunk of peeled ginger. Don't add any salt because it toughens the lentils. Bring to a boil, then reduce the heat and simmer until the lentils are soft and falling apart. Scoop out the ginger and let the lentils cool slightly.

If you prefer a smooth dal, process it in a blender at this point; it's up to you how you'd like the texture and consistency to be. I like to give half the lentils a quick blend, then mix it with the more coarse-textured dal in the pan. Add a splash more water, if you feel the lentils need it, and season with salt and black pepper.

Now the tempering. Heat the oil in a small skillet and toss in the cumin seeds followed by the red pepper flakes. Swirl them around for about 20 seconds, until they darken. Add the onion and sauté until lighly browned. Stir in the ginger and garlic and cook for another minute. Now add the tomato and garam masala and continue sautéing for two minutes, or until the tomato has softened.

Transfer this masala to the hot dal and add the cilantro (if using). Stir well and serve with brown rice or whole-wheat flatbread. Fresh chutney and some plain yogurt are good alongside.

also try ... **a south indian version** Omit the cumin from the tempering spices and cook 2 teaspoons mustard seeds in the oil for 30 seconds (until they pop), then add about 8 curry leaves and ¼ teaspoon fenugreek seeds. Add the onion and continue to cook as in the main recipe. This usually has 5–6 cups shredded spinach leaves (coarse stems removed) added at the end; they will wilt in the heat.

divine dal

"My daughter is coming home," sighs my friend Roopa, "We ought to be having something celebratory to eat but she says, 'Mama, all I want is *dal chawal*'." I understand Roopa's daughter. "Dal chawal" is just dal and rice. My comfort dish from childhood is ground beef and potatoes. To a child of Indian heritage it is *dal chawal*. And I yearn for it, too. Seat me in an Indian restaurant and *tarka dal* —the most basic, mellow, earthy lentil dish—will be the first thing I order.

There are loads of bean and lentil dishes in this book, but not because they're healthy or because they're a good alternative to meat (offer me a tenderloin steak or a bowl of dal and I'd have real trouble choosing). They're here because I love them. They are primarily earthy and comforting, but not always. Black lentils tossed with watercress, mango, and a creamy Indian dressing is more of a Bollywood number than a gentle lullaby. And mashed chickpeas, the (garbanzo) beans crushed with sautéed onions, loads of garlic, cumin, lemon, and a big dollop of harissa, isn't mellow either. Beans, or legumes, are, in fact, good for you (that's their bonus). They make you feel full, they're "good" carbs and they're a great source of protein. They're cheap, too. My particular love, in this world of dried things, is Indian dals.

The word "dal" simply denotes a split legume, but in India it has come to mean all dried beans and lentils, as well as dishes in which they are the principal ingredient. Apart from the not very specific "tarka dal" (always on the menu in Indian restaurants), dals were a mystery to me. So I took some instruction from Roopa and can now dal-dance all over India. There is a world of dals and, despite their humble constituents, some of the dishes are, to me anyway, utterly luxurious. They are also simplicity itself. The key thing is creaminess—that's what makes dal such a soothing dish—and long, slow cooking delivers that. In fact, the best dals in India are found at roadside shacks. Big pots—called *patilas*— of lentils are cooked on top of the tandoor ovens overnight (so the heat of the oven isn't wasted), ready to eat the next morning.

Dals can be as thin as a brothy soup, or as thick as oatmeal. They don't require stock, just water. As their distinctiveness lies in the spicing, there is no need for extra flavoring from stock. Vegetables—spinach or zucchini—can be added, too (leafy vegetables go in at the end). Once you have the consistency you prefer (simply add more water or keep cooking to get there), the tempering, or *tarka,* is what both finishes and "makes" the dal. Spices, red onions (and sometimes tomatoes) are sautéed, then sprinkled on top and stirred in. In Southern India, the flavorings are curry leaves, fenugreek seeds, and mustard seeds; in the Punjab, cumin, ginger, garlic, chile, and onion.

Now you just have to track down the various beans and lentils (the only difficult thing), so find an Indian grocery store. Then there's the huge pleasure of unloading packages whose names evoke hot Delhi days and cool Bombay nights. Urad dal, chana dal, toor dal, moong dal … a world of comforting exoticism awaits.

indian-spiced spinach and mushrooms with black lentils and paneer

This is not at all authentic. I wanted something that had Indian spicing and ingredients but that kept its shape and had separate, although integral, parts and this is the result. You don't have to use paneer, it's good without it, but it adds another texture. And I love its creaminess against the lentils.

SERVES 6

3½ tablespoons peanut oil, plus extra for the paneer

2 onions, chopped

2 small red chiles, seeded and finely chopped

2 inch cinnamon stick

1 cup black lentils

salt and black pepper

juice of 1 lime

2 tablespoons finely chopped cilantro leaves

3 garlic cloves, finely chopped

1 inch piece of ginger root, peeled and finely chopped

1¼ lb cremini mushrooms, sliced

1 tablespoon unsalted butter (optional)

¾ teaspoon ground cumin

¾ teaspoon ground coriander

2 large tomatoes, chopped

2 (5 oz) packages baby spinach

4 oz paneer, cut into squares (optional)

1 teaspoon garam masala

3½ tablespoons plain yogurt

Heat 1 tablespoon of the oil in a saucepan and add one of the chopped onions. Sauté until soft and golden brown, then add one of the chiles and the cinnamon and cook for a minute. Add the lentils, cover with plenty of water, and bring to a boil. Reduce the heat and simmer for 15–30 minutes, depending on the age of the lentils, until the lentils are tender. Quickly drain the lentils and return to the warm pan. Season well with salt and black pepper and stir in the lime juice and cilantro. Cover to keep warm.

Meanwhile, sauté the remaining onion in a sauté pan in another 1 tablespoon of oil. When the onion is pale gold, add the garlic, remaining chile, and the ginger and cook for another minute.

In a separate skillet, using the remaining oil, sauté the mushrooms briskly over medium-high heat, in batches, until they are a good color. Add them to the onion mixture. Add the butter (if using, it is really for flavor) and cook for another few minutes, then stir in the ground cumin and coriander and the tomatoes. Sauté until the tomatoes are soft. Reduce the heat and cook for about 10 minutes, until the tomatoes are almost collapsing and have reduced. Add the spinach, in batches, and turn it over in the mixture; the leaves will wilt and give off moisture. Whack up the heat to boil off some of the liquid if it's watery.

Brush the cubes of paneer with a little oil and either grill them in a ridged grill pan or quickly brown them in a skillet.

Stir the garam masala and the yogurt into the mushrooms and heat through, but do not let boil. Check for seasoning. Serve the mushrooms with the paneer sprinkled on top and the lentils spooned around the side.

pilaf of mixed grains, sweet potato, and fennel with avocado "cream"

This is wonderful but pretty starchy when served as a main course, even with the puree. It needs a spicy vegetable dish alongside and plenty of fresh salad greens. It works as a good side dish with meat, too. The quinoa doesn't have to be red, but it does look good if you can find it.

SERVES 4 AS A MAIN DISH,
6–8 AS A SIDE

2 sweet potatoes, peeled

3 tablespoons olive oil

1½ tablespoons balsamic vinegar

salt and black pepper

2 small fennel bulbs

½ cup wild rice

½ cup red quinoa

1 onion, finely chopped

2 garlic cloves, finely chopped

2 red chiles, seeded and
finely chopped

⅔ cup bulgur wheat

1¾ cups chicken stock or
vegetable stock

FOR THE AVOCADO CREAM

2 ripe avocados

juice of 2 limes

1 red chile, seeded and
finely chopped

1 garlic clove, crushed

1 tablespoon olive oil

¼ tablespoon sherry vinegar,
or more to taste

Preheat the oven to 375°F. Cut the sweet potatoes into 1½ inch chunks. Put these in a roasting pan and toss with 2 tablespoons of the oil, the balsamic vinegar, and seasoning. Put into the hot oven and cook for one hour.

About halfway through, trim the tips from the fennel (reserve any feathery leaves), quarter the bulbs, and remove any tough or discolored outer leaves. Carefully cut out the core at the bottom of each (don't cut off so much that the fennel falls apart). Add to the sweet potatoes for the last 20 minutes of their cooking time, tossing in the juices. When ready, both should be tender and slightly charred.

Meanwhile, put the wild rice into a saucepan and cover with water. Bring to a boil and cook for 45 minutes, or according to the package directions.

Toast the quinoa in a dry skillet for two minutes. Put the remaining 1 tablespoon of oil into a saucepan and sauté the onion until soft and lightly browned. Add the garlic and chiles and cook for a couple of minutes, then add the toasted quinoa, bulgur, and stock. Season. Bring to a boil, then reduce to a simmer, cover, and cook for 15 minutes. You should have a panful of dry-ish, fluffy grains.

Drain the wild rice, rinse in boiling water, and gently fork it into the quinoa and bulgur with the vegetables. Check for seasoning.

Prepare the avocado just before serving, because it discolors if it sits for long. Halve, pit, and scoop out the flesh, then mash it with all the other ingredients until smooth. Taste for seasoning (you may want a little more vinegar). Serve with the pilaf.

try this ... with minted yogurt
Mix together 1 cup Greek yogurt, 1 crushed garlic clove, about 20 mint leaves, coarsely chopped, and 2 tablespoons extra virgin olive oil. Serve instead of, or as well as, the avocado cream.

fall menu go east, my friend

persimmon and avocado salad | burmese chile fish | citrus compote with ginger snow

Eating more healthily has drawn me deeper and deeper into the cuisines of the East, particularly the food of Vietnam and Japan. The ingredients are healthy, the flavors are clean, hot or mouth-puckeringly citrusy, and attack the front of your mouth. You quite often leave the table feeling that you've had a jog around a forest. The food is usually very pretty, too, your pleasure starts as you look at your plate. This menu is a perfect illustration of why the east is a good hunting ground for dishes that are irresistible and good for you.

japanese persimmon and avocado salad with ginger

I serve the dressing on the side here for guests to add their own, because the plate topped with snowy white daikon furls just looks so beautiful as you take it to the table. It's hard to find perfectly ripe persimmons, so you need to think ahead: buy them in advance and let them ripen at home.

SERVES 4

FOR THE DRESSING

1 tablespoon rice vinegar,
or to taste

juice of ½ lime

2½ tablespoons ginger syrup from
a preserved ginger jar, or to taste

2 tablespoons peanut oil

2 teaspoons dark soy sauce,
or to taste

1 inch piece of ginger root, peeled
and grated, or to taste

FOR THE SALAD

2 large, just-ripe avocados

juice of 1 lime

salt and black pepper

3 just-ripe persimmons

6 oz daikon, peeled

2 cups mizuna and baby leaves

4 teaspoons black sesame seeds

To make the dressing, just whisk everything together. Taste for a balance of hot, sour, salty, and sweet, adjusting the ginger, vinegar, soy, or syrup as you prefer.

Halve the avocados and remove the pits (hit the blade of a wide knife into the pit, twist, and pull the pit out; it should attach to the blade). Cut into thin slices and carefully peel each slice (I find this approach produces the most intact, neat slices). Immediately squeeze on some lime juice and season; you always seem to get a better salad if you season the avocado separately.

Halve the persimmons and cut out the calyxes. Cut into slices and carefully peel each slice. Squeeze lime juice on these, too.

For the daikon, you can do one of two things: either shave into slices (use a mandoline slicer or a sharp knife); or cut into furls by shaving off slices, using your knife in a circular movement (the results look a little like pencil shavings instead of slices).

Spread the greens in a wide, shallow bowl, then arrange slices of persimmon, avocado, and daikon on top. Sprinkle with the sesame seeds and serve immediately with the dressing on the side.

burmese chile fish with hot-and-sour salad

This is adapted from a recipe in Naomi Duguid's *Burma: Rivers of Flavor*, one of my favorite cookbooks. It's a great quick dish.

SERVES 4

1¾ lb fish fillets, such as porgy, halibut, or red snapper, skinned

2 teaspoons turmeric

½ teaspoon salt

8 shallots, finely chopped

½ teaspoon sea salt flakes

1 inch piece of ginger root, peeled and chopped

4 garlic cloves, peeled and chopped

1½ tablespoons peanut oil

1 dried red chile, crumbled

1 tablespoon Thai fish sauce

lime juice, to taste

FOR THE HOT AND SOUR SALAD

¼ head of savoy cabbage

8 shallots

10 radishes, trimmed

1 red chile, seeded and finely sliced

3 tablespoons Thai fish sauce

3 tablespoons lime juice

1 teaspoon superfine sugar, or more to taste

Rinse the fish, pat dry, and feel along the surface for any little bones that may be left. Pull out any you find. Cut the fish into 2 inch pieces and toss it in a bowl with the turmeric and salt. Turn the fish to coat and set aside for 15 minutes.

Pound the shallots in a large mortar with half the sea salt flakes (the salt acts as an abrasive) until you have a paste, remove, then do the same with the ginger and garlic, using the rest of the salt.

Make the salad so that it's ready to go once the fish is cooked. Remove and discard any discolored or tough outer leaves and the core of the cabbage and shred the leaves finely. Put into a serving bowl. Slice the shallots as finely as you can (use a mandoline slicer if you have one) and do the same with the radishes. Add to the bowl with the chile. In a small bowl, mix the fish sauce, lime juice, and sugar, stirring to help the sugar dissolve. Taste; you may want a little more sugar. Toss the vegetables with the dressing. (There should be plenty of dressing; all the vegetables should be coated.)

Heat ½ tablespoon of the oil and sauté the ground shallots over medium heat until soft and starting to turn golden brown. Add a little more of the oil, the pounded garlic and ginger, and the dried chile and cook for another couple of minutes, until the whole mixture is soft and golden brown. Add a little more oil (you may not need all of what remains) and the fish and cook for 1½ minutes, then turn the pieces over and cook for another minute or so on the other side. It should be lovely and golden brown. Add the fish sauce and taste; you may want to add more. Squeeze in some lime and serve with the hot-and-sour salad and some brown rice.

citrus compote with ginger snow

This is magical—the granita does look like snow—and cleansing. It's so thirst quenching it makes me think of the little boy, Nene, in Leonardo Sciascia's novel *The Wine-dark Sea*. Nene tells his traveling companions that when he gets to Catania he is "going to eat a bucketful" of granita. He must have had this one in mind.

It might seem like a lot of citrus fruit but, as you remove the segments, a lot of the fruit gets left behind. (If you prefer not to segment the fruit, you can slice them instead and use only four of them.) You don't have to make a syrup for the fruit at all, of course. You can just remove the segments and serve them with the granita.

SERVES 4–6

FOR THE GINGER SNOW

¾ cup granulated sugar

finely grated zest of 2 limes (removed with a zester), plus the juice of 3

½ cup peeled and grated ginger root

FOR THE COMPOTE

2 pink grapefruits

2 red grapefruits

2 oranges or white grapefruits

½ cup granulated sugar

juice of 2 limes

To make the granita, mix the sugar, zest, and ginger in a saucepan, pour in 2½ cups of water, and gently bring to a boil, stirring to help the sugar dissolve. Once it's come to a boil, reduce the heat and simmer for two minutes. Let the liquid cool.

Strain the liquid, add the lime juice, and pour the mixture into a freezer-proof shallow container, preferably a metal one. Put it into the freezer. Once the liquid has started to set, stir it with a fork to break up the crystals. Do this three or four times during the freezing process; you should be left with a wonderful mixture of glassy shards.

For the compote, cut the tops and bottoms from all the fruits so they have a flat bottom on which to sit. Using a sharp knife, cut the peel and pith from each, working around the fruit and cutting it away in wide strips from top to bottom. Working over a bowl, remove the segments by inserting a knife between the membrane surrounding each. Let the segments drop into the bowl.

Carefully drain off the citrus juice from the bowl into a saucepan. Add ⅓ cup of water, the sugar, and lime juice and heat, stirring from time to time to help the sugar dissolve. Bring to a boil, then reduce the heat and simmer gently for five minutes. Let cool, strain, and put into the refrigerator until well-chilled.

Put the fruit segments into a serving bowl and pour the cold syrup over them. Serve with the granita spooned on top.

roasted tomatoes, hummus, and spinach on toast

Roasted tomatoes and hummus are good things to make ahead and have on hand in the refrigerator for lunch for one, or for breakfast. (And as you're putting the oven on you might as well roast some bell peppers to keep in the refrigerator as well.) If you are into pushing the boat (and why not?), then a poached egg perched on top is just great and makes the dish more substantial.

SERVES 4

FOR THE TOMATOES, SPINACH, AND TOASTS

6 large plum tomatoes

1½ tablespoons olive oil

1½ teaspoons balsamic vinegar

about ½ teaspoon harissa, if you prefer some heat (optional)

1 teaspoon sugar

salt and black pepper

4 slices whole-wheat bread

½ cup baby spinach leaves

FOR THE HUMMUS

15 oz can of chickpeas

¼ cup tahini

2 fat garlic cloves, crushed

juice of 1 lemon, or to taste

½ teaspoon ground cumin

3 tablespoons extra virgin olive oil, plus extra to serve

1 tablespoon Greek yogurt (optional)

Preheat the oven to 375°F.

Halve the tomatoes and lay them in a single layer in a small roasting pan or ovenproof dish. Mix together the regular olive oil, balsamic vinegar, and harissa (if using) and pour the oil mixture over the tomatoes. Turn the tomatoes over to make sure they are well coated, ending with them cut side up. Sprinkle with sugar and season. Roast in the hot oven for 45 minutes, or until the tomatoes are caramelized and slightly shrunken.

For the hummus, drain and rinse the chickpeas and put them into a food processor. Add the tahini, garlic, lemon juice, cumin, salt, and extra virgin oil with 3 tablespoons of warm water. Blend to a puree. Taste and add the yogurt if you want (I like it). Taste again and see whether you want to add more lemon juice or not. You may want to add more water to thin the mixture a little more as well. Scrape into a bowl, cover, and put in the refrigerator until you want it.

To assemble, just toast the bread and drizzle a little extra virgin oil on it. Put the spinach on top, add a good spoonful of hummus, then arrange three tomato halves on top of that. Serve.

scallops with anchovy and caper dressing

A real treat for two. And a healthy one. Protein, omega-3 fatty acids, and vitamin B_{12}, they're all here. The richness of scallop flesh makes them filling, too. You can serve this with some lightly dressed greens; bitter chicory is good against the sweetness of the scallop flesh, or go with arugula.

SERVES 2

6 large scallops

2 tablespoons extra virgin olive oil

2 garlic cloves, sliced

3 anchovies, drained of oil, finely chopped

1 tablespoon capers, rinsed of salt or brine

2 tablespoons lemon juice

olive oil

salt and black pepper

1½ teaspoons coarsely chopped flat-leaf parsley leaves

Prepare the scallops. Look at the side and you may see a little firm piece that is whiter and a different texture to the rest of the flesh. (It's a little piece of muscle and some fish dealers leave it on.) Pull or cut it off. Dry the scallops by blotting them with paper towels (wet scallops don't brown so well).

Prepare the dressing. Heat the extra virgin oil and gently sauté the garlic, but don't let it brown (about 30 seconds). Add the anchovies and cook gently for another 45 seconds or so, pressing them with the back of a wooden spoon to help them disintegrate a little. Add the capers and lemon juice and let the dressing sit in its pan while you quickly cook the scallops.

Brush the scallops all over with a light coating of the regular olive oil and season. Heat a skillet or ridged grill pan until really hot and cook the scallops for a minute on each side—you want a good golden brown color—then reduce the heat and cook for 30 seconds. The scallops should be cooked on the inside, but be careful not to overcook because it makes them rubbery. Take a look inside one of them with the tip of a small sharp knife to check how they are.

Reheat the dressing—it doesn't have to be hot, just warm—and add the parsley. Put the scallops on two plates, drizzle with the pan juices, and spoon the dressing on top. Serve immediately. This is even better with some bread on the side to mop up the juices.

squid with smoky almond tarator, bell peppers, freekeh, and spinach

A big unarguable-with plateful. Of all the grains, freekeh is the one that can cope best with big flavors, so it's perfect with squid, bell peppers, and smoked paprika. If you can't find freekeh, use wheat berries or kamut (see page 224 for how to cook those).

SERVES 6

FOR THE BELL PEPPERS AND SQUID

3 red bell peppers

olive oil

salt and black pepper

2 lb squid, cleaned weight

juice of ½ lemon, plus lemon wedges to serve

2 red chiles, seeded and shredded

2 tablespoons chopped cilantro leaves

FOR THE FREEKEH

1¼ cups freekeh (whole grains, not broken freekeh)

2 tablespoons olive oil

3 tablespoons coarsely chopped flat-leaf parsley leaves

juice of 1 lemon

3½ tablespoons extra virgin olive oil

2 cups baby spinach

FOR THE TARATOR

1 slice country-style bread, crusts removed

¼ cup milk

⅓ cup blanched almonds

¾ teaspoon smoked paprika

¼ teaspoon cayenne pepper

2 garlic cloves

½ cup extra virgin olive oil (Greek is good for this)

juice of ¾ lemon, or more to taste

Preheat the oven to 350°F. Brush the bell peppers with regular olive oil, season, and put into a roasting pan. Cook the peppers for 35–40 minutes. They should be completely tender and slightly blistered. I don't skin them because I love the charred skin, but do so if you prefer. Slice into strips once cool enough to handle.

Make the tarator. Soak the bread in the milk for 15 minutes. Puree in a food processor with the almonds, smoked paprika, cayenne, garlic, and seasoning, adding the extra virgin oil and lemon juice as you work. Add ⅓ cup of water and blend again. It should be thick but not stiff, so add more water if you need to. Taste and adjust the seasoning. You could need more lemon.

Put the freekeh into a saucepan with plenty of water, ½ teaspoon salt, and the regular olive oil. Bring to a boil. Cover with a tight-fitting lid, reduce the temperature, and simmer for 20–25 minutes. It should be tender but will retain a firmness in the middle. Drain and toss with the parsley, lemon juice, and extra virgin oil and season. This is nice warm, so cover while you cook the squid.

Wash the squid, removing any whitish gunge from inside, and pat dry. (If it's damp, it won't cook well.) If they're small, leave them whole. Otherwise, cut the little wings off and put them aside with the tentacles. Cut the bodies down one side to open out. If they are big, halve the bodies lengthwise and score them on the inside with a crosshatch. Put in a bowl with olive oil to moisten.

Heat a ridged grill pan until really hot. Season the squid and cook it on both sides, in batches, pressing it down to pick up the ridge marks. It needs only about 20 seconds on each side to turn opaque and a nice golden brown. As soon as each batch of squid is ready, transfer to a plate and squeeze lemon juice over it. Add the chiles and cilantro once it's all cooked and toss together.

Toss the spinach with the freekeh and divide among plates or spread out on a serving plate or a wide, shallow bowl, top with the squid and bell peppers, and put a dollop of tarator on the side of each plate, serving the rest in a bowl. Serve with wedges of lemon.

smoked mackerel, beet, and poppy seed relish with molasses bread

I love this kind of food. It's partly Scandinavian, partly Irish. The bread is sweet and cakelike (it's a form of soda bread). I like the slight sweetness contrasting with the saltiness of the mackerel but, if you want something lower in carbs, use plain rye bread instead.

The bread recipe here is enough to make two small loaves. Just halve it if you only want one, but it always seems a little pointless to put the oven on for just one loaf.

SERVES 4

FOR THE BREAD

4 cups whole-wheat flour

1⅓ cups all-purpose flour

¾ cup plus 1 tablespoon rolled oats

1 teaspoon salt

2½ teaspoons baking soda

3½ tablespoons butter, cut into small cubes, plus extra for the pans

¼ cup molasses sugar

¾ cup stout

⅓ cup molasses

1¾ cups buttermilk

steel-cut oats, for the top

FOR THE REST

1 apple

1 tablespoon cider vinegar

¼ red onion, finely sliced

1½ tablespoons olive oil

3 large savoy cabbage leaves

1 teaspoon packed light brown sugar

2 teaspoons poppy seeds

salt and black pepper

3 small cooked beets

a few microgreens, ideally red-veined (optional)

4 smoked mackerel fillets

To make the bread, preheat the oven to 350°F. Mix the flours and oats with the salt and baking soda. Add the butter and rub it in with your fingertips. Stir in the sugar. Make a well in the center of the mixture and gradually pour in the stout, followed by the molasses and then the buttermilk. Mix these liquids in with a butter knife as they are added. You will end up with a pretty wet mixture and won't believe it will ever turn into bread. Divide it between two small buttered loaf pans (each should measure 7½ x 3½ x 2 inches and they should be 2 inches deep), and sprinkle each with the large steel-cut oats.

Put into the oven and bake for 40–50 minutes. To test whether the loaves are ready, remove one of them from the pan and tap the bottom. If it sounds hollow, it is ready. If not, return to the oven for a little while longer. Be sure not to overcook, however, or it will be dry. Turn out of the pans and let cool on a wire rack.

Peel the apple, core, and cut the flesh into matchsticks. Put immediately into a bowl with the vinegar and mix to coat. Sauté the onion gently in 1½ teaspoons of the olive oil for about 1½ minutes. You don't want to brown or even soften it much, just take the raw edge off it. Add to the bowl with the apples. Remove the thick central rib from each of the cabbage leaves, then roll the leaves up and cut them into shreds. Add them to the bowl with the remaining olive oil, sugar, poppy seeds, and seasoning.

Peel the beets and cut into matchsticks. Add to the bowl at the last minute (if you add them earlier, they will bleed over the other ingredients; a little of this is fine, but it looks better when it hasn't gone too far), then spring the salad with microgreens (if using).

Serve the smoked mackerel with the bread and salad.

porgy with ginger, soy, and scallions

One of the cleanest, simplest recipes in the book. If you're trying to cut down your fat intake for whatever reason, you don't have to fry the chile and ginger, though the contrast in texture with the steamed flesh of the fish is wonderful. You can just steam them on top of the fish fillets along with the rest of the ginger instead.

SERVES 4

3½ tablespoons soy sauce

3½ tablespoons rice wine

4 teaspoons superfine sugar

4 (6 oz) porgy fillets (or similar; sea bass is beautiful, but more expensive)

1 inch ginger root, peeled and shredded

⅓ cup peanut oil

2 red chiles, seeded and shredded

8 scallions, trimmed, cut in half horizontally, then julienned

Mix the soy sauce, rice wine, and sugar. Put the porgy fillets on a plate and sprinkle ¼ cup of the soy sauce mixture and half the ginger over them. Let stand for 15 minutes.

Pour water into a large saucepan on top of which a steaming basket will fit. Bring the water to a boil. Set the steamer basket on top and put the fish in, on its plate (you can shake the soy mixture off, but leave the ginger). Cover tightly. Steam for seven minutes, remove from the heat, and let cook in the residual heat for one minute. Check to see that the fish is cooked through.

Heat the oil and quickly sauté the chiles and the rest of the ginger until pale gold. Serve the fish with the scallions strewn over them, then pour in the hot oil with the chiles and ginger. Spoon on some of the remaining soy sauce mixture and put any that remains in a bowl for guests to help themselves at the table.

another way ... scallops with ginger, soy, and scallions

Chop a 1½ inch piece of peeled ginger root into matchsticks. Divide about one-third of it among 4 clean scallop shells, then top each with 3 scallops and their roes. Chop 6 trimmed scallions on the diagonal and sprinkle them over the scallops with ⅓ cup soy sauce. Get a two-tiered steamer ready and put two shells in each of the levels. Steam for six to eight minutes, depending on their size (you should ideally swap the tiers halfway through to make sure they all cook at the same rate). Heat 1 tablespoon peanut oil in a skillet and sauté the rest of the ginger and 2 finely sliced garlic cloves. The garlic should be pale gold and the ginger like little golden shreds. Scoop out and drain on paper towels. Plate the scallops and sprinkle the top with the fried ginger and garlic, adding a drop of toasted sesame oil. Serve immediately. This makes a substantial appetizer or, with rice and stir-fried greens on the side, a main course for serving four.

sashimi

Raw fish isn't to everyone's taste, and you do have to get spankingly fresh stuff (you need an excellent fish dealer), but it quickly grows on you. In fact, I find it addictive (except for the squid option). It isn't a cheap dish—unless you make it with only mackerel—but it is incredibly filling (a massive hit of protein) and wonderful if you're watching your weight.

Wasabi varies greatly in quality. It comes in tubes, in powder form to mix yourself, and as the fresh root (see a photo of the root on page 59). Fresh is the best option, but it's difficult to find; it can be grated on a special Japanese grater. Japanese soy sauce is lighter and more refined than others and doesn't overwhelm the taste of the fish.

SERVES AS MANY AS YOU LIKE

about 3 oz sushi-quality skinned fish fillets per person (tuna, salmon, sea bass, mackerel, sardine)

TO SERVE

shredded daikon

julienned carrots

sprigs of cress or microgreens

finely chopped scallions

finely sliced radishes

pickled ginger

wasabi

Japanese soy sauce

Using a sharp knife—preferably a fish filleting knife—cut the fish at an angle into slices about ⅛ inch thick and 1 inch wide. You shouldn't need to "saw" the fish, just slice through it.

Arrange each type of fish—slightly overlapping—in a line. You can serve the various vegetable possibilities (daikon, carrots, greens, scallions, radishes) in little piles on the plate, although when it comes to arranging everything you can do your own thing. One of the thrills of serving and eating sashimi is just how simple and beautiful a plateful can look.

Serve other accompaniments—ginger, wasabi, and soy sauce—in little bowls.

mackerel with hazelnut picada

Picada is generally used as a thickener in Catalan cooking, added to braises at the last minute, but some Spanish cooks now use it as a final flourish in much the same way that Italians use gremolata.

A bitter green salad and some lentils are perfect with this.

SERVES 4

FOR THE PICADA

¼ cup extra virgin olive oil

2 (½ inch) slices chewy bread, crusts removed

⅓ cup unblanched hazelnuts

zest from ½ orange, removed with a zester, then finely chopped

1 garlic clove, finely chopped

2 tablespoons finely chopped flat-leaf parsley leaves

1 tablespoon sherry vinegar, or to taste

salt and black pepper

FOR THE FISH

4 large (5½ oz) mackerel fillets, or 8 small fillets

2 tablespoons olive oil

good squeeze of orange juice

To make the picada, preheat the oven to 375°F. Pour 3 tablespoons of the oil into a small skillet and set over medium-low heat. To test for the correct temperature, dip a piece of bread in the oil. If it sizzles a bit, reduce the heat slightly and add the bread in a single layer. Cook for two to three minutes, until the bread is a pale caramel. Remove the bread and spread out on paper towels to cool.

Toast the hazelnuts in a roasting pan in the oven for 10 minutes, or until the skins have darkened but not burned. Put them in a dish towel and rub while they are still warm to remove most of the skins. Finely chop the nuts. Break the bread into chunks, put them in a paper bag, and crush them into coarse crumbs, using a rolling pin. Add the rest of the ingredients, including the remaining 1 tablespoon of virgin olive oil, season to taste, and mix together.

For the fish, season the mackerel fillets. Heat the regular olive oil in a nonstick skillet, then quickly cook the fillets over medium heat for three minutes on each side, skin side down first if you have larger fillets. Put on warm plates, skin side up, and squeeze over orange juice. Spoon some picada on top and serve.

more mackerel ... japanese mackerel with mushrooms I think the Japanese might call this "dying leaves in rain." (You have to put yourself in a Zen place not to snigger at that, I know … get yourself to that place!) It's a beautiful mix of golden mushrooms and shimmering mackerel skin. Heat 2 tablespoons canola oil in a saucepan and cook 4 (4 oz) mackerel fillets, skin side down, for about 3 minutes, until golden brown. Turn and cook for 3 minutes on the other side. Remove. Add 2 finely sliced garlic cloves and cook for 1 minute, then add 3½ oz shiitake, halved or sliced (depending on size), and 3½ oz enoki mushrooms. Cook briskly for 3 minutes, then return the mackerel with ¼ cup sake or dry sherry and 1 tablespoon soy sauce and heat through. Sprinkle with some black or white sesame seeds. Serves 4.

hot chile-ginger stir-fried squid

Hot, quick, good for you, and relatively cheap as well. Seriously, what more could you want?

SERVES 4

1 lemon grass stalk, trimmed, coarse outer leaves removed

1 tablespoon peanut oil

2 garlic cloves, finely sliced

¾ inch piece of ginger root, peeled and finely chopped

1–2 red chiles, seeded and shredded

2 lb cleaned and prepared squid, cut into rings

4 scallions, chopped

1 teaspoon superfine sugar, or to taste

splash of Thai fish sauce

salt and black pepper

juice of ½ lime, or to taste

2 tablespoons chopped cilantro or mint leaves

Chop the lemon grass and bash it in a mortar with a pestle. Heat the oil in a wok or skillet and add the lemon grass, garlic, ginger, and chiles. Cook over medium heat for one minute.

It's important that the squid is dry, otherwise it won't cook properly, so pat it dry with paper towels. Add to the pan and cook over high heat for one minute.

Reduce the heat, add the scallions, sugar, fish sauce, salt and black pepper, and lime juice. Cook for another 30 seconds or so, quickly taste to check the seasoning (and sweet-tart balance, adjusting the levels of sugar and lime if you want), toss in the herbs, and turn out onto warm plates.

Serve with brown rice and a salad or stir-fried greens.

more superquick seafood ... shrimp with lime and bok choy

Heat 1 tablespoon peanut oil in a wok and throw in a ¾ inch piece of ginger root, peeled and finely chopped, 1 lemon grass stalk, coarse leaves removed and tender heart finely chopped, 1 red and 1 green chile, seeded and shredded, and 4 scallions, trimmed and chopped on the diagonal. Cook over medium heat until the ginger is soft and beginning to brown. Increase the heat and add 1 lb raw, shelled and deveined jumbo shrimp (ideally organic). Cook until they start to turn opaque, then add the juice and finely grated zest of 1 lime, 1 tablespoon Thai fish sauce, and 1 tablespoon superfine sugar. Cook until the shrimp are pink. Scoop them out with a slotted spoon and add ⅓ head of bok choy, sliced lengthwise, to the wok. Let it wilt and the sauce reduce. Chuck the shrimp back in with ½ cup coarsely chopped cilantro and ¼ cup torn basil leaves. Taste for sweet-tart (sugar-lime) balance and serve immediately. You can eat the dish on its own or with brown rice. Offer wedges of lime. Serves 4.

warm duck salad with plum-ginger dressing and sesame

Gourmet food stores may stock Japanese pickled plum paste, sometimes known by it's Japanese name of umeboshi. Its fresh, sour quality is great in dressings and marinades. I remove the skin and fat from the duck breast; it still makes a wonderful salad, however, you can leave the skin on if you prefer.

SERVES 4

FOR THE DRESSING

3½ tablespoons mirin (Japanese rice wine) or dry sherry

2 tablespoons rice vinegar, or to taste

2½ tablespoons peanut oil

2½ tablespoons olive oil

2 teaspoons pickled plum paste, or to taste

2 teaspoons packed light brown sugar, or to taste

½ piece of preserved ginger in syrup, finely chopped

FOR THE SALAD

2 avocados

salt and black pepper

10 sweet, mild radishes (preferably French Breakfast)

2 large duck breasts, skin and fat removed

1 tablespoon peanut oil

1½ cup green beans, tops trimmed but not the bottoms (or sugar snap peas, or a mixture)

4½ cups baby spinach

2 tablespoons sesame seeds (preferably black sesame)

Preheat the oven to 425°F.

Make the dressing by simply whisking everything together. The pickled plum paste won't completely blend in; there will still be little pale pink pieces in the dressing. Taste for a balance of sweet and tart, adjusting the sugar, vinegar, and plum paste accordingly.

Get the vegetables ready. Halve, pit, and slice the avocados, peel each slice, and immediately season and toss with some of the dressing. Wash the radishes, trim, and slice lengthwise thinly.

Season the duck breasts. Heat the oil in a skillet and brown the duck breasts on both sides, then put them in a roasting pan and cook in the hot oven for 5 minutes. (You can check whether the meat is done by slicing through the center of a breast. It should be pink, like rare steak.) Remove the duck breasts, cover with aluminum foil to insulate, and let rest for three or four minutes.

Meanwhile, steam or boil the green beans until tender, then immediately rinse in cold water. Slice the duck breasts and season, then combine with all the other ingredients (except the sesame seeds) and toss with the dressing. Arrange on a large plate or divide among four plates. Sprinkle the sesame seeds on top and serve immediately.

thai-style chicken and mango salad

To be strictly Thai, you can omit the watercress and increase the quantity of herbs. If you can't find green mangoes, or prefer to eat ripe ones, you can use 1 ripe mango and 1 tart green apple (core removed). As well as sourness, the green mangoes provide crunch, so apple is a fine substitute.

SERVES 4 AS A MAIN COURSE

salt and black pepper

4 skinless boneless chicken breasts or thighs

⅓ cup peanut oil

6 scallions, trimmed and sliced on the diagonal

8 garlic cloves, peeled and finely sliced

2 green mangoes, peeled

3 red chiles, seeded and shredded

2 tablespoons Thai fish sauce

1½ tablespoons superfine sugar

juice of 1½ limes

2 cups cilantro leaves

1 cup mint leaves

¼ bunch of watercress leaves, coarse stems removed

1½ tablespoons coarsely chopped roasted peanuts

Lightly season the chicken and sauté in 2 tablespoons of the oil until cooked through. Let cool. (Or you can use the same amount of leftover chicken, shredded.)

Sauté the scallions, using ½ tablespoon more oil, in the same pan, then put them in a wide, shallow bowl. Quickly sauté the garlic until golden brown; be careful not to burn it. Add to the bowl too.

Slice the flesh from the mangoes and cut it into lengths about the thickness of two matchsticks. Put these in the bowl with the chiles, fish sauce, sugar, and lime juice.

Finally, cut the chicken into strips and add to the bowl with the herbs, watercress, and the remaining 2½ tablespoons of oil. Mix everything together. Sprinkle the peanuts over the top and serve.

and also … burmese-style chicken salad Soak 2 sliced shallots in cold water for 10 minutes, then drain. Put these in a dish with 1½–2 cups shredded cooked chicken (but use whatever you have, I generally make this with leftovers). Add the juice of 3 limes, ½ green chile, seeded and shredded, and a really generous handful of cilantro and mint leaves. Slice another 4 shallots and sauté them in 2 tablespoons peanut oil until golden brown. Pour them over the salad, season, and toss. Sprinkle with about 1 tablespoon of chopped roasted peanuts, if you want. I also sometimes add matchsticks of carrot or shredded cabbage, especially if I am short of chicken. Serves 2 as a light main course.

shawarma chicken with warm chickpea puree and sumac onions

This is a great mixture of flavors and temperatures and people always love it. You can prepare the puree in advance, then all you have to do is grill the chicken. The puree is also excellent with lamb or with roasted Mediterranean vegetables.

SERVES 4

FOR THE CHICKEN AND MARINADE

4 garlic cloves, crushed

1 teaspoon ground ginger

1 teaspoon allspice

½ teaspoon turmeric

2 teaspoon ground cumin

3 tablespoons olive oil

juice of 1 lemon

salt and plenty of black pepper

8 skinless boneless chicken thighs

FOR THE PUREE

1 onion, finely chopped

1 tablespoon olive oil

4 garlic cloves, finely chopped

1 tablespoon ground cumin

½ teaspoon ground allspice

15 oz can of chickpeas, drained and rinsed

⅔ cup extra virgin olive oil

2 tablespoons tahini

juice of 1 lemon, or to taste

FOR THE ONIONS

½ small red onion, peeled and finely sliced

seeds from ½ pomegranate

½ teaspoon sumac

TO SERVE

really fresh sprigs of cilantro

Greek yogurt

lemon wedges

Prepare the marinade by mixing everything together (except the chicken) in a shallow, nonreactive dish that will hold the chicken pieces in a single layer. Put them in this, turning them over to make sure they are well coated. Cover. Ideally, let chicken marinate for a couple of hours in the refrigerator (or put it in the refrigerator in the morning and let marinate all day), but I let it marinate for 30 minutes when pushed. Turn the chicken every so often.

To make the puree, sauté the onion in the regular olive oil until soft and golden brown. Add the garlic and cook for another two minutes, then add the spices for another minute. Toss in the chickpeas and heat them through, tossing them with the onions and spices. Transfer all this to a food processor with the extra virgin oil, tahini, lemon juice, salt, and black pepper, adding ⅓–½ cup water. Puree and taste; you may want to add more lemon juice or seasoning (it needs good, assertive seasoning). You might also need to add more water to get the right texture (if you do, adjust the seasoning again). Scrape out into a clean saucepan so you can reheat the puree (though you can serve it at room temperature if you want).

Put the red onion into a bowl of cold water and let stand for about 15 minutes, until crisp.

Lift the chicken out of the marinade and season with salt. Heat a skillet or ridged grill pan until hot, then cook the chicken for 1½ minutes on each side (you don't need to add any oil). Reduce the heat and cook for another 2½ minutes on each side. The chicken will be golden brown and gorgeously singed in places.

Drain the red onion, pat dry, mix with the pomegranate seeds, and sprinkle with sumac.

Reheat the puree if you prefer it hot. Serve the chicken thighs with some of the puree, add the sprigs of cilantro, and top with the pomegranate and red onion mixture. Provide a bowl of yogurt and some lemon wedges, too. You can offer flatbread or bulgur wheat on the side but you really don't need it; a salad of bitter greens (endive or radicchio) is better.

chicken and pumpkin with soy and star anise

This is slightly adapted from an excellent American book (*All About Braising*, by Molly Stevens). It quickly became one of the most cooked dishes in my house, because it's easy and children love it. You might feel that there isn't enough soy but, as the chicken exudes its juices, you end up with enough liquid.

Don't be tempted to add more star anise; one really is enough. It's a powerful spice.

SERVES 4

1 tablespoon peanut oil

8 bone-in chicken thighs

2 tablespoons soy sauce

2 tablespoons rice vinegar

2 tablespoons Thai fish sauce

2 tablespoons packed dark brown sugar

1 red chile, seeded and shredded

1 inch piece of ginger root, peeled and finely chopped

3 garlic cloves, finely chopped

8 scallions, trimmed and chopped on the diagonal

2 lb of pumpkin or 1 butternut squash, peeled, seeded, and cut into chunks

3 strips of orange zest

1 star anise

2 tablespoons orange juice

black pepper

Preheat the oven to 350°F.

Heat the oil in a casserole, dutch oven, or sauté pan (something in which all the chicken thighs can lie in a single layer). Remove the chicken skin, if you prefer, then brown the chicken on both sides. Don't try to turn the thighs until they are easy to move, because pulling will tear them. Take the chicken out of the pan and set aside. Pour the fat out of the pan into a cup.

Mix the soy sauce, vinegar, and fish sauce with the sugar and stir. Put 1 tablespoon of the reserved fat back in the pan, heat it, and add the chile, ginger, and garlic. Reserve some of the greener parts of scallion to sprinkle on at the end and add the rest to the pan. Cook over medium heat for a couple of minutes, until the garlic is lightly browned, then add the soy sauce mixture. Return the chicken, along with any juices that have seeped out, plus the pumpkin, orange zest, star anise, orange juice, and 3–4 tablespoons of water. Grind over some black pepper. Cover and put in the hot oven for 40 minutes in total. After 15 minutes' cooking time, turn the chicken pieces over, then cover once more. After 30 minutes' cooking time, uncover and return to the oven to cook for the remaining 10 minutes.

Sprinkle with the reserved scallion greens and serve. Any grain is good on the side: brown rice, kamut, quinoa, or wheat berries (see pages 223–224 for how to cook them). Just season the grain well and toss it with plenty of chopped cilantro leaves and some lime juice.

spiced pork chops with ginger and mango relish

Don't keep this relish just for chops, because it's wonderful with any spicy meat (and broiled salmon and mackerel, too). I've called it a relish but it's chunky, almost like a salad, and people usually end up filling a third of their plate with it (and asking for more). You can treat chicken in the same way as the chops. If you prefer to cut down on fat, then remove it from the chops, or let guests do it for themselves, but not until after cooking (you need it for the flavor).

SERVES 6

FOR THE CHOPS

2 tablespoons peanut oil

juice of 3 limes

2 red chiles, seeded and chopped

2 garlic cloves, crushed

¾ inch piece of ginger root, peeled and grated

6 pork loin chops

FOR THE RELISH

2 mangoes

finely grated zest and juice of 1 lime

1 tablespoon peanut oil

10 garlic cloves, grated

1¼ cups peeled and grated ginger root

2 teaspoons whole-grain mustard

superfine sugar, to taste (about 1 teaspoon)

salt and black pepper

1 green chile, seeded and shredded

1 red chile, seeded and shredded

leaves from a small bunch of cilantro, coarsely chopped

Mix everything for the chops (except the meat itself) together to make a marinade and place in a shallow, nonreactive bowl. Put the chops into it, turn to coat, cover, and marinate in the refrigerator for a couple of hours. Turn the chops over every so often.

Peel the mangoes and cut the flesh from each side of the pits. Remove whatever flesh you can slice off into neat strips from the mango pits. Cut the mango sides pieces into wedges about the thickness of a nickel and toss with the lime zest and juice.

Heat the oil in a skillet and add the grated garlic and ginger pastes. Cook over medium-low heat until it smells cooked and no longer raw. Pull off the heat and stir in the mustard, then stir this mixture into the mangoes. Gently stir in the sugar, salt, black pepper, chiles, and cilantro.

Heat a skillet until it is really hot and take the chops out of the marinade. Scrape the marinade off the chops and back into the bowl in which they were lying. Season the chops. Cook them over high heat for about three minutes, or until nicely browned, then turn and do the same on the other side. Now reduce the heat to low and continue to cook until completely cooked through; this takes at least 10 minutes. There should be no pink juices when you pierce them with the tip of a sharp knife. When you get toward the end of the cooking time, add the marinade and let it glaze the pork chops and simmer in the pan until reduced. Serve the chops with the ginger and mango relish.

crazy grains

It's great when a previously unglamorous and relatively cheap ingredient becomes the *dernier cri*. I love an underdog making it to the top, so I have to smile when I think that whole grains—once the domain of the sandal-wearing granola brigade—are now eaten by minxes shod in Christian Louboutin. Whole grains are hip. And don't assume they're all chewy and taste of straw. Quinoa has small grains and a delicate flavor, bulgur is gently nutty. I especially like the stronger grains—deeply earthy rye berries and smoky, sexy freekeh—and they've all made me more inventive as a cook.

The consensus is that they're good for us, certainly preferable to processed grains that have had most of their nutrients stripped away. Refined carbohydrates are quickly converted by our bodies into sugar, and the surges and dips in blood sugar this causes provoke a rise in insulin. High levels of insulin are increasingly blamed for weight gain and obesity (and their attendant problems). Whole grains, on the other hand, don't produce such spikes. A meal of slowly digested whole-grain carbohydrates and proteins smooths out the blood sugar-insulin roller coaster. Whole grains make you feel fuller for longer and also send the "satiety" signal to your brain relatively quickly, so you feel full sooner. Fans also see them as a good alternative to meat and point out how important fiber is in our diet.

I am pretty convinced by the findings of The Nurses' Health Study, one of the longest-running, most intensive investigations into health and nutrition ever conducted. (Started in 1976 with funding from the National Institutes of Health in the United States, it is still going, with the nurses' children now taking part as well.) It has looked at the whole question of fiber, and found that participants who ate most fiber from whole grains (about 7.5 g a day) were 30 percent less likely to develop type-2 diabetes than those who ate less (2.5 g), while those who ate two servings of whole grains a day were 30 percent less likely to develop heart disease than those who ate only one serving a week. There's no arguing with that.

There are negative murmurings. The investigative food journalist Joanna Blythman, in her book *What to Eat*, argues that all the vitamins and minerals in whole grains are found in greater quantities in meat, fish, and eggs (although for various reasons animal proteins are not always an option and some grains—such as buckwheat, kamut, oats, quinoa, rye, and spelt—provide good levels of protein). The anti-carbists aren't enthusiastic about them either, because although they're "good carbs," they're still carbs.

Whole grains are so filling you're not going to gorge yourself on them, however, so unless you have real problems with carbohydrates, I'd put them on the menu. And I'm not saying never have a bowl of white rice with your Chinese again, just not too often. Besides, you'll get to love the brown stuff … honest.

barley

Banish all thoughts of sensible barley soup, barley has been liberated and is now found in trendy salads everywhere. Pearl barley is the type most commonly available. This has been processed—the germ and some of the bran removed—but, unlike most grains, barley's fiber is found right through the kernel. Pearl barley cooks in 25–30 minutes. Drain, dress in vinaigrette, and use as a salad base, or make a pilaf with it by the absorption method (cooking it in stock and other flavorings, letting the liquid become absorbed as the grain cooks), or cook it like risotto rice, stirring so it becomes creamy. The unprocessed type, pot barley, sometimes called Scotch barley, takes an hour to cook (and needs overnight soaking).

brown long-grain rice

This retains a certain firmness after cooking. Cook it in boiling water for about 25 minutes, or make it by the absorption method (see above). It doesn't need presoaking. Because the grains stay separate (like many whole grains), it makes a great salad base.

buckwheat

A staple in Russia and Eastern Europe, both buckwheat groats and roasted buckwheat (also known as kasha) have a robust, "beefy" flavor (particularly the roasted variety). Start with the unroasted type and sauté it in oil before adding water and cooking for 15 minutes.

bulgur wheat

This, much used in Middle Eastern food, is a boon, it's so quick to prepare. It is produced when wheat (usually durum) is boiled, dried, and cracked. Cook in boiling water or stock: the time depends on the size of the grain (medium, the type I mostly use, takes 15 minutes). For salads, where it requires a less fluffy texture, just soak it in water for 15 minutes.

farro

An ancient grain, believed to have sustained the Roman legions, also known as emmer wheat. It's pale brown, has a real hazelnutty flavor and makes a superb salad base. Most commonly available is semi-pearled; this doesn't need soaking and cooks in 20–25 minutes. Use the unpearled type if you prefer; it needs overnight soaking and cooks in one hour. I used to cook farro only in fall and winter, but a summery farro salad in Rome—containing tomatoes, olives, basil, and grassy Tuscan oil—won me over to using it all year round.

freekeh

Freekeh is assertive. Smoky. Chewy. It's roasted young green wheat, cooked mostly in the Middle East, and is the coolest grain around. It stands up well to big flavors such as preserved lemons, pomegranate molasses, and oily fish. Boil it in water for 20–25 minutes, drain, and use in salads, or cook in stock by the absorption method (see page 223). You can substitute it with wheat berries, bulgur wheat, or quinoa if difficult to find.

kamut

The brand name for khorasan, an ancient variety of wheat that's still under the radar. Flavor isn't its chief attraction—it's fairly bland—but the large, honey-color kernels make a great salad base. Soak overnight, then cook for 50–60 minutes. Spelt is a suitable substitute.

oats

See page 240 for everything you need to know about oats.

quinoa

This pseudo grain—really a seed—is a health wonder. It's a complete protein (rare in the plant world). In texture and size it's somewhere between couscous and bulgur and is great hot or cold. Toast it for a few minutes in a dry saucepan—it helps the flavor—then add 3 cups liquid for every 1¾ cups quinoa and cook for 15 minutes for plump, dry grains. It can be cream, black, or red, so you also get to be a painter when you use it.

rye berries

The cold grain, easily grown in the wet and chilly north. I love it for its deep, dark, fruity flavor. It's fantastic teamed with other "northern" ingredients; try it with beets, smoked fish, dill, caraway, and buttermilk. Soak the grain overnight and cook it for 50–60 minutes.

spelt

Because the name sounds rather austere (just say it out loud), I usually team spelt with "northern" Scandinavian ingredients, such as smoked foods and buttermilk. Spelt is often used interchangeably with farro, but pearl spelt, the type most commonly available, is more refined (and makes a better risotto, nice and creamy) than semi-pearl farro. Pearl spelt cooks in 20–25 minutes. Substitute nonpearl spelt, the whole grain version, if you want—find it online—except for in risottos (soak it overnight and cook for about one hour).

wheat berries

Both soft and hard types are available (the latter is more chewy) and both need to be soaked overnight. Soft wheat cooks in 40 minutes; hard wheat can take about 90 minutes.

wild rice

This is the grain from a native American water grass. It stays firm and is great mixed with quinoa, red rice, or brown rice, mainly because of its color but also texture (on its own, I find it too chewy and robust, it's better as a "mixer"). It's ready in about 45 minutes.

grilled chicken, kale, and farro with creamy garlic and anchovy dressing

You won't get this at all until you taste it, but I think of it as healthy chicken Caesar. It's got all the same elements, but with the addition of grains. And it uses great greens. The farro can be substituted with spelt. You don't have to use grilled chicken. Just roast a whole chicken, carve the meat, and serve it on the grains and greens.

SERVES 4

1 cup farro

2½ tablespoons olive oil

1 small onion, finely chopped

8 oz kale

1½ teaspoons extra virgin olive oil

good squeeze of lemon, plus lemon wedges to serve

4 boneless chicken thighs

FOR THE DRESSING

6 anchovies, drained of oil

¼ cup pine nuts or blanched almonds

1 fat garlic clove

salt and black pepper

2 tablespoons extra virgin olive oil

juice of ½ lemon

1½ teaspoons finely chopped flat-leaf parsley leaves

Put the farro in a saucepan and cover with plenty of water. Bring to a boil, then reduce the heat to a lively simmer and cook for 20–25 minutes, or until the farro is just tender. (It doesn't completely soften like rice, but retains a slight "bite.")

Meanwhile, for the dressing, put the anchovies, nuts, garlic, and some black pepper into a small food processor. With the motor running, add the extra virgin oil, lemon juice, and 2 tablespoons of water. Process until smooth. You can add a little more water if you would like the dressing to be thinner; it should be about as thick as heavy cream (though not as smooth). Scrape into a bowl and stir in the parsley.

Heat 1½ tablespoons of the regular olive oil in a skillet and cook the onion over medium-low heat until lightly browned and soft. Set aside.

Remove the ribs from the kale and discard, then tear the leaves into pieces. Put it into plenty of boiling water and cook for four minutes. Drain really well and add to the onion in the pan. Set over medium heat once more, stirring the kale to make sure it gets coated in the oil. It should be deep green and glossy.

Rinse the farro in boiling water, then immediately toss with the kale, extra virgin oil, and lemon juice. Season to taste (but remember you will be adding a really punchy dressing).

Brush the chicken thighs on both sides with the remaining regular oil and season. Heat a ridged grill pan until really hot, then cook the chicken for two minutes on each side. Reduce the heat and cook for another two minutes on each side, or until the chicken is cooked through (there should be no trace of pink in the center).

Divide the farro and kale among four plates and drizzle with the dressing (serve the rest on the side). Put the chicken on top; you can slice it or leave the thighs whole. Serve with lemon wedges.

fall menu indian warmth

lentil, roasted tomato and saffron soup | indian-spiced beet, pumpkin, and spinach | mangoes

The is the kind of menu that surprises people. There's no meat, but diners don't realize it until they've finished. You certainly don't feel anything is missing. I crave Indian spices as soon as the weather starts to get cold. They render food warming in a sweet, fragrant, "alive" kind of way. For dessert, simply serve perfectly ripe mangoes and good juicy limes. Let people cut their own mangoes into slices and squeeze the lime over them. A bowl of fresh litchis would be good, too. If you want to serve a "proper" dessert, Citrus compote with ginger snow (see page 200) would be wonderful.

lentil and roasted tomato soup with saffron

The tomatoes give real depth. It makes a hearty opener, but the main course is deceptively light.

SERVES 6

10 plum tomatoes, halved

¼ cup olive oil

2 teaspoons harissa

salt and black pepper

2 teaspoons brown sugar (optional)

2 teaspoons cumin seeds

1 teaspoon coriander seeds

1 tablespoon peanut oil

1 large onion, chopped

4 garlic cloves, chopped

½ teaspoon turmeric

good pinch of saffron stamens

¾ inch piece ginger root, chopped

1 green chile, finely chopped

1 cup split red lentils

3¾ cups vegetable stock

¼ cup chopped cilantro leaves

plain yogurt (optional)

toasted slivered almonds

Preheat the oven to 375°F. Put the tomatoes in a roasting pan in which they can lie in a single layer. Mix together the olive oil, harissa, and salt and black pepper in a small bowl and pour the mixture over the tomatoes. Turn over to coat, ending with the tomatoes cut side up. (If your tomatoes aren't the best, sprinkle the brown sugar over them, but their natural sweetness comes out as they roast.) Cook for 45 minutes, until slightly shrunken and charred in places. Set aside the six nicest looking tomato halves.

Toast the cumin and coriander seeds for two minutes in a dry pan. Grind them in a mortar and set aside. Heat the peanut oil in a saucepan and sauté the onion until soft and golden brown. Add the garlic, all the spices, ginger, and chile and cook for two minutes. Add the lentils, stirring to coat in the cooking juices, tomatoes with their juices, and the stock. Season well. Bring to a boil, reduce the heat to a simmer, and cook for 15–20 minutes, or until the lentils have collapsed into a puree. The tomatoes should have disintegrated, too. Now either puree the soup or keep it chunky. Check the seasoning and stir in most of the cilantro. Serve each bowlful with a swirl of yogurt (if you want), a reserved tomato half, a few toasted almonds, and some of the remaining cilantro.

indian-spiced beet, pumpkin, and spinach

This started out as a thoran, a stir-fry from Kerala with the key flavorings of mustard seeds, curry leaves, and coconut. But then I decided I wanted something more substantial, so it's not an authentic dish, but it is delicious. One of the boons is that it doesn't use many spices. You can buy curry leaves in Indian grocery stores and online. They freeze well. If you can't find them, just omit them (don't substitute dried). It won't be the same, but it will still be good.

SERVES 6

1½ tablespoons peanut oil

4 teaspoons mustard seeds

handful of curry leaves (about 30)

1 tablespoon dried red pepper flakes (or more, depending on how hot you want it)

2 small red onions, sliced

1½ inch piece of ginger root, peeled and shredded

1 teaspoon turmeric

3 beets, peeled and cut into chunks

3 cups peeled and seeded pumpkin or butternut squash chunks

salt and black pepper

2 russet potatoes, peeled and cut into chunks

6 oz baby spinach leaves, washed well

juice of 1 juicy lime

⅓ cup freshly grated coconut

Heat the oil in a large wok or saucepan set over medium heat. Toss in the mustard seeds followed by the curry leaves and red pepper flakes. Swirl everything around until the leaves and mustard seeds stop spluttering. Reduce the heat to low.

Add the onions and ginger and cook for five minutes, until they have softened. Add the turmeric and cook for another minute.

Add the beets and pumpkin. Stir well to coat them with the spices. If you have bought a fresh coconut to make this recipe, add the coconut water to the pan, plus another ⅓ cup of water. If you don't have any coconut water, just add about ½ cup of water to the pan. Season well. Bring to a boil, then reduce the heat, cover, and cook over gentle heat for about 15 minutes. Stir in the potatoes and continue to cook until all the vegetables are tender. Keep an eye on the pan to make sure the vegetables don't catch on the bottom and add a little more water if you need to, though this dish should end up quite "dry."

When the vegetables are soft add the spinach, mix together, and cook, stirring a little to help incorporate the spinach, until wilted (this only takes a few minutes). Add the lime juice and check the seasoning. Sprinkle with the coconut before serving. Offer brown rice alongside, and some plain yogurt.

crazy salad

This is one of my favorite dishes in the book. I wanted to come up with a salad, especially one that would be good in the colder months, that was robust, really healthy, and irresistible ("accidentally healthy"). When I served this, the kids said "Crazy, mom," because they said it was hippy salad reborn. I wasn't sure whether that was a criticism or a compliment, and then sat back and watched them eat platefuls of it.

This recipe is a starting point. Cook other grains—kamut or wheat berries (see page 224 for how to cook them)—and add peas, cucumber, crumbled feta cheese, and mint, other beans, black or red lentils instead of Puy, blueberries, or chopped apples instead of pomegranates. There are all kinds of things you can do if you start off with a cooked grain as a salad base. As long as you stick to the basic quantities for the dressing (1 tablespoon vinegar, ¼ cup oil), you can flavor it differently, too.

SERVES 6 AS A SIDE DISH

FOR THE SALAD

½ cup semi-pearl farro or pearl spelt

¼ cup Puy or green lentils

2 carrots, cut into matchsticks

⅔ cup drained and rinsed, cooked chickpeas

2 tablespoons mixed seeds (sunflower, pumpkin, sesame, whatever you have)

seeds from ½ pomegranate

a handful of watercress, coarse stems removed

FOR THE DRESSING

1 tablespoon white balsamic vinegar, or to taste

½–1 teaspoon harissa, or to taste

¼ cup extra virgin olive oil

½–1 teaspoon honey

¾ tablespoon pomegranate molasses

salt and black pepper

Put the farro or spelt into a saucepan and cover with water. Bring to a boil, reduce the heat to a simmer, and cook for 20–25 minutes, or until the grain is cooked but still has a nutty bite. Cook the lentils at the same time, again in water, until they are tender. (Cooking time varies depending on their age, so it could take as little as 15 or as much as 35 minutes.)

Meanwhile, make the dressing by mixing all the ingredients together, seasoning well. Drain the grains and lentils, run cold water through them to cool them down, shake the strainer vigorously to get rid of as much water as possible, and transfer to a serving bowl. Season and add half the dressing.

Toss in all the other ingredients (if you want to assemble the salad ahead of time, don't add the watercress until just before serving) and add the rest of the dressing. Taste for seasoning: You might want a little more salt, black pepper, or harissa, or you may even want more white balsamic vinegar.

pears poached in earl grey

These pears end up a wonderful rich toffee color and, if you are able to leave them sitting in the reduced syrup overnight before serving, they will absorb more of the subtly smoky tea flavor. Serve them with Greek yogurt.

SERVES 4

4 Earl Grey tea bags

¾ cup granulated sugar

juice of 2 lemons, plus 2 wide strips of lemon zest

2 wide strips of orange zest

4 pears, peeled, halved, and cored

Put three of the tea bags into a heatproof bowl with 4 cups of boiling water and let brew. Discard the tea bags and pour the tea into a saucepan wide enough to take all the pear halves in a single layer. Add the sugar.

Stir over medium heat to dissolve the sugar, then add the lemon juice, lemon and orange zests, and the pears. Bring the liquid to a simmer, then reduce the heat and gently cook the pears until tender. How long this takes depends on how ripe your fruit is. Keep checking, sticking the tip of a sharp knife into the flesh. Once the pears are ready, scoop them out with a slotted spoon and set them in a dish where they are not touching each other, so they can cool down and stop cooking (if you pile them on top of each other, the heat will continue to soften them).

Remove the zest from the poaching liquid and bring it to a boil. Add the final tea bag and simmer until the liquid is reduced to about 1 generous cup. The syrup will thicken more as it cools. Let cool completely, strain, then put the pears into a serving dish and pour it over the syrup.

turkish quince sorbet

Quince flesh is so honeyed that I think it needs a little help from acidity, hence the tart apples and lemon juice here. You need to allow a decent amount of time for the sorbet to soften before serving because it sets pretty solid, due to the high proportion of pectin in it. You can replace some of the water with pomegranate juice (pure stuff, not sweetened or "pomegranate juice drink") for a beautifully colored sorbet with a slightly different flavor.

SERVES 8

1 tart crisp apple
(I use Granny Smith)

4 quinces

1⅔ cups granulated sugar

juice of 1 lemon

1–2 teaspoons flower water
(rose or orange), optional

seeds from 1 pomegranate,
to serve (optional)

Peel and core the apples and quinces and chop the flesh into chunks. Put in a saucepan and add enough water to just cover. Cover and cook the fruit gently until soft—it could take as much as 30 minutes because quince flesh is so hard—by which time there should be little liquid left. (Keep a careful eye on it to make sure it doesn't boil dry, but don't add too much water because it will affect the sorbet. If you really need it, add only 1–2 tablespoons at a time.)

Make a sugar syrup by gently dissolving the sugar over medium heat in 1⅓ cups of water. Set aside to cool.

Puree the apple and quince flesh in a food processor or blender, then push it through a nylon strainer (quince is so fibrous you really have to do this to get a decently smooth sorbet). Add the lemon juice, then a small amount of flower water and taste; brands vary in strength, so you might want a little more. Add the sugar syrup, too, then chill in the refrigerator. Freeze in an ice cream machine according to the manufacturer's instructions. If you don't have an ice cream machine, put the mixture in a shallow, freezer-proof container in the freezer. When it has frozen around the edges but is still slushy in the middle, churn the mixture in a food processor (or use a fork and beat vigorously). Repeat three or four times during the freezing process.

Serve sprinkled with the pomegranate seeds.

blackberry and red wine gelatins

This may seem like a lot of gelatin, but alcohol inhibits its setting qualities, so you do need the amount given. This is not a dessert for every day (that alcohol!), but a weekend treat. It's best to make the gelatins the day before serving, so they have time to set.

SERVES 6

5 large or 10 small sheets gelatin (about generous ½ oz in total)

2 cups red wine

¾ cup granulated sugar

2¾ cups blackberries

Put the gelatin into a shallow bowl and cover with water. Soak for five minutes, until completely soft. Scoop up the gelatin and gently squeeze out the excess water. Meanwhile, heat the wine and sugar with ¾ cup of water, stirring gently to help the sugar dissolve. The wine shouldn't get any hotter than lukewarm. Add the soaked gelatin and stir to dissolve. (Gelatin can't go into boiling liquid or it will lose its setting properties.)

Divide the berries between six glasses and pour the liquid over them. Put in the refrigerator to set. There is a lot of fruit here, so it shouldn't bob too much to the top because it is tightly packed. Let stand overnight to set before serving.

more fruit gelatin please … cardamom-scented plum gelatins

Make these in early fall before the plums disappear. Halve and pit 1½ lb red-fleshed plums and put them in a saucepan with 1¾ cups apple juice, ½ cup water, ⅔ cup sugar, and the ground seeds of 4 cardamom pods. Heat gently, stirring to help the sugar dissolve and, when nearly boiling, reduce the heat to a simmer and cook until the fruit is completely soft and falling apart. Let cool a little, then puree in a blender or food processor. Measure how much you have and make up the quantity to 4 cups with either more apple juice or water. Put 4 large or 8 small sheets of gelatin in a bowl and cover with cold water. Let stand for 10 minutes, until it turns completely soft. Meanwhile, heat some of the plum puree to lukewarm (it must be hot enough to melt the gelatin but not so hot that it destroys its setting properties). Squeeze the excess water out of the gelatin and put it into the warm puree. Stir to dissolve, then add it back to the rest of the puree. Pour into six glasses and let stand in the refrigerator to set overnight. Serve with some Greek yogurt sweetened slightly with sugar. Serves 6.

date, apricot, and walnut loaf cake

This is not so healthy that you can eat it with abandon (it is full of dried fruits, which are high in sugar, not to mention the stuff that comes in a bag), but it uses good whole-grain flours and has plenty of good-for-you nuts and seeds in it, too. It's a great Saturday or Sunday afternoon treat because it's so easy and quick to make (mix, scrape into the pan, put it in the oven). My kids like it just as much as chocolate cake. They eat it warm spread with butter … what's not to like?

SERVES ABOUT 10

1½ sticks unsalted butter, plus extra for the pan

1 cup chopped pitted dates

⅔ cup chopped dried apricots

⅓ cup apple juice

⅔ cup firmly packed dark brown sugar

finely grated zest of 1 orange

1 egg, lightly beaten

¾ cup all-purpose flour

1 cup whole-wheat flour

1 teaspoon baking powder

good pinch of allspice

really generous grating of nutmeg

½ cup chopped walnuts

2 tablespoons pumpkin seeds, plus extra for the top (optional)

2 tablespoons sunflower seeds

1 tablespoon sesame seeds (optional)

Butter a loaf pan measuring 9 x 4½ x 2½ inches and line the bottom with parchment paper. Put the dates and apricots in a saucepan with the apple juice and 3–4 tablespoons of water. Bring to a boil, then reduce the heat right down and simmer for 15 minutes. You will have something that looks like a puree. Let cool. Melt the butter and let it cool, too. Meanwhile, preheat the oven to 350°F.

Add the butter to the dates and apricots with the sugar, zest, and egg. Sift the flours into a bowl, then add the bran caught in the sifter back into the bowl. Add the baking powder, allspice, nutmeg, nuts, and pumpkin and sunflower seeds. Add the date and egg mixture, stirring it into the dry ingredients. Make sure everything is combined, but don't overwork the dough. Scrape into the pan and sprinkle with the sesame seeds and extra pumpkin seeds (if using).

Bake in the hot oven for 1¼ hours, until a toothpick inserted into the middle comes out clean. Let cool for 10 minutes, then turn out onto a wire rack, remove the paper, and turn the right way up. Let cool. Eat in slices, either plain or, if you prefer, with butter.

ballymaloe brown bread

My reliable loaf from the celebrated Ballymaloe House. It's fantastic—very easy—and I've been making it for years. It doesn't even require kneading. Darina Allen from Ballymaloe writes that, "white or brown sugar, honey, golden [light corn] syrup, treacle or molasses may be used. Each will give a slightly different flavor to the bread. Different flours produce breads of different textures and flavors ... the quantity of water should be altered accordingly. The dough should be just too wet to knead." At Ballymaloe, their favorite variation uses whole-wheat with a little added rye flour.

MAKES 2 SMALL LOAVES

butter or light oil, for the tins

1 (2 oz) cake plus ½ (⅔ oz) cake fresh yeast or 3½ teaspoons dried yeast

3–3½ cups lukewarm water

2 tablespoons black molasses

8 cups whole-wheat flour

2 teaspoons salt

2 tablespoons sesame seeds

Lightly butter or oil two 9 x 4½ x 2½ inch loaf pans. Mix the yeast with 1 cup of the water and the molasses and let rest in a warm place until frothy. This will take 10–15 minutes.

Sift the flour and salt into a bowl. Make a well in the center and pour in the yeast mixture. Bring the flour into the well and mix, adding enough of the remaining water to make a wettish dough (however, it shouldn't be so wet that it won't come together).

Divide the dough in two and put in the pans. Let rise in a warm place, loosely covered with a couple of cloths, for about 30 minutes. Preheat the oven to 450°F.

Sprinkle with the sesame seeds and cook in the hot oven for 45–50 minutes, but take them out of their pans after 30 minutes and put them on a shelf in the oven to finish cooking. When they are cooked, they should sound hollow when you tap the bottom.

clare's wheaten bread

Everyone in Northern Ireland has a recipe for wheaten bread—a no-knead bread made with buttermilk and baking soda—and it is the quickest and easiest bread in the world. Versions vary in sweetness and oatiness and you can embellish them by mixing in other ingredients (as in the version at the bottom of this page). This recipe is from my sister-in-law, Clare Henry.

MAKES 1 LOAF

5 tablespoons cold butter, cut into little chunks, plus extra for the pan

2 cups whole-wheat flour

1 cup all-purpose flour, plus extra if needed

1 teaspoon baking soda

3 tablespoons packed light brown sugar

1¼ cups buttermilk, plus extra if needed

a little whole milk, if needed

sesame seeds and oats, for the top

Preheat the oven to 350°F and butter a 7½ x 3½ x 2 inch loaf pan.

Sift the flours and baking soda together into a large bowl, mix in the sugar, and rub in the butter with your fingers.

Add the buttermilk. You may find you need a little more liquid than suggested here. If you don't have anymore buttermilk, then normal milk will do. On the other hand, you may need a little more flour, so have more available.

Bring everything together with your hands—this is a sticky dough, not one you could ever hope to knead even if you had to—and put it into the prepared pan. Smooth the top. Sprinkle with sesame seeds and oats and bake in the oven for 50 minutes.

a fruity version Make as above but add 1 cup chopped, dried figs (snip the stems off) or the same amount of chopped apricots or dried cranberries, plus ¾ cup blanched hazelnuts (leave them whole). Add them to the mixture before you start mixing in the buttermilk. Bake the fruit version—which will turn out a little larger—in a 9 x 5 x 3 inch loaf pan.

breakfast in the cold months

Some of our best breakfast dishes were made for cold weather. It's good—as it is in the warm months—to get some protein under your belt to keep you going, but cold weather requires you to heat your body, too. Oatmeal settles in your insides like a soft, warm blanket. Fruit—dried or fresh—can be baked or stewed and served warm instead of cold. A dish of smoky kedgeree or bosky mushrooms topped with a poached egg reflect the season outside. Those dark frosty mornings can be grim and a "good" breakfast isn't merely nutritionally sound, but gives you pleasure and makes you feel cared for as well. A bowl of cold cereal just doesn't cut it. The next few pages offer a few better ways to start those cold days.

roasted tomatoes and avocado on toast

Cooked tomatoes are one of the healthiest things you can eat. I roast tomatoes even in the winter. The heat condenses their flavor and sweetness. I nearly always have them in the refrigerator to form the basis of breakfast or lunch dishes. Double the amount of tomatoes and you have enough for two breakfasts (if you're putting the oven on for 40 minutes, it's best to make good use of it).

SERVES 2

6 large plum tomatoes

1½ tablespoons olive oil

½ tablespoon balsamic vinegar

a little harissa (about ½ teaspoon), if you prefer some heat

½ teaspoon sugar (only if your tomatoes aren't very sweet)

salt and black pepper

1 ripe avocado

2 slices of whole-grain bread

about 2 tablespoons avocado oil, or extra virgin olive oil

lemon or lime juice

Preheat the oven to 375°F.

Halve the tomatoes and put them in a single layer in a small roasting pan or ovenproof dish. Mix together the olive oil, balsamic vinegar, and harissa (if using) and pour the mixture over the tomatoes. Turn the tomatoes over with your hands to make sure they get well coated, and leave them cut side up. Sprinkle with the sugar (if using) and season. Roast in the hot oven for 45 minutes, or until the tomatoes are caramelized in patches and slightly shrunken.

Halve and pit the avocado and scoop out the flesh. Toast the bread, then drizzle it with some of the avocado oil, spread the avocado flesh coarsely on each piece, sprinkle with the lemon or lime juice, season, then put the tomatoes on top. Drizzle with some more of the avocado oil and serve.

multigrain porridge with blueberries and honey

You don't have to use the grains suggested; you can get loads of different flakes these days, so use any mixture you want as long as they add up to the same amount. (Make mixtures up in advance and keep them in the cupboard.) And, of course, the topping can be whatever and wherever your taste, budget, cupboard, and refrigerator take you.

SERVES 4

FOR THE PORRIDGE

⅓ cup rye flakes

½ cup spelt flakes

½ cup quinoa flakes

1 cup barley flakes

5 cups milk, or water, or a mixture, plus extra to serve (optional)

soft light brown sugar, to taste

TO SERVE

4 big tablespoons Greek yogurt

3 tablespoons honey

1 cup blueberries

1 tablespoon sunflower seeds

Toast the flakes in a dry skillet for a minute. Transfer to a saucepan and add the milk for a creamier porridge, or water, or a mixture. Bring to a boil, then reduce the heat and simmer, stirring from time to time, for about 20 minutes, until the mixture is thick and soft. Add sugar to taste.

Divide among four bowls and add a drizzle of milk, if you prefer. Top with the yogurt, honey, blueberries, and sunflower seeds.

spelt and oat porridge with pomegranates and pistachios

Porridge and then some, this is breakfast for a lumberjack. Replace the spelt with farro, if you prefer. Cook the grains the night before, stick them in the refrigerator, then finish off in 10 minutes the next morning. Use any topping (this is quite fancypants). Spelt feels "northern", so I also like this with Shaken currants (see page 158), or stewed apples with honey.

SERVES 4

½ cup pearl spelt

¾ cup steel-cut rolled oats

1¼ cups milk, or mixed milk and water

light brown sugar, to taste

seeds from 1 pomegranate

1½ tablespoons chopped pistachios

Put the spelt into a saucepan and cover with plenty of water. Bring to a boil, reduce the heat, and simmer for 20–30 minutes. Drain.

Return the spelt to the pan with the oats, milk (or milk and water), and sugar, bring to just under a boil, reduce the heat, and simmer for 10 minutes, stirring all the time. It will be thick and creamy.

Top with the pomegranate seeds and pistachios, or whatever other topping you prefer.

proper slow-cooked oatmeal with maple apples

Having only tasted joyless oatmeal that was surely meant to punish (made with salt, I know many Scots like it, but I can't take such a dour start to the day), I eventually tasted the kind that lulled Goldilocks to sleep. Now I like oatmeal so much I limit it to a couple of times a week (I know it's made of healthy oats and has a low GI, but if you like it as much as I do, you'll eat too much of it).

Here's the knowledge. Freshly harvested oats contain about 14 percent moisture, so they have to be dried and lightly toasted. Their outer casing is then removed by grinding to remove the groat or kernel. Pinhead and steel-cut oats (they're the same thing) are produced by passing them through steel cutters, which chop them. These are the ones I like, they make a good chunky oatmeal.

Rolled oats are whole or split groats that are steamed and flattened to make oat flakes, which we call "porridge oats" in the UK. Whole flakes are called "jumbo" oat flakes and are popular in the United States. These make quick oatmeal, derided by oatmeal aficionados: they have a slightly pappy texture and less flavor, but cook in a fraction of the time… and we do live in the real world.

During the weekend, do whatever you like (as far as I'm concerned weekends are for treats), adding a splash of cream and topping with soaked dried fruit in winter or fresh raspberries in the summer and early fall. And you can add a dash of whiskey. (Pretend that, in the middle of a healthy cookbook, I didn't really say that last part … but boy, it's good.)

SERVES 2–3

FOR THE OATMEAL

1 cup steel-cut oats

1¾ cups mixed milk and water, or just water

light brown sugar, to taste (optional)

FOR THE APPLES

2 apples, peeled

maple syrup, to taste

TO SERVE

milk, plain yogurt, maple syrup, flaxseed (all optional)

Put the oats into a bowl and cover with half the milk and water, or water. Let stand overnight soak. (You can omit the soaking, but then you'll need to add about 10 minutes to the cooking time.)

Slice the apples into a small saucepan until you have worked your way through to the cores, then throw away the cores. Add about 4 tablespoons of water and set over medium heat. Keep an eye on the apple and, once you can see that it is hot and starting to cook, reduce the heat and cover. Let cook, stirring and pressing the mass with a wooden spoon every so often, until completely soft. Let cool, then sweeten with maple syrup to taste.

Put the oats into a saucepan and add the remaining liquid. Slowly bring to a boil, then reduce the heat to low and cook, stirring (you can stir just occasionally, but I prefer to stir nearly all the time as it produces a creamier oatmeal) for 20 minutes. Add more water if needed (I tend to add only water once it is cooking, otherwise it is quite a rich oatmeal). Add some sugar if you want to.

Divide among two or three bowls. You can pour a little more milk over the top to cool it if you want, then add yogurt and a big dollop of the apples. Drizzle with a little more maple syrup if you want to, or sprinkle with some flaxseed, and eat immediately.

toasty rye muesli with hazelnuts and dried cranberries

This makes a change from regular muesli or granola, but you can use the same basic quantities and substitute oats or quinoa flakes instead and use whatever nuts you prefer. I have to admit I do add a little brown sugar (½ teaspoon per bowl) or a drizzle of maple syrup, but you do what you prefer. Or you could increase the quantity of dried fruit. Another nice touch—though it won't be to everyone's taste—is to add some toasted and crushed caraway seeds. Very Scandinavian.

The muesli can be eaten plain with cold milk, or heated with milk as instructed in this recipe.

MAKES ABOUT 6½ CUPS

1 cup rye flakes

1 cup spelt or barley flakes

2 cups toasted malted wheat flakes

½ cup wheat bran

2 tablespoons sesame seeds

⅓ cup sunflower seeds

1 tablespoon flaxseed

1 tablespoon hemp seeds

½ cup unblanched hazelnuts

½ cup dried cranberries or dried sour cherries

2 tablespoons raisins

2 tablespoons poppy seeds

TO SERVE

milk

Greek yogurt and chopped fresh fruit (both optional)

Preheat the oven to 350°F. Put all the flakes, the bran, the sesame, sunflower, flaxseed, and hemp seeds into a roasting pan and spread them out. Bake for about 15 minutes, turning the contents over a couple of times. (You can also do this in a dry skillet if you prefer; it just takes minutes. You'll smell the toasty aroma.)

Coarsely chop the hazelnuts and put them into a roasting pan, too. Bake for about four minutes (you can also do these in a dry skillet and, in fact, it's easier to make sure they don't burn that way).

Mix all the ingredients for the muesli together. You can store it in an airtight container for up to two weeks.

To cook, put ½ cup of the muesli mix and ⅓ cup milk per person into a saucepan. Heat until almost boiling, stir gently, then cover and let sit for five minutes so that the ingredients can soften.

Serve the muesli and milk, and add yogurt and fresh fruit as well, if you want. I especially like blueberries with the rye flavor.

soy mushrooms with egg ribbons and black sesame

These are shamelessly stolen from Caravan, a London restaurant that has made a name for itself in the breakfast department. I have no idea how they make them, but this is my take. The omelet strips are a little Japanese touch. The strange thing is that the mushrooms don't taste at all Eastern, just deeply savory. A lip-smacking serving of umami.

SERVES 1

1 tablespoon peanut oil or sunflower oil

6 oz portobello or button mushrooms, sliced

1½ teaspoons soy sauce

1½ tablespoons crème fraîche

black pepper

tiny pat of butter

1 egg, lightly beaten

white or black sesame seeds, to serve

Heat the oil in a skillet and cook the mushrooms over high heat, stirring with a wooden spoon to make sure they get a good color all over. As soon as they are a lovely golden brown (about two minutes), add the soy sauce and let it simmer for a few seconds, then immediately add the crème fraîche and black pepper. Stir it in and as soon as it is warmed through—a matter of seconds—remove it from the heat.

Melt the butter in a small, nonstick skillet. Season the egg with black pepper, add it to the pan, then swish it around and cook as you would an omelet, but don't fold one half on top of the other; instead, slide it onto a board and cut into ribbons. Serve the mushrooms with the egg ribbons and sprinkle with sesame seeds.

winter

eating in winter

This is the season we profess to dread. We think gray skies mean brown food. But it's not true; flick through these pages for proof. Fruit and vegetable counters are splattered with color: glowing persimmons, mandarins and clementines, and candy-pink early rhubarb. And let's not forget those bitter leaves: this is the time for crimson chicories and magenta raddichio, too.

Cold weather makes us crave internal central heating and we want psychological succour, too, so our appetites become conservative. Although it's a fantasy, we feel we need to eat for survival. We bolster ourselves with mashed potatoes and buttery white rice, but we don't have to. Beans and grains—spiced or well-seasoned—are deeply satisfying, better for you and keep you feeling full for longer. You can get sleepy after a dish of pommes dauphinoise, but a bowl of spicy dal, or cranberry beans tossed with a garlicky anchovy puree, will both sooth and invigorate. So don't just think about the fruit and vegetables that are available, remember all those beans that can be cooked to softness and comfort.

early winter

broccoli
brussels sprouts
cauliflower
celeriac
chard
chicory
fennel
horseradish
jerusalem artichoke
kale
leek
mâche
parsnip
radicchio
rutabaga
sweet potato
turnip
winter squash

clementine
grapefruit
kiwi fruit
lemon
mandarin
oranges
persimmon
pommelo
tamarillo
tangerine

duck
partridge
pheasant
rabbit
venison

late winter

blood oranges
rhubarb

crimson and white

Delicate and very pretty. You can increase the amount of feta cheese used, but it's better not to mess about with this dish too much. It's one of those salads where you taste every ingredient because it isn't complicated. It does look wonderful if you can get microgreens, or find the seeds to grow them yourself (try www.burpee.com). It's easy. Really.

SERVES 6 AS AN APPETIZER

2 pink grapefruits

5½ oz mild, sweet radishes (preferably French Breakfast)

1 head of red Belgian endive

1 small fennel bulb

juice of 1 lemon

½ teaspoon sugar

¼ cup extra virgin olive oil

salt and black pepper

1 cup crumbled feta cheese, ideally barrel-aged

handful of crimson microgreens (if available)

leaves from 5 sprigs of mint, torn

To cut the grapefruits into segments, cut a slice from the bottom and top of each fruit so they have a flat bottom on which to sit. Using a sharp knife, cut the peel and pith off each grapefruit, working around the fruit and cutting the peel away in wide strips from top to bottom. Working over a bowl, slip a sharp, thin knife in between the membrane on each side of each segment and ease the segment out.

Cut the leaves from the radishes (if they are really fresh and perky, set them aside to add to the salad). Trim off and discard the unsightly part from the bottom of each radish, then wash really well. Using a knife or a mandoline slicer, cut into wafer-thin slices.

Discard any blemished outer leaves from the endive and cut the remaining leaves, lengthwise, into slices. Trim the tips from the fennel (keep any little feathery leaves for the salad) and quarter. Remove the tough outer layer of leaves and cut a little slice off the core. Again using a knife or mandoline slicer, cut the fennel into thin slices. As soon as you cut each piece, toss it with half the lemon juice (otherwise the fennel will discolor).

Whisk together the rest of the lemon juice with the sugar, extra virgin oil, and salt and black pepper to make the dressing and taste.

Arrange all the fruits and vegetables you've prepared on individual plates—or one large plate—and add the feta, the microgreens (if you're able to get any), and the mint. Spoon the dressing on top and serve immediately.

eat your greens (and your reds and your pinks)

When I was little, I was given the *Ladybird Book of Trees*. It had pictures of all the major species, so I could recognize them and remember their characteristics. I loved the book but refused to take it "tree spotting," arguing that too much information would ruin my enjoyment of trees. I have always felt much the same about food. I don't want to sit down to chunks of nutrients, but to a meal. I take a particular joy in soft-boiled eggs with antipasti (the recipe's on page 30). Salty, melting anchovies and sweet baby broccoli mollified by a rich, runny egg yolk, it gives mouthful after mouthful of pleasure. Taking the dish apart, however—labeling its properties—or cooking it only because it's "healthy," would kill it completely. So I've always been vague about what fruits and vegetables do for you. But when I started looking at my eating, I found there was an additional pleasure in knowing about the health-giving properties of this or that, even if it's just being able vaguely to remember what's good about tomatoes. And just as with the *Ladybird Book of Trees*, I can have the knowledge, then put it away.

I'm not going to list the properties of everything from apples to yams. If you want those details, consult Joanna Blythman's book *What to Eat*, a great reference on the health-giving properties of foods. Fruits and vegetables are the things most nutritionists and doctors agree on and governments encourage us to eat. Why? The report on food and cancer by the World Cancer Research Fund (2007) is clear: eat more fruits and vegetables. "Eat mostly foods of plant origin" is the specific advice. There's one slight downer in the report. Studies since the mid-1990s have indicated that fruit and veg *may* help us fight cancer rather than that they definitely do. There's a lot of work still to be done. The good news, however, is that fruits and vegetables may help reduce the risk of developing heart disease, hypertension, and diabetes as well as cancer because they're full of phytochemicals and antioxidants. Phytochemicals are naturally occurring chemicals, found in plants, which have properties that protect us from disease. Plants produce these to protect themselves, but research shows they can protect us, too. The action of phytochemicals varies by the color and type of food, so it's best to eat as wide a range (and as many colors) of fruits and vegetables as possible.

Phytochemicals can act in the same way as antioxidants, and may even stop carcinogens (cancer-causing agents) from forming. Well-known phytochemicals are lycopene—found in cooked tomatoes—which appears to reduce the risk of heart attacks and cancer, and lutein—found in leafy greens—which seems to protect us against heart disease and breast cancer.

Antioxidants are a good thing, because they protect us from the damaging impact of free radicals. (Free radicals—by-products of the body's normal chemical processes—can attack healthy cells, damaging DNA and allowing tumors to grow). Antioxidants aren't yet completely understood, but because they appear to heal and protect (instead of harm), it makes sense to eat plenty of them. Foods strong in antioxidants are blueberries, cranberries, blackberries, raspberries, strawberries, apples, cherries, plums, avocados, oranges, red grapes, and grapefruit (and there's nothing on that list I wouldn't eat with pleasure).

Cancer researchers Professor Richard Béliveau and Dr. Denis Gingras, from the University of Montreal in Canada, have written the clearest, most authoritative work I have found on the link between nutrition and cancer. They list key "good" foods in their book *Foods to Fight Cancer*, giving top marks to the following fruits and vegetables: cabbage and other cruciferous (cabbage family) vegetables, such as broccoli; garlic and other alliums (those in the onion family); berries; tomatoes; citrus fruit; dark greens, such as spinach; and other dark-color vegetables such as beet. (Other foods are soybean products, such as tofu; turmeric; green tea; oily fish; chocolate; and wine. Yes, you read that right, chocolate and wine!)

Looking at food this way can seem somewhat removed from the joy of eating. And it's easy to throw your hands up when every day new claims are made for particular foods. I'm skeptical about expensive "superfoods." Acai berries, chia seeds ... let's see how they pan out in the long term. Anyway, good health comes from eating well across the board, not from sticking a handful of expensive berries on your muesli.

It's much easier to appreciate what a particular food can do if you enjoy it, or see how it's grown. I wasn't sure about watercress (was it another hyped food?) until I saw its cultivation in Hampshire in the UK. As I stood with Dr. Steve Rothwell, the scientific brains behind much of what is grown there, he picked and ate watercress constantly. Nothing could have looked healthier than those dark green beds with spring water flowing through them, and, indeed, research carried out at the University of Ulster found that a daily portion of watercress (about 3 oz, or 3 cups chopped) reduced DNA damage to cells and increased the ability of those cells to resist additional DNA damage caused by free radicals. I also discovered that watercress is at the top of something called the Aggregate Nutrient Density Index, a list collated by an American doctor that scores fruits and vegetables from one to one thousand for their nutrient qualities. Watercress has more vitamin C than oranges, more calcium than milk, more vitamin E than broccoli, and more folate than bananas. I liked watercress anyway, but since my visit to Hampshire, I eat it every day and it's been easy to incorporate. Experts I've talked to say you don't need to eat vegetables raw (light cooking is best for cruciferous vegetables, for example), but if you apply a mixture of approaches—raw, roasted, and steamed—just as you eat a range of colors, you will get the most out of them.

We don't yet fully understand the relationship between fruits and vegetables and health, but it seems a good idea to eat stuff that will probably help protect us from cancer and heart disease. And some major experts don't think five a day is enough; their advice is to eat them "in abundance." I wouldn't eat vegetables for health reasons alone, just as I don't down spoonfuls of cod liver oil. I eat them because I love them. Often, when I've eaten a vegetable dish from this book, I think, "Meat; who needs it?" A piece of meat is, well, a piece of meat. There's a limit to what you can do with it. But vegetables? Color, texture, flavor, the different cooking methods they can take ... they're a marvel. Eat the rainbow.

roasted pumpkin, labneh, walnut gremolata, and pomegranates

One of my favorite dishes. Instead of pumpkin, you can use carrots or beets (or a mixture of the two) and you can also replace the spinach leaves with watercress, if you prefer.

SERVES 4

FOR THE LABNEH

1¼ cups Greek yogurt

1 garlic clove, crushed

good pinch of salt

FOR THE PUMPKIN AND SALAD

2¾ lb of pumpkin or butternut squash or other winter squash

¼ cup olive oil

½ teaspoon ground cinnamon

½ teaspoon cayenne pepper

2 inch piece of ginger root, peeled and finely chopped

black pepper

juice of ½ small lemon

4 cups baby spinach leaves

small bunch of cilantro leaves

seeds from ¼ pomegranate

FOR THE GREMOLATA

⅓ cup walnut pieces

zest of 1 lemon (removed with a zester)

2 garlic cloves, finely chopped

2 tablespoons chopped flat-leaf parsley

FOR THE DRESSING

2 teaspoons pomegranate molasses

smidgen of Dijon mustard

¼ cup extra virgin olive oil

pinch of sugar (optional)

squeeze of lemon

Make the labneh the day before you want to serve the dish, as on page 104, using the yogurt, garlic, and salt.

Preheat the oven to 375°F. Halve the squash and scoop out and discard the seeds and fibers. Cut into slices about 1 inch thick at the thickest part. (If you are using a long butternut squash, you can halve it horizontally as well as lengthwise before cutting the wedges, otherwise you could have long slices.) Peel each slice if you want, or you can leave the skin on if you don't mind discarding it when you are eating the dish. (Sometimes it is actually thin enough to eat.)

In a small saucepan, heat the regular olive oil, cinnamon, cayenne, and ginger. Put the wedges of squash into a roasting pan and pour the spicy mixture over them, using your hands to make sure the squash gets well coated. Season with salt and black pepper.

Put into the hot oven and roast for 35 minutes, or until tender and slightly caramelized, basting every so often. Put into a serving dish and squeeze the lemon over the top.

Make the gremolata by toasting the walnuts in the oven for five minutes (keep an eye on them because they burn easily). Now simply chop everything for the gremolata together.

Take the drained labneh out of its cheeseclothand gently break it up into nuggets.

Put the pomegranate molasses, mustard, and salt and black pepper into a small bowl and whisk in the extra virgin oil. Taste and add the sugar (if using) and lemon; you really have to work on this dressing to get a good sweet-sour balance, so use your taste buds.

Using about three-quarters of the dressing, gently toss the spinach, cilantro, and pumpkin together in a wide, shallow bowl.

Dot nuggets of labneh over the salad. Sprinkle with the gremolata and pomegranate seeds, drizzle the rest of the dressing over the top, and serve.

beet and carrot fritters with dill and yogurt sauce

The beets make these an amazing color but, if you prefer something mellower in tone, use parsnips or butternut squash instead. You can make different versions too: add 1⅓ cups crumbled feta cheese to make Greek-style fritters; or add a chopped, seeded chile, 2 teaspoons ground cumin, 2 teaspoons ground ginger, and 1 teaspoon ground coriander to the onions and sauté for a couple of minutes to make Indian-spiced fritters. (Use cilantro leaves in the yogurt if you make the latter.)

SERVES 4 (MAKES 8 FRITTERS)

FOR THE FRITTERS

2½ tablespoons peanut oil

1 small onion, finely chopped

2 garlic cloves, crushed

1 large ruuset or Yukon gold potato

3 large carrots

2 large beets

2 eggs, lightly beaten

salt and black pepper

FOR THE SAUCE

1 cup Greek yogurt

2 garlic cloves, crushed

1 tablespoon extra virgin olive oil

1 tablespoon chopped dill leaves, plus extra to serve

Heat ½ tablespoon of the peanut oil in a large nonstick skillet and gently sauté the onion until it is soft but not browned. Add the garlic and cook for another two minutes. Put into a bowl.

Coarsely shred all the other vegetables, keeping them separate. After you finish shredding each type of vegetable, put into a dish towel and squeeze out excess moisture. (Better use paper towels for the beets because they will really stain your dish towel.) Add the vegetables to the onion with the eggs, season well, and mix together. Make the sauce by mixing all the ingredients together.

Heat another 1 tablespoon of peanut oil in the skillet. Spoon enough mixture into the pan to make a batch of fritters each about 3½ inches in diameter. Cook over medium heat until a crust forms on one side, then carefully turn each over and cook on the other side, again until a crust forms. Don't overbrown or they will burn on the outside before they are cooked inside. After the crust forms, reduce the heat right down and cook for four to five minutes on each side, or until the vegetables are cooked through. (You'll know from the taste whether they are cooked right through. The potato becomes sweet.) You can keep the cooked fritters in a low oven while you finish the others, adding more oil to the pan to cook them, if necessary.

Serve the fritters with the yogurt sauce, sprinkled with more dill.

japanese family chicken, egg, and rice bowl (oyaka domburi)

This is a classic Japanese dish. It has a lovely name: "oyaka" means "parent and child." It's not quite clear whether my interpretation of that—calling it "family soup"—is right, or whether the name is a play on the fact that the dish has both chicken and egg (which is the parent, which the child?)

This recipe does require dashi (Japanese stock), but making dashi is easy and quick, so don't be daunted. Dried bonito flakes are expensive, but you don't need much. Follow the instructions for making it carefully; the temperature and the stage at which you do things is important, or it can turn out slightly bitter, or too fishy. Dashi can be kept for three or four days in the refrigerator, but doesn't freeze well (it tends to impair the flavor).

Traditionally this dish is made with white rice, but brown produces a good deep flavor. All the Japanese ingredients you need can be bought online.

SERVES 4

FOR THE DASHI

5 inch square of kombu

1 cup bonito flakes

FOR THE REST

¾ cup brown rice

4 eggs

1¾ cups dashi

2 tablespoons soy sauce

1 teaspoon sugar

1 tablespoon sake or dry sherry

6 oz skinless chicken breast, cut on the diagonal into slices about ¼ inch thick

1 onion, cut into fine slices (almost shaved)

8 large sprigs of watercress, coarse stems removed

1 sheet of toasted nori, crumbled (optional)

To make the dashi, put the kombu into a saucepan with 4 cups of water. To get the maximum flavor, let soak for 15 minutes, then place over medium heat. As soon as little bubbles appear on the surface and at the sides, take the pan off the heat. Sprinkle the bonito flakes onto the water and let them sink by themselves. After four minutes, pour the stock through a strainer lined with a coffee filter. (If you leave the bonito flakes too long, the stock becomes fishy.) Discard the solids.

Cook the rice in plenty of boiling water until it is tender (a matter of 25–30 minutes), then drain and return it to the pan. Cover to keep warm.

Beat the eggs lightly; the Japanese like to see streaks of white in the finished dish.

Put the measured dashi into a deep skillet or a sauté pan with the soy sauce, sugar, and sake and gently heat. When bubbles start to appear, add the chicken and onion and poach for about two minutes. The chicken will turn white.

Pour the eggs over the poaching chicken and cook for about a minute, or until you can see that the egg is set but still moist. You are basically making an omelet but in a little liquid instead of fat. The omelet should come away from the sides of the pan. Break it up into four.

Divide the rice among four bowls and put the chicken and egg mixture on top, spooning it onto the warm rice. Garnish with the watercress and the nori (if using) and serve immediately.

winter greens with crispy onions, tahini, and sumac

Savoy and cavolo nero (or kale) are really good together because the first is quite sweet and the second robust and bitter. You could also add cooked lentils to this at the last minute (just toss them in the pan and heat through when you are sautéing the cavolo nero). I know it seems like a pain to cook the two vegetables differently, but they do require different treatments before being tossed together. If you don't want to have the crispy fried onions, just omit them.

SERVES 6 AS A SIDE DISH

FOR THE TAHINI DRESSING

¼ cup tahini

2 tablespoons extra virgin olive oil, plus extra if needed

juice of ½ lemon

2 tablespoons plain yogurt

2 small garlic cloves, grated

salt and black pepper

FOR THE GREENS

½ savoy cabbage (or any other soft-leaf winter cabbage)

12 oz cavolo nero or kale (or a mixture)

3½ tablespoons olive oil

1 onion, very finely sliced

4 garlic cloves, finely sliced

1 teaspoon dried red pepper flakes, or to taste (you might want a little more)

small pat of unsalted butter

good squeeze of lemon juice

½ teaspoon sumac

To make the tahini dressing, beat the tahini (just use a fork) and then gradually add ¼ cup of water, the extra virgin oil, lemon juice, yogurt, and garlic. It might look, at some stages, as if it's going to split, but just keep going, it will come together. Taste and season with salt and black pepper. You may also want to add a little more water or extra virgin oil to thin the mixture. Different brands of tahini have different consistencies, so you have to alter the amount of water and seasonings you add. Your finished mixture should be about the thickness of heavy cream.

Remove the hard core from the savoy cabbage. Keeping them separate, tear the leaves of the savoy and the cavolo nero from their tough central ribs and cut the leaves into strips. Plunge the cavolo nero into boiling water for five minutes, then drain well.

Meanwhile, heat 1½ tablespoons of the regular olive oil and sauté the onion over fairly high heat until golden brown and crispy. Set aside.

Heat the rest of the regular olive oil in a saucepan that has a lid and sauté the savoy cabbage for one minute with the garlic and red pepper flakes. Now add 1 tablespoon of water, salt and black pepper, and the butter. Put the lid on and cook over medium heat for about two minutes, shaking the pan every so often. Remove the lid, add the drained cavolo nero, season to taste, and cook for another couple of minutes, until everything is hot. The garlic should be golden brown. Squeeze on the lemon juice. Put on a serving plate and drizzle with the tahini dressing (serve the rest on the side), top with the crispy onions, and sprinkle with the sumac.

spinach, pomegranate, and bulgur soup

This is based on an Azerbaijani soup, but I've taken liberties with the amount of pomegranate molasses (their version is very sweet-sour) and cooked the vegetables for much less time. The result manages to be grounded and earthy—all those beans, loads of greenery—yet with plenty of "top" notes (the fruity acidity of pomegranates, the cleanness of dill and mint). You don't have to make the chunky walnut and garlic relish for the garnish; you can just sprinkle with chopped toasted walnuts and pomegranate seeds, if you prefer.

SERVES 6

FOR THE SOUP

2 tablespoons olive oil

1 large onion, finely sliced

2 garlic cloves, finely chopped

2½ teaspoons ground cumin

¼ teaspoon ground cinnamon

½ cup yellow split peas

½ cup brown lentils

4 cups vegetable stock,
chicken stock, or water,
plus extra if needed

⅓ cup bulgur wheat

⅓ cup pomegranate molasses

salt and black pepper

4 cups torn spinach leaves
(coarse stems removed)

¼ cup chopped dill leaves

¼ cup torn mint leaves

¼ cup coarsely chopped flat-leaf
parsley leaves

TO FINISH

1 garlic clove, chopped

sea salt

¼ cup coarsely chopped
toasted walnuts

2 tablespoons extra virgin olive oil

2 tablespoons torn dill leaves, and/
or mint or flat-leaf parsley leaves

seeds from ½ pomegranate

Heat the regular olive oil in a heavy saucepan and sauté the onion for about 10 minutes, until it is soft and lightly browned. Add the garlic and cook for another couple of minutes, then add the cumin and cinnamon and cook for another minute. Add the split peas, lentils, and stock or water and bring to a boil. Reduce the heat, cover, and simmer for about 25 minutes.

Add the bulgur wheat, pomegranate molasses, and 1¼ cups of water and season. Return to a boil, then reduce the heat and simmer once more for 15 minutes.

Now add the spinach and all the herbs and heat through. Traditionally, this is cooked for about 20 minutes, but the soup is much fresher tasting—not to mention greener looking—if you give it only a couple of minutes now, just enough time for the spinach to wilt. (If you're making the soup in advance, add the spinach and herbs when you are reheating the soup.)

Adjust the thickness if you need to by adding more water or stock. It's a thick soup, but it's not supposed to be like a puree. Taste for seasoning as well.

To finish the dish, put the garlic and a little sea salt in a mortar and grind to a paste. Add the walnuts and pound to a coarse mixture, then stir in the extra virgin oil. Put spoonfuls of this on each bowl of soup and strew with herbs and pomegranate seeds.

kale, salmon, and barley soup with buttermilk

I grew up with vegetable and barley broth—it's both filling and restorative—and this is just a Scandinavian version. The fish is supposed to season the dish, it's not the main attraction. If you prefer something richer, serve it with sour cream mixed with dill instead of buttermilk. You can omit the potato if you prefer and increase the amount of barley by ⅓–½ cup.

SERVES 6–8

7 cups fish stock or light chicken stock, plus extra if needed

½ cup pearl barley

1 large carrot, finely chopped

1 large leek, trimmed, chopped and washed

2 small Yukon gold or white round potatoes, peeled and cut into small cubes

salt and black pepper

⅔ cup torn kale leaves (tough ribs removed and discarded

7 oz raw or hot-smoked salmon, skinned and cut into chunks

⅔ cup buttermilk

1 tablespoon lemon juice

1 tablespoon chopped dill leaves

Put the stock, barley, and carrot into a saucepan and bring to a boil. Reduce the heat and simmer for 15 minutes. Add the leek, potatoes, and seasoning and cook for another 30 minutes.

If your stock has really reduced, top off with water. In the last five minutes, add the kale and, in the last two minutes, add the salmon and cook gently (this will cook the raw salmon, or warm through the hot-smoked fish). You can add more stock or water if it seems too thick.

Mix the buttermilk with the lemon juice and dill and season. Serve each bowl of soup topped with a generous spoonful of the dilled buttermilk, and offer the rest in a bowl on the side.

winter menu jewels in cold weather

red lentil kofte | spiced quail with blood orange and date salad | yogurt and apricot compote

A grand meal—it's so beautiful it's almost regal—although the only big expense is the quail. The blood oranges used in the main course salad aren't in season for long, so grab them while you can.

red lentil and carrot kofte with pomegranates, cilantro, and tahini

Really easy to make, pretty, and addictive. If you can't get Turkish pepper paste—which has a really vibrant flavor—use harissa. (Find a recipe for Turkish pepper paste in my book *Salt Sugar Smoke.*)

MAKES ABOUT 30 (SERVES 6)

2 tablespoons tahini

juice of 1¾ lemons

4 garlic cloves, crushed

salt and black pepper

⅓ cup extra virgin olive oil

½ cup red lentils

⅓ cup bulgur wheat

3 large carrots

pinch of sugar

⅔ cup carrot juice or water

1 tablespoon olive oil

1 red onion, finely chopped

1 tablespoon ground cumin

1 teaspoon ground paprika

1 tablespoon Turkish pepper paste

1 tablespoon tomato paste

leaves from 2 bunches of cilantro, finely chopped

seeds from 1 pomegranate

1 cup baby salad greens

To make the tahini sauce, mix the tahini with ⅓ cup of water, then the juice of ½ lemon, 1 crushed garlic clove, salt and black pepper, and 2 tablespoons of the extra virgin oil. Taste for seasoning. You need to get the consistency right so you may need more water. It should end up about as thick as heavy cream.

Put the lentils in a saucepan with 1 cup of water. Bring to a boil, reduce the heat to a simmer, cover, and cook for 20 minutes, until completely soft. Remove from the heat and add the bulgur, stir, cover, and let stand for 20 minutes so the grains can plump up.

Cook the carrots with the sugar and salt and black pepper in the carrot juice or water (the carrot juice intensifies their flavor). When completely soft, drain, mash, and mix with the lentil mixture.

Heat the regular olive oil and sauté the onion for about seven minutes, until completely soft. Add the cumin, paprika, and remaining garlic and cook for another two minutes. Stir in the pepper paste and tomato paste and cook for 30 seconds. Stir the pepper and tomato mixture into the lentil and carrot mixture. Mix in the juice of 1 lemon, half the cilantro, seasoning, and 2 tablespoons of the extra virgin oil. Taste for seasoning.

Shape the kofte mixture into balls the size of a walnut in its shell, with an indentation in one side. Put on a serving plate. Fill each indentation with pomegranate seeds. Toss the remaining cilantro and baby greens with the remaining extra virgin oil and lemon, put on a plate, and drizzle with tahini. Serve the kofte with the salad.

spiced quail with blood orange and date salad

Sweet, sour, and juicy. If you find dates too sweet, you can cut the amount. Or temper the sweetness by tossing shaved raw fennel in with the blood oranges and dates.

SERVES 6

FOR THE MARINADE

⅓ cup olive oil

3 tablespoons pomegranate molasses

1½ teaspoons ground cumin

½ teaspoon ground cinnamon

2 tablespoons harissa

4 garlic cloves, crushed

4 teaspoons packed light brown sugar

¼ cup lemon juice

salt and black pepper

FOR THE QUAIL AND SALAD

12 quails

6 blood oranges

12 medjool dates, pitted and quartered lengthwise

2 red chiles, seeded and shredded

leaves from 1 bunch of cilantro)

leaves from 12 sprigs of mint

seeds from ½ pomegranate (or buy a package and use 2 heaping tablespoons)

FOR THE DRESSING

2 garlic cloves, crushed

⅓ cup extra virgin olive oil (fruity instead of grassy)

⅓ cup blood orange juice

¼ cup pomegranate molasses

2 teaspoons honey

drop of orange flower water (really, just a tiny splash)

To make the marinade, just mix everything together. Put the birds into a nonreactive shallow dish and pour the marinade over them, turning them to make sure they are coated. Cover with plastic wrap and put in the refrigerator for a few hours (overnight is even better if you have time).

When you're ready to cook, preheat the oven to 375°F. Put the birds into a small roasting pan and pour the marinade over them. Season with salt and black pepper. Roast for 25 minutes.

Meanwhile, make the salad (or make it immediately before you cook the appetizer). Slice the ends off the oranges so they have a flat bottom on which to sit. Using a sharp knife, cut the peel and pith off each, working around the fruit and cutting the peel away in wide strips from top to bottom. Working over a bowl, slip a sharp, thin knife in between the membrane on each side of each segment and ease the segment out. Put them into a bowl with the dates, chiles, herbs, salt, and black pepper.

Whisk all the dressing ingredients together. Pour two-thirds of teh dressing over the orange salad.

Spoon the salad onto six plates and sprinkle with the pomegranate seeds. Put the spicy quail on top and pour the rest of the dressing over the birds. Serve with bulgur wheat or couscous on the side.

yogurt with honeyed saffron syrup, almonds, and apricot compote

A really simple dessert that looks beautiful. If you don't usually like saffron, try it anyway—it's quite subtle and provides much of the visual impact.

SERVES 6

FOR THE COMPOTE

2 cups dried apricots

⅓ cup apple juice

juice of 1 lemon

wide strip of lemon zest

wide strip of orange zest

¼ cup agave syrup

crushed seeds of 8 cardamom pods

FOR THE HONEYED SYRUP

good pinch of saffron stamens

½ cup honey (ideally orange blossom honey)

2–3 teaspoons orange flower water, or to taste

TO SERVE

1 cup Greek yogurt

2 tablespoons toasted slivered almonds

The night before you want to eat it, put all the ingredients for the compote in a saucepan with generous 1 cup of water and bring slowly to a boil. Immediately reduce the heat to a simmer and cook for 10–15 minutes. It's important that you keep an eye on them, because some dried apricots are much softer than others and you don't want them to all fall apart (although it's fine if some do). Sometimes it takes 10 minutes for them to soften and plump up, sometimes a lot longer. You should end up with fat apricots in a syrup. If the syrup is a little thin (it depends how long the apricots have cooked), remove the apricots with a slotted spoon and boil the juices until they get thicker before returning the apricots. Let cool in the syrup, then put into a bowl, cover, and let stand overnight (remove the strips of peel before serving). You can keep the apricots, covered, in the refrigerator for a week.

It's best to prepare the honeyed syrup the day before, too, because the saffron continues to flavor it. Put 2 tablespoons of boiling water into a teacup or coffee mug and add the saffron. Stir well to release the saffron's color and flavor, then add to the honey with the orange flower water. Mix together, then cover, and let stand overnight.

To serve, put the apricot compote into little glasses or bowls, top with some of the yogurt, then spoon the saffron honey over the top. Sprinkle with some almonds and serve.

mustardy farro and roasted winter vegetable salad

This dish has beautiful muted colors, and it's really adaptable. You can serve it as a side dish with a vegetable or meat main course, or as a main course in its own right, adding sautéed mushrooms (wild if you have them), toasted walnuts or hazelnuts, crumbled goat cheese, or shavings of Gouda. Spelt or wheat berries can be used instead of farro (see page 224 for how to cook them). Those of you on a carb watch can omit the parsnips and increase the quantity of the other vegetables.

**SERVES 6 AS A SIDE DISH,
4 AS A MAIN COURSE**

FOR THE SALAD

6 carrots, trimmed, peeled and halved lengthwise (quartered if very fat)

3 parsnips, prepared as for the carrots

½ head of celeriac, peeled and cut into wedges

½ head of cauliflower, broken into small florets (use the core to make soup)

3 tablespoons olive oil

salt and black pepper

1 cup semi-pearl farro

1 tablespoon extra virgin olive oil

2 teaspoons white balsamic vinegar

2 teaspoons mixed seeds: hemp, sesame, sunflower, and pumpkin seeds are all good

FOR THE DRESSING

1 teaspoon whole-grain mustard

1–2 teaspoons honey

5 teaspoons cider vinegar

½ cup extra virgin olive oil (fruity instead of grassy)

2 garlic cloves, crushed

pinch of dried red pepper flakes (optional)

1 tablespoon finely chopped flat-leaf parsley leaves

Preheat the oven to 375°F. Put the carrots, parsnips, celeriac, and cauliflower into a roasting pan in which they can lie in a single layer: you want them to roast, not sweat. Drizzle with the regular olive oil, season, and turn over to make sure they all get well coated in the oil. Roast for about 40 minutes, or until tender and slightly burnished in patches.

Meanwhile, cook the farro. Put it into a saucepan and cover with plenty of cold water. Bring to a boil, then reduce the heat and cook for 20–25 minutes, until tender (even when cooked it retains a bite in the center). Drain and immediately dress with the extra virgin oil, white balsamic vinegar, and seasoning (this keeps the grain moist and seasons it thoroughly).

To make the dressing, put the mustard, honey, and vinegar into a small bowl, season well, and, using a fork, whisk in the extra virgin oil in a steady stream. Now mix in all the other dressing ingredients and taste.

Gently toss all the vegetables together with the farro and the dressing, adding any seeds you prefer.

also try this raw ... Make this with raw vegetables, omitting the parsnips. Raw cauliflower should be in small florets. Shave the carrots into ribbons, chop the celeriac into matchsticks (immediately squeeze lemon juice all over to stop it from discoloring) and cut 3 beets (a range of colored beets is especially lovely) into thin disks or matchsticks. Cook the farro and toss with the vegetables and dressing. You can add watercress, too.

quinoa, black lentil, mango, and smoked chicken salad with korma dressing

I love the look of this dish, it is such a fantastic array of strong colors. Use regular chicken if you don't like smoked, or flaked cooked salmon, or even sliced raw salmon that you've marinated in the juice of two limes for five minutes.

SERVES 4 AS A MAIN COURSE

1½ cups black lentils

1½ cups cream-colored quinoa

1 just-ripe mango

1 cup watercress leaves (coarse stems removed)

12 oz smoked chicken, skinned and neatly sliced

¼ cup torn mint leaves,

2 tablespoons olive oil

juice of ½ lime

FOR THE DRESSING

juice of 1 lime

½ teaspoon superfine sugar, or to taste

1 teaspoon fairly hot curry paste

¼ cup peanut or canola oil

salt and black pepper

3 tablespoons light cream

Put the lentils in a saucepan and cover with water. Bring to a boil and cook for 15–30 minutes, or until the lentils are tender but not falling apart (the length of time it takes depends on the age of the lentils). Meanwhile, toast the quinoa in a dry skillet for about two minutes, then put it into a separate saucepan, add boiling water, cover, and cook for 15 minutes.

Peel the mango and cut the side sections away from the central pit. Carefully cut the side sections into slices about the thickness of a nickel. It is difficult to remove the flesh nearer the pit neatly, so just use the side sections for this dish and use the remaining flesh for something else (or eat it).

Make the dressing. Using a fork, whisk everything together except the cream, then whisk that in, too. Taste for seasoning.

Drain the lentils, quickly rinse them in hot water, then toss in a serving bowl with the drained quinoa, the mango, watercress, chicken, mint, olive oil, lime juice, and seasoning (taste and adjust it if you need to—grains and lentils need assertive seasoning). Drizzle on the creamy korma dressing just before serving.

a veggie version If you want a vegetarian dish, replace the chicken with 3 avocados and add 3 finely chopped scallions.

carrot love

Yes, three carrot salads (and there are more in the pages that follow, too). Since I first tasted *salade de carottes râpées* (grated or julienned carrots tossed with vinaigrette) on an exchange trip to France, I have thought them a wonderful salad ingredient. Crunch. Texture. Sweetness. Color. And more filling than leaves. Carrot salads span the globe, too, so they take you places. And what about health? Carrots are rich in vitamins C and E, which help neutralize the damage done to cells by free radicals, and are a great source of betacarotene (the deeper the orange the more betacarotene they contain), which converts to vitamin A. And it's thought they help protect vision against degenerative conditions (such as cataracts), too. So carrots do (among other things) help you see. Get crunching.

moroccan carrot salad

There are salads in Morocco (some very sweet), made with raw or cooked carrots. The cooked carrot versions, while good, have a slightly "boiled carrot" flavor instead of a fresh taste. I prefer to cook the carrots halfway. They are no longer raw, they retain bite, but are certainly not tender. Herbs are optional; sometimes cilantro and mint make every Moroccan dish you cook taste the same, so add herbs—or not—depending on what else you are serving with this dish.

SERVES 4

8 carrots (about 1 lb)

2 garlic cloves, bruised

2 tablespoons lemon juice

salt and black pepper

¼ teaspoon harissa

½ teaspoon light brown sugar

good pinch of ground cinnamon

¼ teaspoon ground cumin, or to taste

¼ teaspoon sweet paprika, or to taste

2 tablespoons extra virgin olive oil

2 tablespoons chopped cilantro leaves (optional)

torn leaves from 4 sprigs of mint (optional)

Peel and trim the carrots and cut them into circles or batons. Put them into a saucepan, cover with water, and add the garlic. Bring to a boil and cook the carrots until they are no longer raw but not cooked. They should still have bite (but not be crunchy). I can't give you an exact time for this because it will depend on how you have cut the carrots, so keep checking the texture.

Meanwhile, mix together the lemon juice, salt and black pepper, harissa, sugar, and spices with the extra virgin oil. Drain the carrots as soon as they are ready and immediately add the dressing. Taste for seasoning and spicing. Add the herbs (if using) and serve.

japanese carrot and daikon salad

Very simple. I like this with boiled brown rice and a watercress salad—it is very addictive—but you can use it as an accompaniment to plenty of the Eastern dishes in the book, such as the Japanese rice bowl, Japanese ginger and garlic chicken, Seared tuna with avocado and wasabi puree, or Avocado, raw salmon, and brown rice salad (see pages 43, 63, 291, and 306).

SERVES 4–6

1 cup rice vinegar

3 tablespoons superfine sugar

2 daikon radishes (about 1½ lb)

12 carrots (about 1½ lb)

1½ teaspoons salt

Heat the vinegar and sugar together gently in a saucepan, stirring a little to help the sugar dissolve. Let cool completely.

Peel and trim the daikon and carrots, keeping them separate, and cut into matchstick-size pieces. Put them into colanders (or strainers). Mix 1 teaspoon of the salt into the daikon and ½ teaspoon into the carrot, mixing it well with your hands. Let stand for 10 minutes, then squeeze out the excess water from both. Put both vegetables into a clean bowl and mix in the sweet vinegar mixture. Keep in the refrigerator and serve nice and cold. It will be fine for about five days.

spiced carrot, date, and sesame salad

I never tire of this. It's great on its own, or have it with brown rice or hummus. If you don't have dates, raisins or dried apricots are good. Add extra seeds, such as pumpkin or sunflower, they provide great crunch. (They're good for you, too.)

SERVES 4

4 carrots, peeled

juice of 1 lime (some can be dry, so you may need 2)

4 pitted medjool dates, sliced

2 tablespoons coarsely chopped cilantro or mint leaves

1 tablespoon black or toasted white sesame seeds

2 tablespoons canola or olive oil

1 teaspoon cumin seeds

1 teaspoon mustard seeds

pinch of dried red pepper flakes

2 small garlic cloves, finely sliced

1 cup chopped baby spinach

Shredd the carrot coarsely into a bowl (or cut it into matchsticks, which takes longer but does produces a great texture). Add the lime juice, dates, herbs, and sesame seeds.

Heat the oil in a small skillet and add the cumin and mustard seeds. Cook over medium heat until they just start to splutter, then add the chile and garlic and reduce the heat. Cook gently until the garlic is lightly browned (about two minutes). Toss the flavorings immediately into the rest of the salad and add the spinach. Taste before adding any salt.

carrot and daikon salad with peanut-chile dressing

Whenever I serve meat with this, I wonder why I bother; nobody ever cares about the meat bit, this is what they want. It's fresh, crunchy, hot, and addictive. Have it on its own with brown rice or soba noodles or with other vegetable dishes, such as Japanese eggplants with miso (see page 188).

SERVES 6 AS A SIDE DISH

FOR THE SALAD

½ daikon radish

1 large carrot

6–10 pink radishes, depending on size

1 cup bean sprouts

¼ cup cilantro leaves

1 cup mizuna or watercress

1 tablespoon rice vinegar

juice of 1 lime

1 teaspoon superfine sugar

FOR THE PEANUT-CHILLI DRESSING

1½ tablespoons peanut oil

3 shallots, sliced

2 garlic cloves, finely chopped

¾ inch piece of ginger root, peeled and finely chopped

1 red chile, seeded and cut into slivers

¼ cup coarsely crushed peanuts

2 teaspoons superfine sugar

juice of 1 lime

1½ teaspoons soy sauce

2 tablespoons sesame oil

Peel the daikon and carrot, trim the tops and bottoms, and cut into fine batons. Put into ice-cold water, because this helps them to become crisp, while you make the rest of the salad.

Trim the radishes, then either slice them finely (on a mandoline slicer if you have one) or cut into matchstick-size pieces. Throw into the cold water as well.

For the dressing, heat the peanut oil in a skillet and add the shallots. Cook over medium heat until they are golden brown, then add the garlic, ginger, and chile and cook for another minute. Add the peanuts and sugar and stir for a couple more minutes. You should see and smell that the sugar is caramelizing. When this happens, take the pan off the heat and add the lime juice and soy sauce. Add 1–2 tablespoons of water (judge how much by the strength and consistency of the dressing), then the sesame oil.

Drain and dry the daikon, carrot, and radishes and put into a wide, shallow bowl with the bean sprouts, cilantro, and mizuna or watercress. Mix the rice vinegar with the lime juice and sugar, stir to dissolve the sugar, then toss this with the salad. Spoon the peanut dressing over the top and serve immediately.

winter menu spices and smoke

mandalay carrot salad | spiced smoked haddock stew | blood orange and cardamom sorbet

Sometimes you want to give your friends something grand, sometimes you just want a menu that uses everyday ingredients but uses them well. So it is with this. Carrots, lentils, and smoked fish are about as down-to-earth as you can get. A good dinner for a wet November night.

mandalay carrot salad

A very usable salad— easy to make and cheap—but quite addictive. It's wonderful on its own with brown rice (and some dal or lentil salad), or used in sandwiches along with spinach and chicken, or with some kind of earthy bean puree.

SERVES 4–6

2 teaspoons chickpea (besan) flour

8 carrots, coarsely shredded

juice of 2 limes

1 tablespoon Thai fish sauce, or more to taste

1 green chile, seeded and finely chopped

1 teaspoon superfine sugar

½ teaspoon salt

6 shallots

2 tablespoons peanut oil

1 tablespoon chopped roasted peanuts

2 tablespoons chopped cilantro leaves

2 tablespoons chopped mint leaves

Put the flour into a small, dry skillet over medium heat. Stir until it smells toasty and has turned a shade darker (don't take it too far). Transfer to a bowl. Put the carrots in another bowl and add the lime juice and fish sauce. Press the carrots with the back of a wooden spoon to crush them a little. Spoon them into a serving dish, add the toasted chickpea flour, chile, sugar, and salt and toss.

Cut the shallots lengthwise into thin slices. Heat the oil in a skillet over medium-high heat. Add the shallots and cook for about 10 minutes, until they are golden brown. If they start to brown before that time, reduce the heat. Lift out of the pan with a slotted spoon onto paper towels. Separate any clumps so that excess oil can be absorbed properly and let dry for about 10 minutes, until crispy and cool.

Just before serving, add the peanuts, crispy shallots, and herbs to the carrot mixture.

smoked haddock with indian scented lentils

This, with its English and Indian flavors, was inspired by kedgeree. There is a little cream in it. You can either reduce it if you're worried about your fat intake, or increase it a little if you're not. And if you're not sure whether you're worried, first read pages 284–285 to see if that helps.

SERVES 4–6

2 large onions

1 tablespoon butter

1 tablespoon curry powder

¼ teaspoon turmeric

½ teaspoon ground ginger

½ teaspoon cayenne pepper

ground seeds of 10 cardamom pods

2 small Yukon gold or white round potatoes, peeled (if you can be bothered) and cut into chunks

⅔ cup bulgur wheat

4 cups well-flavored chicken stock (preferably homemade)

salt and black pepper

¾ cup Puy or green lentils

1 bay leaf

¼ cup heavy cream

1 lb smoked haddock fillet, skinned, cut into big chunks

2 tablespoons chopped cilantro leaves

1 tablespoon peanut oil or sunflower oil

1 teaspoon dark brown sugar

juice of ½ lime, plus lime wedges to serve

Finely chop one of the onions and cut the other into fine slices.

Heat the butter in a saucepan and sauté the chopped onion until soft and slightly browned. Add the spices and cook for another two minutes. Add the potatoes, bulgur, and stock and bring to a boil. Season. Reduce the heat to medium and let simmer gently until the potatoes are tender.

Meanwhile, put the lentils into a saucepan on their own and cover with water. Bring to a boil, add the bay, then reduce the heat and simmer the lentils until just tender. This could take 15 minutes, it could take 30 (it depends on the age of the lentils). When they are ready, drain them and season well. Add the lentils and the cream to the potato and bulgur wheat "broth" to heat through, then add the fish and let it poach gently for about two minutes, until cooked. Stir in most of the cilantro.

While the fish is cooking, quickly sauté the sliced onion over high heat in the oil until golden brown. Add the sugar and let it caramelize while the onions get darker. Squeeze in the lime juice. Divide the stew among warmed dishes, spoon the caramelized onions on top of each serving, and sprinkle with the remaining cilantro. Offer wedges of lime alongside.

blood orange and cardamom sorbet

This can vary a lot in color, depending on what the flesh of your blood oranges is like; sometimes it's an orangey red, others more pinky. If you don't like cardamom, just omit it. It does, however, tie the dessert to the other two dishes in the menu.

SERVES 4–6

⅔ cup granulated sugar

8 cardamom pods, crushed

finely grated zest of 1 blood orange or regular orange

1 cup blood orange juice

juice of ½ lemon

pistachios, to serve (optional)

Put ⅔ cup of water and the sugar in a saucepan and heat, stirring to help the sugar dissolve. Add the cardamom, zest, and juices and bring to a boil. Take off the heat and let cool.

Strain and put the liquid into an ice cream maker to churn, or pour into a wide, shallow freezer-proof container and put in the freezer. If you choose the latter method, when the sections around the outside become firm, mix everything up together again with a fork. Do this three or four times during the freezing process to break up the crystals and make sure you have a smooth sorbet. If you don't want to do it by hand, you can put it in the food processor and blend briefly, but I can never be bothered with the cleaning up.

Serve the sorbet with some pistachios—crushed or chopped—on top of each portion (if using).

also try ... orange and rosemary sorbet. Make this in exactly the same way (using regular or blood oranges) and put a sprig of rosemary into the syrup instead of the cardamom. Strain to remove it before churning. Citrus works wonderfully with rosemary. Lavender—to which rosemary is related—is also good (although only available in season in the summer).

kale pesto with wholewheat linguine

Yes, I know. This sounds really holier than thou. But it isn't. In fact, I prefer it to basil pesto (which I've always found a bit perfumed and slightly cloying). If you're not the biggest fan of kale, this is the way to eat it; it's seasoned and enriched. You can also make this with cavolo nero or black kale in exactly the same way. I find whole-wheat pasta a tough one. I can barely eat the shapes, they just seem chewy and punishing. But linguine and spaghetti are a different matter.

Toss steamed broccoli into this (yes, I mean it!) for a double dose of greens.

SERVES 4

1 lb whole-wheat linguine

sea salt

12 oz kale (about 4 cups leaves once you've remove the tough stems)

2 tablespoons butter

¼ cup extra virgin olive oil (grassy instead of fruity)

¼ cup flat-leaf parsley

2 good-quality anchovies, drained of oil

2 garlic cloves, coarsely chopped

½–¾ cup grated Parmesan or pecorino

really good pinch of dried red pepper flakes (optional)

Put the linguine into a large saucepan of boiling slightly salted water and boil according to the package directions until it is cooked but still al dente.

At the same time, make the pesto. Wash the kale well and strip the fibrous leaves from their stems. Bring a large pot of water to a boil, plunge the leaves in, and cook for five minutes. Drain well. Put the cooked kale into a food processor with the butter, extra virgin oil, parsley, anchovies, garlic, and ½ cup of the cheese. Add the red pepper flakes (if using). Process, using the pulse-blend button. I like this pesto when it isn't completely pureed but still has quite large flecks in it, so don't overdo it.

Taste, adding the rest of the cheese if you want. To be honest, I don't need any extra; it has a great rich strong taste without it. But you decide.

Drain the linguine, then return it to the pan with a little of its cooking water. Mix in the pesto and serve immediately.

more greens please … **watercress pesto** Excellent with whole-wheat linguine and a poached egg. And good for you. Put 2 cups watercress, ¼ cup flat-leaf parsley (or basil) leaves, ¼ cup grated pecorino, 1 garlic clove, ⅓ cup toasted pine nuts (or sweeter cashews), ⅓ cup extra virgin oil, and seasoning into a food processor and pulse-blend. Serves 4 with pasta.

calabrian pesto Even my fussy kids like this. Heat 2 tablespoons olive oil and cook 1 finely chopped red bell pepper and ½ onion, chopped, for 10 minutes, until lightly caramelized. Add ⅔ cup finely chopped eggplant and cook for 10 minutes, then add 1 chopped plum tomato, 1 chopped garlic clove, and a good pinch of dried red pepper flakes for five minutes. Pulse-blend with ¼ cup ricotta, ⅓ cup almonds, 2 tablespoons extra virgin oil, seasoning, and ¼ cup basil leaves. Serves 4 with pasta.

good fat bad fat

The battle of the fats—saturated, polyunsaturated, monounsaturated—has been waged for more than fifty years. I used to ignore it. I couldn't keep up. I didn't understand the terms. And I love butter. But looking into it has been an eye opener. You could be eating stuff the World Health Organization, no less, labels toxic (no mincing of words here). So read on.

Butter was banned in our house—except for making cakes and pastry—in the mid-1970s. Mom put us all on low-fat spread. It seemed like the healthy option. Scientists had first sounded alarm bells about heart and circulatory disease in the 1950s. By the 1960s, these were big killers, and they still are. Saturated fat—found in butter and red meat—and cholesterol in the diet became the fall guys. The thinking on cholesterol has since changed. (Raised blood cholesterol is a risk factor for heart disease, but there is no direct correlation between cholesterol in your diet and levels of blood cholesterol.) Furthermore, it's now accepted that margarines and spreads made by the hydrogenation process—the means by which polyunsaturated fats were made solid—are bad for us ("toxic," as the WHO says). The process creates artery-clogging transfats that are a likely cause of heart disease. Producers now use a different process (called interesterification) to make low-fat spreads, but transfats are still around. *And you can't see them.* Factory-made cookies, cakes, and pastries, takeouts, and processed foods may contain transfats (they are cheap and extend shelf life). Some health organizations would like transfats eliminated and, until they are, be on the alert. Check labels (look for "hydrogenated vegetable oil," "partially hydrogenated vegetable oil," "vegetable shortening," and "margarine") and don't buy takeouts. This is the fat I can be clear on.

So where does this leave saturated fat? Plenty of people don't believe that fat equals heart disease. The French, they point out, eat red meat and cheese and don't have the high rates of heart disease found in the United States or Britain. The jury is out. There may be a correlation between saturated fat and heart disease but it's not as strong as that between, for example, tobacco and lung cancer. When we were instructed to watch saturated fat, the link was described as cause and effect. Some doctors specializing in obesity claim the emphasis on cutting fat has actually made us more overweight, because when we cut fat we tend to eat more refined carbohydrates. Experts also point out that foods high in fat fill you up, helping you eat less (which diets rich in refined carbs, with their blood sugar spikes, do not).

We've significantly reduced our intake of fat, eating thirty-three percent of our calorie intake as fats compared with forty percent in the 1960s. But heart disease is still a huge problem and obesity rates are soaring. There's clearly something wrong with the way we eat, but is fat the *main* villain?

Before you dive into that chunk of butter, consider the research on high-fat diets, such as Atkins. An American study in 2002 found people on a diet where they consumed sixty percent of their calories as fats lost more weight, and had better cholesterol overall, than others on The American Heart Association diet, which is low in fat and relatively high in carbs. Five years later, another American study found that Atkins dieters had "increased levels of LDL ('bad') cholesterol." Researchers also declared that the diet may be "potentially detrimental" for cardiovascular health. Confused? Me too. But it looks as though keeping an eye on saturated fats—until we know more—is sensible. And we shouldn't replace saturated fats with refined carbs, otherwise we're dealing with one problem but creating another.

What about polyunsaturated fats, most often seen in cooking oils? We thought they were healthy, but corn, sunflower, safflower, and grapeseed oils are high in omega-6 fatty acids and, used excessively, are now thought to be harmful. The good news is that research suggests olive oil (mainly monounsaturated fat) lowers blood pressure and the level of bad fats in the blood, and protects against heart disease. Two other monounsaturated fats— canola and avocado oils—are good, too (avocado oil is luscious, gorgeously green with a rich, buttery flavor). Cold-pressed walnut, hazelnut, and flaxseed oil are also good (though they're for dressings, not cooking).

Don't confuse omega-6 fatty acids with omega-3 fatty acids. Research clearly shows that omega-3 fatty acids, found in oily fish, help prevent strokes and heart disease and improve brain function. Everything good you've heard about oily fish seems to be true. So fill your plates with them! (Though the modern caveat has to be, "as long as they are sustainable.")

Trying to come to a clear conclusion, I went to the British Heart Foundation Web site. It's unequivocal. "Avoid saturated fats wherever possible." They also advise you to watch your intake of all fats, although many experts vehemently disagree with this last part, advising us instead to replace saturated fat with good fats (such as olive oil).

Me? I'm cutting out "low-fat" products—low-fat yogurt, low-fat cheese—because these often have something less healthy, usually sugar (which is *definitely* bad, see pages 24–26) added to replace the fat. I'm watching how much butter and cheese I eat (you'll know if you eat "balanced" quantities or not). Red meat isn't a problem because I don't eat much. I enjoy it, but love vegetables and grains, too, and the ecological considerations of eating too much meat (the planet can't support its production) are important to me. I don't eat much polyunsaturated fat—except for some frying—and use loads of monounsaturated fat (mainly olive oil). It's as wonderful as butter, and more varied, so I'm glad it gets approval.

What seems clear is that adulterated foods—such as hydrogenated oils—can be a disaster. Spreads may be made differently now but, given our experience, I'm not inclined to be trusting. It's also clear that cooking your own food instead of buying foods where fats are hidden, is the way to go. Some mornings I may put butter on my toast, another day it might be a slug of extra virgin olive oil and mashed avocado. Both sound great to me. And in each case I know what I'm eating and exactly how much.

Here's a thought to end on. The biggest source of fats in the UK, and particularly of saturated fats, is processed products such as hamburgers, sausages, and pies. Cookies and cakes are the next biggest source, then milk, and, finally, butter. Perhaps it's not the butter on our toast we should be worrying about.

leek, spelt, and goat cheese risotto

It's now usual to make "risottos" with barley, farro, and spelt, as well as with risotto rice. Pearl spelt is the most successful because it becomes very creamy. Semi-pearl farro is delicious (and better for you), but the grains remain firmer and are less creamy. Use the same quantities of spelt and stock and you can make all kinds of risottos. You could also add kale to this recipe at the end; just remove the thick stems, blanch in boiling water for five minutes, and drain.

SERVES 4 AS A MAIN COURSE

4 cups vegetable stock or chicken stock

2 tablespoons olive oil or canola oil

½ onion, peeled and finely chopped

4 leeks, trimmed, washed, and cut into ¾ inch-thick circles

2 garlic cloves, finely chopped

1⅔ cups pearl spelt

3 oz goat cheese, crumbled

black pepper

Put the stock in a saucepan, bring to a simmer, then reduce the heat to low.

Heat the oil in a large saucepan over medium heat. Add the onion and leeks and sauté gently for about 10 minutes, until soft. Add the garlic and cook for another couple of minutes, then stir in the spelt. Cook gently for a minute or two, stirring the grains in the fat and juices, then start adding the stock half a ladleful at a time, stirring often and letting each lot of stock become absorbed before you add the next. It should take about 35 minutes for the spelt to become tender with a little bite still in the center of each grain. If you run out of stock, add a splash of boiling water.

Gently stir in most of the goat cheese. Add black pepper. Taste for seasoning (you shouldn't need any salt if you've used chicken stock, you might if you've used vegetable stock). Serve immediately with the remaining goat cheese sprinkled over the top of each plate.

a barley version ... pumpkin and chestnut risotto

Heat 2 tablespoons olive oil in a saucepan and sauté 3 cups of peeled, seeded, and chopped pumpkin, butternut squash, or other winter squash, in two batches if you need to, until caramelized in patches. Set aside. Add another tablespoons of oil and sauté 1 small finely chopped onion, 2 chopped garlic cloves, and 1 chopped celery stick until pale gold. Add 1½ cups pearl barley and stir to coat in the juices. Add 4 cups hot chicken or vegetable stock a ladleful at a time. (You don't have to stir continually, only from time to time.) In 30 minutes, it will soften and become creamy. Return the pumpkin after 15 minutes and add 6 cooked, halved chestnuts five minutes before the end. Season. Add 1 tablespoon chopped parsley or sage leaves, check the seasoning, and serve with grated Parmesan. Serves 4.

fruited rye berries with gorgonzola

There's a mixture of warm and cold in this recipe, but it works nonetheless and is adaptable; you can sauté the pear slices, if you prefer (in which case use two pears and cut them into slices about ¼ inch thick).

If you want this dish as a side to go with other dishes, you can omit the pears and serve it in a big bowl, or it can be more of a carefully constructed salad served on individual plates. You can use raw radicchio or red Belgian endive instead of warm red cabbage, and wheat berries or brown rice instead of the rye berries, if you prefer.

The whole is gorgeously nutty. The key thing is to get your seasoning right.

SERVES 6–8 (DEPENDS IF IT IS AN APPETIZER OR SIDE SALAD)

FOR THE SALAD

4 cups rye berries

salt and black pepper

juice of 1 lemon, plus extra for the dressing

⅓ cup dried cranberries

1 fat, perfectly ripe pear

1½ teaspoons olive oil

1½ cups ¾ inch-wide red cabbage strips

1½ cups watercress leaves (coarse stems removed)

4 oz Gorgonzola or other blue cheese, crumbled

½ cup pecans, toasted and coarsely chopped

1½ teaspoons sunflower seeds

1½ teaspoons poppy seeds

FOR THE DRESSING

1 tablespoon balsamic vinegar

1¼ teaspoons Dijon mustard

1¼ teaspoons maple syrup

¼ cup walnut oil or hazelnut oil

1¼ tablespoons extra virgin olive oil (fruity instead of grassy)

Soak the rye berries overnight, then rinse well. Put in a saucepan with plenty of water to cover, then bring to a boil. Reduce the heat a little and cook for 50–60 minutes, until tender. Check during this time to make sure there's plenty of water in the pan and add boiling water if you need to. Drain it, season the rye, and add the juice of ½ lemon. Put the dried cranberries in a small bowl, cover with boiling water, and let soak for 15 minutes, then drain.

Meanwhile, halve and core the pear and cut into thin slices. Squeeze the juice of ½ lemon over the slice to stop them from discoloring.

To make the dressing, mix together the vinegar, mustard, maple syrup, and some seasoning, then whisk in the oils with a fork. Add lemon juice to taste.

Heat the regular olive oil and sauté the red cabbage over medium heat for about three minutes; it will wilt. Season. Put the rye into a wide, shallow dish (or divide it among plates) and add the rest of the ingredients (except the poppy seeds). Gently toss the various components together (try not to crush the cheese) with the dressing. Check the seasoning again—grains do need a lot—and sprinkle the poppy seeds on top. Serve while still warm.

radicchio and red onions on white bean puree

It is truly amazing what you can do with a couple of cans of beans. Here, they are transformed into a pretty classy dish (if you choose the right plate to serve it on, it even looks painterly). Bitter leaves, sweet onions, earthy beans, the different components work well together.

Eat as a main course or with a range of vegetables. Italian dishes are best alongside: try Beluga lentil, roasted grape, and red Belgian endive salad, though use watercress instead of red endive as the leafy component, or Roasted Jerusalem artichokes and pumpkin with agresto (see pages 172 and 178). It's also good with meaty fish.

SERVES 6

FOR THE BEAN PUREE

2 tablespoons olive oil

½ onion, coarsely chopped

1 garlic clove, crushed

2 (15 oz) cans cannellini beans, drained and rinsed

⅔ cup chicken stock or water

salt and black pepper

¼ cup extra virgin olive oil, plus extra to serve

good squeeze of lemon

FOR THE REST

2 large heads of radicchio

2 red onions, peeled

3 tablespoons olive oil

¼ cup balsamic vinegar

For the bean puree, heat the regular olive oil in a saucepan and gently cook the onion until it is soft but not browned. Add the garlic, the beans, stock or water, and seasoning. Cook over medium heat for about four minutes.

Process the beans and their cooking liquid in a blender or food processor with the extra virgin oil and lemon juice. Taste and adjust the seasoning. You can set the puree aside to reheat later, or serve it at room temperature.

Now for the rest. Halve each head of radicchio, then cut each half into four sections. Trim the bottom and a little of the white heart from each piece, without letting the sections fall apart. Halve the onions and trim the bottom of each. Cut each half lengthwise into semicircle wedges, about ¾ inch wide at their thickest part. (Or just slice them horizontally, if you prefer.)

Mix the regular olive oil, balsamic vinegar, and seasoning together in a dish and put the onions and radicchio in it. Gently turn over to coat, then let stand for about 10 minutes.

Heat a ridged grill pan until really hot and cook the onions quickly until well browned on both sides. Reduce the heat to low and let the onions cook until they are soft, turning frequently.

Meanwhile, spoon the bean puree into a serving dish, reheating it gently first if you want to.

Increase the heat under the ridged grill pan and add the radicchio. Let it brown on each side—this will happen quickly—and wilt. Put the radicchio and onions on top of the bean puree. Season and serve with a little extra virgin oil drizzled over the top.

uzbeki carrots

It's just carrots, but not as you've ever had them before. You can, honestly, eat this just with rice or couscous and be happy. Add a dollop of yogurt, too. If you want another vegetable dish to serve alongside, make sure it contrasts, so definitely not something sweet.

SERVES 6

1 tablespoon canola oil or peanut oil

1 onion, finely sliced

2 tomatoes, peeled and cut into thin wedges

4 garlic cloves, finely chopped

2 green chiles, seeded and shredded

¼ teaspoon ground cinnamon

½ teaspoon ground cumin

10 carrots (about 1¼ lb), cut into batons

½ cup dried currants

1 tablespoon dried barberries

¼ teaspoon saffron stamens

1½ cups vegetable stock or chicken stock, or water, plus extra if needed

1 tablespoon tomato paste

2 teaspoons honey, or to taste

salt and black pepper

1 tablespoon shelled unsalted pistachios, coarsely chopped

2 tablespoons chopped cilantro or mint leaves

Heat the oil in a large saucepan and sauté the onion over medium heat until golden brown, then add the tomatoes and cook until they are beginning to soften (about three minutes). Add the garlic and chiles and cook for another minute, then the cinnamon and cumin and cook for another minute. Add everything else, except the pistachios and herbs, and bring to a boil.

Reduce the heat and simmer the carrots until totally tender, about 25 minutes. The mixture should remain moist but not be swimming in juice. If it gets too dry, add a little more stock or water. If it is too sloppy, turn the heat up and boil off some of the liquid.

Taste for seasoning and balance; the mixture should be sweet and savory. Stir in the pistachios and herbs and serve.

seared tuna with avocado and wasabi puree

Ready in minutes, filling, zingy … everything you could possibly want.

SERVES 4

FOR THE TUNA

2 tablespoons olive oil

3 garlic cloves, crushed

¼ cup soy sauce

black pepper

4 (6 oz) tuna steak

pickled ginger, to serve

FOR THE PUREE

2 completely ripe avocados

1 teaspoon wasabi paste, or to taste

juice of 1 lime, or to taste

salt

Mix the olive oil, garlic, soy sauce, and black pepper. Put the tuna steaks in a dish and pour the marinade over them, turning to coat. Let marinate for 30 minutes.

To make the puree, halve and pit the avocados and scoop out the flesh with a spoon. Mash with the wasabi and lime juice, add salt, and taste. Add more wasabi, salt, or lime, as you think is needed.

Heat a ridged grill pan until it's really hot. Lift the tuna out of the marinade and gently shake off the excess. Grill the tuna for about one minute on each side (this gives you a moist interior that is raw in the center).

Serve the tuna with the avocado puree, with pickled ginger on the side. Offer brown rice as well, if you like.

try this with … leeks with miso mustard

Remove the tough outer leaves from 6 leeks and discard. Slice the bottom from each leek and trim the dark green leaves from the top end. Cut the leeks into 1½ inch lengths. Wash really well, making sure you get rid of any grit or soil inside the layers. Steam over boiling water for four to six minutes. They should be completely tender to the middle; test with the tip of a knife. Transfer to a clean dish towel and gently pat to soak up excess moisture. Whisk together ½ tablespoons Dijon mustard, 1½ tablespoons brown miso, 2 tablespoons white miso, 1 tablespoon honey, and 1½ tablespoons rice vinegar with a fork. Gently toss the dressing with the leeks and sprinkle with sesame seeds. Serves 4.

cranberry beans and kale with anchovy and rosemary sauce

If you are in a hurry, you can make this with a couple of cans of drained and rinsed cranberry beans and it will still be good. But home-cooked beans just have that unctuousness and depth of flavor that canned beans don't. In summer, fresh cranberry beans would also be wonderful (use about 3 cups shelled). Just shell the fresh beans and cook in simmering water for 30–40 minutes, or until tender, and replace the kale with 1 lb of spinach, adding the leaves to the dish at the end of cooking just long enough to wilt them.

This is a "meaty" dish, despite there being no meat in it. It's wonderful with farro (see page 223 for how to cook it). If you are in a meat-eating mood, it's also great with roasted lamb (and not bad with roasted chicken). The anchovy sauce is definitely a recipe to keep. It's excellent with meaty fish, such as monkfish.

SERVES 4 AS A MAIN COURSE, 6 AS A SIDE DISH

FOR THE BEANS AND KALE

1 cup dried cranberry beans, soaked overnight and drained

½ head of garlic (halved horizontally), plus 2 garlic cloves, finely sliced

a few parsley stems

1 dried chile, crumbled

1 carrot, coarsely chopped

1 bay leaf

3 celery sticks

½ cup extra virgin olive oil

juice of 1 lemon

salt and black pepper

1 lb kale

¼ teaspoon dried red pepper flakes

FOR THE SAUCE

1 teaspoon rosemary leaves

6 cured anchovies, drained of oil

juice of ¼ lemon, or to taste

2½ tablespoons extra virgin olive oil

Put the cranberry beans into a heavy saucepan with enough water to cover, the ½ head of garlic, parsley stems, chile, carrot, bay, two of the celery sticks, each broken in half, and ¼ cup of the the extra virgin oil. Bring to a boil, then reduce the heat to its lowest, cover, and cook for an hour or until the beans are tender but not falling apart. Drain the beans and remove the garlic, parsley stems, carrot, bay, and celery. Return the beans to the pan with another 2 tablespoons of the extra virgin oil and the juice of ½ lemon, salt, and black pepper.

To make the sauce, pound the rosemary in a mortar, then add the anchovies and crush to a paste. Gradually add the lemon juice and then the extra virgin oil, a little at a time, grinding as you work. You aren't making a mayonnaise, so don't expect it to emulsify. You'll be left with a lumpy sauce, but the pounding just melds all the elements together. Add black pepper and set aside.

Rip the kale leaves from their coarse ribs (discard the ribs), then plunge the leaves into a saucepan of boiling water. Cook for five minutes, then drain.

Dice the remaining celery stick and heat the remaining 2 tablespoons of extra virgin oil in a large saucepan (preferably a sauté pan). Cook the celery for one minute, or just until it is beginning to soften but hasn't yet lost its bite. Add the sliced garlic and red pepper flakes and cook for another minute, then add the beans and kale. Carefully heat these through without squashing them or overcooking. Check for seasoning, add some more lemon, and serve with the sauce.

soba noodles with chile, baby broccoli, and a fried egg

Made from buckwheat flour, Japanese soba noodles are healthier than regular pasta and have a gently meaty flavor. They can be eaten cold with dipping sauces, or hot (and are especially popular in broths in Japan). I also serve them in Japanese dishes where I would otherwise serve brown rice, such as in a Japanese rice bowl (see page 43). The following recipe makes a perfect lunch for one. Surprisingly filling.

SERVES 1

2½ oz soba noodles

5 baby broccoli stalks

1 tablespoon peanut oil

½ inch ginger root, peeled and finely chopped

1 red chile, seeded and finely sliced

2 garlic cloves, finely sliced

2 tablespoons soy sauce

3 scallions, chopped

1 extra-large egg

black sesame seeds

Put the soba noodles in a saucepan of boiling water. It will take about seven minutes to cook them (but follow the package directions), and you need to have everything else ready.

Trim the bottom of the broccoli stems. Steam the broccoli until tender (two to four minutes, depending on thickness).

Meanwhile, heat half the oil in a skillet and gently sauté the ginger, chile, and garlic until the garlic is pale gold. Add the soy sauce, then drain the noodles and add them to the pan. Toss in the baby broccoli and the scallions. In another small skillet, quickly sauté the egg in the remaining oil. Put the noodles and broccoli into a bowl and slide the egg on top. Sprinkle with black sesame seeds and serve immediately.

sea bass ceviche with avocado and grapefruit

This can be made with spanking-fresh mackerel if you would like a cheaper option than sea bass. It's gorgeous—bright-flavored, slightly sweet because of the grapefruit, and hot—so much so that I can eat the ceviche completely on it's own.

SERVES 4 AS AN APPETIZER OR LIGHT MAIN COURSE

FOR THE CEVICHE

1 lb sushi-quality sea bass fillet

½ small red onion, peeled and sliced wafer-thin

1 red chile, finely sliced

1 garlic clove, peeled and finely sliced

juice of 2 limes

salt and black pepper

2 pink or white grapefruits

2 just-ripe avocados

¼ cup coarsely chopped cilantro leaves,

FOR THE DRESSING

2½ tablespoons olive oil

3 tablespoons verjuice

Place the sea bass fillet skin side down on a board and, with a sharp knife, cut slices on the bias as you would for smoked salmon, leaving the skin behind. Put the fish, onion, chile, and garlic into a nonreactive shallow dish. Mix the lime juice with ¼ teaspoon of salt, pour it in, and gently turn the fish. Cover with plastic wrap and refrigerate for one hour, turning the fish again halfway through.

To cut the grapefruits into segments, cut a slice off the bottom and top of each fruit so they have a flat bottom on which to sit. Using a sharp knife, cut the peel and pith off each grapefruit, working around the fruit and cutting the peel away in wide strips from top to bottom. Working over a bowl, slip a sharp, thin knife in between the membrane on each side of each segment and ease the segment out.

To prepare the avocados, halve and remove the pits. Cut each half into slices, then peel each slice, working carefully to avoid squashing the flesh. Sprinkle with salt and black pepper.

Once the fish is "cooked" in the marinade, strain off the liquid. Whisk the olive oil, verjuice, and a little salt together for the dressing. Arrange the marinated fish (with the onions, chile, and garlic) on plates with the avocados and grapefruit. Spoon the dressing over and sprinkle with the cilantro.

goan baked fish with green chile and coconut chutney

Every so often I buy a fresh coconut and smash it on the front doorstep (watching it bounce off into the lavender bushes), but now you can actually buy little packages of fresh stuff, which is a boon for recipes like this. This is a big impact dish. Everyone smiles as you take it to the table. It kind of smells of exotic vacations.

SERVES 6

FOR THE CHUTNEY

1½ teaspoons peanut oil, plus extra for the fish

½ onion, coarsely chopped

¾ teaspoon cumin seeds

¾ teaspoon mustard seeds

3 garlic cloves, coarsely chopped

leaves from a 4 oz bunch of cilantro, plus extra small sprigs to serve (optional)

4 green chiles, seeded and coarsely chopped

juice of 3 limes

1 teaspoon superfine sugar

1 inch piece of ginger root, peeled and grated

2 x 6 inch piece fresh coconut, trimmed of dark skin and chopped, plus extra coconut, shaved wafer thin, to serve (optional)

salt

FOR THE FISH

6 (10 oz) porgy, scaled, trimmed, and cleaned

wedges of lime, to serve

Preheat the oven to 350°F.

For the chutney, heat the oil in a skillet and gently sauté the onion until softening but not golden brown; you just need to take off the raw edge. Scrape into a food processor. Put the cumin and mustard seeds into the skillet and toast until they become fragrant. Scrape these into the food processor, too, with all the other chutney ingredients. Process, using the pulse-blend button, until you have a coarse paste. Taste for seasoning.

Make two slashes on both sides of each fish. Season the fish inside and out with salt. Push some of the chutney into the slits and inside each fish, too. Put the fish on a lightly oiled piece of aluminum foil or parchment paper on a baking sheet and brush the top of each with a little more oil. Put into the oven and cook for 20 minutes, or until the flesh near the bone is white and has lost its glassy look.

Serve each diner with a whole fish, more of the chutney and lime wedges, sprinkling the fish with coconut shavings and cilantro sprigs (if using). Brown rice is a good side option, as is Kachumber (see page 89).

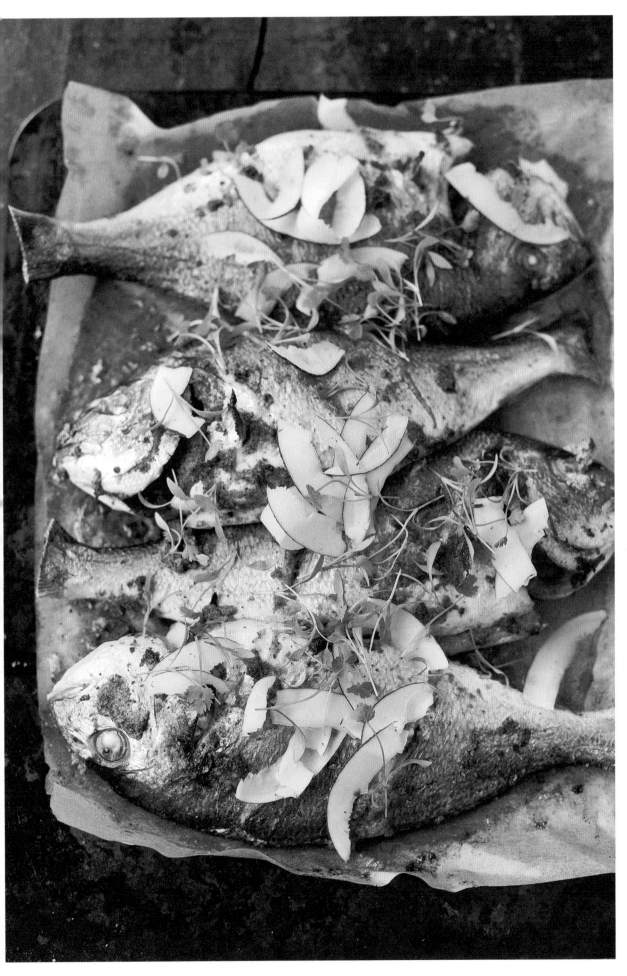

winter menu a painterly dinner

bagna cauda | georgian chicken with walnut sauce | orange and pomegranate cake

A meal of fantastic colors—the bagna cauda on its own looks like an old master—that completely demolishes the notion that wintry food has to be brown.

cold weather bagna cauda

This recipe is from chef Brett Barnes, who cooks at one of my favorite restaurants, Ducksoup in Soho in London. Bagna cauda is a Piedmontese sauce and I've eaten it there plenty of times, but Brett's is by far the best version I've ever tasted: pungent, earthy, and rich. You don't have to use only the vegetables I suggest here; you can serve cooked carrots, Jerusalem artichokes, or cardoons.

Yes, the sauce is high in fat—and saturated fat at that because it's butter—but saturated fat may not be the bogeyman we once thought it was (see pages 284–285). And you don't eat this every day. You can make it with just half the butter given here, or replace the butter with extra virgin olive oil (plenty of bagna cauda recipes are made completely with olive oil). But this is true to Brett's recipe.

SERVES 6

FOR THE BAGNA CAUDA

2 oz can best-quality anchovies

1 head of garlic, cloves separated and peeled

1 cup milk, more if needed

1 slice sourdough bread, crusts cut off

1 stick unsalted butter, diced

FOR THE VEGETABLES

bunch of mild, sweet radishes (preferably French Breakfast), leaves removed, trimmed

two heads of red Belgian endive, leaves separated

1 head of Swiss chard, leaves separated

18 baby broccoli stalks, trimmed

Chop the anchovies. Put the radishes and endive on a plate.

Cook the garlic in the milk over gentle heat for about 10 minutes, until completely soft; be careful not to let it go too far. At this point, the milk should still just cover the garlic.

Take the pan of garlic and milk off the heat and add the bread, torn into really small chunks, then the anchovies. Return to a low heat and simmer for two minutes, whisking constantly (one of those small wire whisks is ideal here). If you find that the mixture is so thick it won't move, add a little milk (only about 2 tablespoons). Once you've cooked and whisked for a couple of minutes you should have a thick, homogenous mass. Whisk in the butter, a little at a time, until you have a creamy yet rough emulsion.

Meanwhile, lightly cook the chard and baby broccoli (steam or boil them for two to four minutes, depending on size).

Put the chard and broccoli on the plate with the other vegetables. Serve with the warm anchovy sauce.

georgian chicken with walnut sauce and hot grated beet

The walnut sauce here is based on a Georgian recipe called *satsivi*. The authentic sauce is thinner (diluted with chicken stock), but I prefer the chunkiness of this version. Bulgur wheat, farro, or brown rice are good on the side (see page 223 for how to cook them). You could stir some greens through the grain—kale or spinach—but don't do anything too fancy, there's enough going on. You can buy the dried marigold flowers used in Georgian cooking online.

SERVES 6

FOR THE BEETS

6 beets

1½ tablespoons olive oil

salt and black pepper

3 garlic cloves, crushed

½ teaspoon ground coriander

½ cup chopped flat-leaf parsley

2 teaspoons red wine vinegar

1½ teaspoons extra virgin olive oil

FOR THE CHICKEN

1 (4lb) chicken

1 teaspoon cayenne pepper

2 tablespoons olive oil

1 lemon, halved

FOR THE SAUCE

2 tablespoons olive oil

1 onion, finely chopped

¾ cup walnut pieces

2 garlic cloves, crushed

¼ teaspoon ground cinnamon

½ teaspoon ground coriander

¼ teaspoon cayenne pepper

¼ teaspoon paprika

good pinch of ground fenugreek

½ teaspoon dried marigold (calendula) flowers, plus extra to serve

1½ teaspoons red wine vinegar

1 cup chicken stock

2 tablespoons chopped cilantro leaves

Preheat the oven to 375°F. Trim the beets and put them on a double-thickness square of aluminum foil. Drizzle with the regular olive oil, season, and pull the foil up and around them, sealing to make a "tent." Place in a small roasting pan and bake for one hour, or until tender to the tip of a sharp knife.

Season the chicken inside and out and sprinkle the cayenne over it. Put into a roasting pan. Drizzle with the regular olive oil, then squeeze the lemon halves over the bird. Put the lemon halves in the cavity and roast the chicken in the oven with the beets for 1¼ hours.

Meanwhile, grind together the garlic, ground coriander, and parsley for the beets until you have a paste.

Make the walnut sauce while the chicken is in the oven. Heat the regular olive oil in a skillet and sauté the onion until soft and pale gold, about 10 minutes. Add the walnut pieces, garlic, spices, and marigolds and sauté for another four minutes or so, stirring frequently. Put the onion mixture into a large mortar and pound to a coarse paste (traditionally this is pounded until smooth, but I prefer to keep some texture). Return to the pan and add the vinegar. Simmer over medium-low heat and gradually add the chicken stock, a little at a time, stirring and letting the mixture thicken. Taste for seasoning and stir in the chopped cilantro.

Check to see whether the chicken is cooked by piercing the flesh between one of the legs and the breast of the bird; the juices should run clear, with no trace of pinkness.

When the beets are cool enough to handle, peel, grate into a bowl, add the ground garlic and herb paste, the vinegar, and extra virgin oil. You can serve at room temperature.

Serve the chicken, sprinkled with a few dried marigold flowers, with the warm walnut sauce and beets.

orange and pomegranate cake

Incredibly easy. Not sugar-free I know but, as cakes go, not bad. And it is for dessert. Serve thin slices with Greek yogurt. It's very, very moist (almost puddinglike) so be careful when you're moving it off the bottom of the cake pan and onto a plate.

SERVES 8

FOR THE CAKE

1 cup fresh whole-wheat bread crumbs

1 cup ground almonds (almond meal)

¾ cup firmly packed light brown sugar

2 teaspoons baking powder

finely grated zest of 1½ oranges

1 cup olive oil, plus extra for the pan

4 eggs, lightly beaten

seeds from ½ pomegranate

FOR THE SYRUP

juice of 1 orange

½ cup pomegranate juice (pure juice, not "pomegranate juice drink")

1 tablespoon pomegranate molasses

2 tablespoons honey

In a bowl, mix together the bread crumbs, almonds, sugar, and baking powder. Add the orange zest, olive oil, and eggs and stir well until everything is amalgamated.

Pour the batter into an oiled 8 inch springform cake pan. Put the pan it into a cold oven and set the heat to 375°F. Bake for 45–50 minutes, or until the cake is browned and a toothpick inserted into the middle comes out clean.

Meanwhile, make the syrup by gently heating all the ingredients together. Stir a little until the honey has dissolved, then increase the heat and simmer for five minutes. You should end up with about ½ cup of syrup.

When the cake is cooked, pierce holes all over the surface and slowly pour the syrup all over it, letting it sink in. Let the cake cool completely in the pan. It will sink a little in the middle but don't worry; it makes a great dip for the pomegranate seeds to lie in. Sprinkle the pomegranate seeds on top just before serving.

avocado, raw salmon, and brown rice salad

A good midweek dinner or lunch dish. If you aren't enthusiastic about raw fish, you can cook it, but there is something very satisfying—and truly filling —about raw fish.

SERVES 4

salt and black pepper

1 cup brown rice

3 tablespoons rice vinegar

1 inch piece of ginger root, peeled and grated

½ cup mild olive oil

1 tablespoon sesame oil

2 teaspoons honey, or to taste

2 avocados

6 oz mild, sweet radishes (preferably French Breakfast), finely sliced

2 scallions, trimmed and finely chopped

¾ bunch of watercress (use only sprigs with fine stems, keep the rest for soup)

pickled ginger

wasabi paste (optional)

soy sauce, to serve

FOR THE SALMON

1¼ lb sushi-quality salmon fillet, skinned, tiny bones removed, sliced about ¹⁄₁₆ inch thick

juice of 2 limes

2 teaspoons superfine sugar

Bring a saucepan of salted water to a boil, then cook the brown rice until tender (it can take up to 25 minutes). While the rice is cooking, mix the rice vinegar with the ginger, olive oil, sesame oil, honey, salt, and black pepper.

You need to marinate the salmon while cooking the rice. The longer you marinate it, the more the lime juice will "cook" it; just toss the salmon in a nonreactive dish with the lime juice, sugar, and salt and black pepper, or you can let it rest for three to four minutes, to taste.

Halve the avocados and remove the pits. Cut each half into slices, then peel each slice.

When the rice is cooked, drain it and toss with most of the dressing (you need to set some aside for dressing the avocado), the radishes, scallions, and watercress. Taste for seasoning; rice does take a lot of seasoning. Spoon the rice mixture onto plates and lay the salmon and the avocado slices alongside. Put some slices of pickled ginger over the salmon and drizzle the rest of the dressing over the avocados. Grind some black pepper on top. Add a little dollop of wasabi to each plate (if using) and offer soy sauce for people to help themselves.

north african spiced mackerel with kamut

Kamut has a nutty flavor and I love its texture—good big grains—but it's quite bland, so needs strong seasoning. It works really well with ingredients that have a good assertive flavor, such as mackerel, and is excellent with Moroccan dishes (read more about it on page 224).

SERVES 4

FOR THE KAMUT

1¼ cups kamut berries or wheat berries

2 tablespoons juice from the preserved lemon jar

2 tablespoons extra virgin olive oil

½ cup pitted and chopped green olives

3 tablespoons chopped cilantro leaves

2 preserved lemons (1 if you are using larger homemade lemons)

FOR THE FISH

1½ teaspoons ground cumin

2 teaspoons cayenne pepper

½ teaspoon dried red pepper flakes

½ teaspoon ground ginger

2 garlic cloves, crushed

¼ cup olive oil

4 mackerel

salt and black pepper

juice of ½ lemon

The day before you are going to eat it, put the kamut to soak in plenty of water in a large bowl. Next day, drain it well.

Put the soaked, drained kamut into a saucepan and cover with plenty of water. Bring to a boil, then reduce the heat to a brisk simmer. Cook for 50–60 minutes, or until tender. The berries will have plumped up and be soft but still "nutty." Keep an eye on the water level and make sure the berries are always covered.

Preheat the oven to 400°F. For the fish, mix together the cumin, cayenne, red pepper flakes, ginger, and garlic with the regular olive oil. Rub the mixture all over the mackerel, inside and out, and season all over, too. Put into a roasting pan and squeeze the lemon all over the fish. Cook in the hot oven for 20 minutes.

Drain the kamut and immediately toss with the preserved lemon juice, extra virgin oil, olives, cilantro, and salt and black pepper. Halve the preserved lemons and scrape out the flesh (discard it). Cut the zest into shreds and add to the kamut, too.

To check the fish for doneness, look at the thickest part of the flesh near the bone; it should be white and not at all glassy. Serve the spiced mackerel with the kamut.

chicken with yogurt and pomegranates

Most of the dishes in this book have big flavors. They aren't subtle. This one is different. Apart from the tart juice of the pomegranates on top, all is creaminess and restraint.

SERVES 4

1½ tablespoons olive oil

salt and black pepper

8 skinless bone-in chicken thighs

1 large onion, finely sliced

1 teaspoon ground cumin

½ teaspoon cayenne pepper

¼ teaspoon dried red pepper flakes

6 garlic cloves, crushed

1¾ cups chicken stock

1 cup Greek yogurt

1 tablespoon all-purpose flour

seeds from ½ pomegranate

1 tablespoon finely chopped cilantro leaves

Heat the olive oil in a wide, heavy saucepan or sauté pan. Season the chicken pieces and brown them on both sides until lightly browned. Remove from the pan and set aside. Add the onion to the fat and cooking juices and cook it until soft and a pale brown. Sprinkle on the cumin, cayenne, red pepper flakes, and garlic and cook for another couple of minutes.

Return the chicken pieces to the pan with any juices that have emerged and add the stock. Bring to a boil, then immediately reduce the heat to low. Cover and cook for 20 minutes, then uncover and cook for another 15 minutes. The liquid will reduce somewhat and the chicken should be cooked through (when you pierce the thickest piece there should be no pink juices). If you have more than about 1 cup of liquid, take the chicken pieces out and boil to reduce the liquid.

Mix the yogurt with the flour (this stabilizes it and stops it from splitting). Add a small ladleful of the cooking liquid to the yogurt and mix well. Now add the yogurt to the pan and mix carefully. If you have removed the chicken to reduce the cooking juices, return it now. Gently heat through, then sprinkle with the pomegranate seeds and cilantro and serve.

lamb with kurdish rhubarb and split peas

The rhubarb and split pea braise here is actually served as a dish in its own right in Kurdistan, with grains on the side. I thought it made a good accompaniment to lamb, but you could try it as a main course, too (we're not used to seeing rhubarb as a savory ingredient, but it's good). My recipe is based on one in a wonderful book called *Silk Road Cooking* by Najmieh Batmanglij.

Cooking this with lamb cutlets means you can make the braise in advance, then cook the lamb at the last minute. The sauce is also good with venison (see below), though that's a bit unorthodox.

SERVES 6

⅓ cup olive oil

1 onion, finely sliced

4 garlic cloves, finely chopped

1 red chile, seeded and finely chopped

½ teaspoon turmeric

½ cup yellow split peas

3⅓ cups chicken stock, lamb stock, or vegetable stock

½ teaspoon saffron stamens

1 large tomato, coarsely chopped

juice of 1 lime

2 tablespoons superfine sugar, or to taste

salt and black pepper

1 lb forced rhubarb, trimmed and cut into 1 inch lengths

¾ cup flat-leaf parsley leaves

leaves from 8 sprigs of mint

¼ cup dill leaves

½ cup cilantro leaves

3 (10 oz) lamb cutlets, trimmed

Heat 2 tablespoons of the olive oil in a saucepan and sauté the onion for about five minutes, until soft. Add the garlic and chile and cook for another two minutes, then add the turmeric and cook for another minute. Stir in the split peas and add the stock and saffron. Bring to a boil, then reduce the heat and simmer for about 30 minutes. Preheat the oven to 400°F.

Add the tomato, lime, sugar, and seasoning to the split pea mixture and stir them in. Return to a boil, reduce the heat to a simmer, and put the rhubarb on top. Cover and cook for 15 minutes. The rhubarb should cook without completely falling apart. Gently stir it into the other ingredients with all the herbs, being careful not to make the rhubarb too mushy. Season and taste for salt, black pepper, and a sweet-sour balance.

Sprinkle the lamb with salt and black pepper and heat the remaining 3 tablespoons of olive oil in a sauté pan. Brown the meat all over, then transfer to a roasting pan and cook in the oven for 10 minutes. Take the lamb out, cover, and keep warm to rest for 10 minutes.

Cut the lamb cutlets into thick slices. Serve with the rhubarb and split pea braise, some Greek yogurt, and grains (bulgur is very good here). A watercress salad is good on the side, too.

try the braise with ... venison. Brush 6 venison steaks (about 6 oz each, cut from the leg or the loin) with olive oil and season with salt and black pepper. Heat a skillet until really hot, then sear the steaks on each side so they get a really good color. Reduce the heat and cook until rare, it should take about 2½ minutes on each side. Cut each steak into four slices, just to reveal the lovely pinkness inside, and serve on warm plates with spoonfuls of the braise alongside. Serves 6.

grilled vietnamese chicken with table salad

Vietnamese table salad isn't a salad as we know it, because the various elements aren't tossed together but are instead offered separately. The diner is supposed to take pieces of chicken and various vegetables, then roll them all up in large lettuce leaves and dip the resulting package in a hot sauce. This is the most wonderful kind of eating. Offer napkins, because you eat this with your hands.

SERVES 4

FOR THE CHICKEN

3 lemon grass stalks, white part only, finely chopped

4 garlic cloves, chopped

salt and black pepper

1 teaspoon superfine sugar

1 tablespoon Thai fish sauce

2½ tablespoons vegetable oil or sunflower oil

4 skinless chicken breasts

FOR THE DIPPING SAUCE

8 garlic cloves

2 red chiles, seeded and finely chopped

¾ inch piece of ginger root, peeled and grated

2 tablespoons granulated sugar

juice of 2 limes

½ cup Thai fish sauce

FOR THE SALAD

1 small, slightly underripe mango

3 carrots, peeled and cut into fine batons

½ cucumber, cut into fine batons

1 cup bean sprouts

leaves from a small bunch of mint

leaves from a small bunch of basil

leaves from ¼ head of Romaine or other large lettuce, washed

First marinate the chicken. Using a mortar and pestle or a small food processor, grind the lemon grass and garlic together with some salt and black pepper. Now work in the sugar, fish sauce, and oil. Put the chicken in a bowl and pour the marinade over it, turning to make sure everything gets well coated. Cover and let stand in the refrigerator for a couple of hours, or overnight.

To make the dipping sauce, using a mortar and pestle or small food processor, pound or process the garlic, chiles, ginger, and sugar together, then add the lime juice and fish sauce. Add ¼–⅓ cup of water (according to how strong you want it) and mix well.

For the salad, peel the mango and cut the sides off from near the pit. Cut the side sections into slices or batons. Remove the rest of the flesh from the mango and do the same with it. The flesh must be intact and not soft or bruised, so keep any parts that are less than perfect for making a smoothie (or eat them).

Now, basically, you just provide the array of fruit, vegetables, and herbs on a plate. You can either toss the ingredients together (except for the lettuce leaves), or keep them separate and let people pick what they want to add to their plates.

Heat a ridged grill pan until hot and take the chicken out of the marinade. Cook each piece on both sides over medium-high heat at first, and then on a lower heat until the chicken is cooked through, turning it every so often.

Serve the chicken with the table salad, the dipping sauce, and some brown rice on the side. Generally, diners put their choice of fruit, vegetables, herbs, and chicken together, roll them up in a lettuce leaf, and dip in the dipping sauce. Let people help themselves.

beef carpaccio with beluga lentils, horseradish, and buttermilk

Delicious, filling, luxurious, this is great for entertaining. Beef tenderloin is expensive, I know, but it is only a small amount per head.

SERVES 6 AS A MAIN COURSE

FOR THE DISH

4 medium or 8 small beets

1 tablespoon olive oil, plus extra for the beets

salt and black pepper

½ red onion, finely chopped

½ celery stick, finely chopped

1 garlic clove, finely chopped

1¼ cups black lentils

⅓ cup extra virgin olive oil, plus extra to serve

1 tablespoon white balsamic vinegar

good squeeze of lemon juice

2 tablespoons chopped dill leaves

1 lb well-aged beef tenderloin, in one piece

1½ inch fresh horseradish, peeled and grated

FOR THE BUTTERMILK DRESSING

½ cup buttermilk

½ garlic clove, crushed

1 tablespoon extra virgin olive oil

For the beets, preheat the oven to 425°F. Remove any leaves from the beets. If they're nice and fresh, keep them (they can go on the plate, too). If they're at all withered, then throw them out. Wash the beets and set them on a double sheet of aluminum foil in a roasting dish (use enough foil to make a kind of tent around them). Drizzle with olive oil and season. Pull the foil up around the vegetables, seal the edges, and put into the hot oven. Cook for about 30 minutes, or one hour if using medium beets, then check for tenderness with the tip of a knife; if the beets aren't tender right through, return them to the oven and cook until they are.

Meanwhile, cook the lentils. Heat the 1 tablespoon of regular olive oil in a saucepan and add the onion and celery. Sauté until the vegetables are soft but not browned. Add the garlic and cook for another two minutes, then add the lentils and enough water to cover by about 2 inches. Bring to a boil, reduce the heat, and simmer until the lentils are tender (check after 15 minutes, as cooking time depends on the age of the lentils). Drain and immediately add the extra virgin oil, white balsamic, lemon juice, salt and black pepper, and dill.

If you have reserved any beet leaves, wash them well, then blanch them in boiling, salted water for three minutes. Scoop them out with a slotted spoon onto a dry dish towel and carefully dry them.

Wipe the meat with paper towels and remove any fat or sinew from the surface. Using a sharp, fine knife—I use a fish filleting knife—cut the beef into very thin slices across the grain. Put these between two sheets of dampened wax paper and beat them with a mallet or rolling pin (do several pieces at once).

Mix all the ingredients for the dressing and season to taste.

Halve or quarter the roasted beets, depending on size and arrange on plates with the beef, lentils, and blanched leaves (if using). Drizzle the beets and leaves with extra virgin oil. Season the leaves. Sprinkle on some of the horseradish and offer the rest in a small bowl, serving the buttermilk dressing in another bowl.

braised venison and beet with horseradish

There are a lot of light, bright, quickly cooked dishes in this book, but you crave dark, mellow stews in winter. They don't have to be rich in wine, however, and vegetables can play as big a role as meat. Venison is great—lean with a strong flavor—and great with whole grain,s such as barley, bulgur wheat, farro, or spelt, on the side (see pages 223–224 for how to cook those). Just make sure to keep checking and stirring, venison can become dry, so you need to keep an eye on it. A dish for a cold Scandinavian day.

SERVES 6

salt and black pepper

3 tablespoons all-purpose flour

2¼ lb braising venison, cut into cubes

1 tablespoon peanut oil or sunflower oil, plus extra if needed

2 onions, coarsely chopped

10 juniper berries, crushed

sprig of rosemary

2 cups beef stock or chicken stock, plus extra if needed

1 tablespoon plum or red currant jelly or preserves

4 beets, peeled

1½ tablespoons chopped dill leaves

fresh grated horseradish, to serve

Preheat the oven to 300°F. Season the flour, then toss the meat in it (you need only a light coating, so vigorously shake off the excess).

Heat the oil in a heavy ovenproof casserole or Dutch oven. Brown the venison all over in batches, removing each once it has browned. Don't crowd the pan, or the meat will steam instead of brown. Sauté the onions in the same pan (you may need a little more oil) until soft and golden brown, then stir in the juniper and rosemary and return the meat. Add the stock and jelly, then season.

Cut the beets into wedges, about ½ inch thick at the thickest part, and add to the pan. Bring to a boil, then reduce the heat to really low, cover, and put into the oven. After 1½ hours, uncover and stir occasionally for up to another 30 minutes; the liquid will reduce and thicken and the venison should become completely tender. If it seems dry, add a little more stock or water. Taste for seasoning. Sprinkle with the dill and horseradish and serve.

for something different ... You can replace the beets with squash and use a little honey instead of red currant jelly. This is good with Walnut gremolata (see page 254) instead of dill and horseradish sprinkled on top. Or replace the beets with mixed fresh and dried wild mushrooms, or regular mushrooms.

litchis in jasmine tea

Subtle and delicately perfumed. Be careful not to let the tea get too perfumed—don't brew it for long—and don't add too much lime juice, or the other flavors will be overwhelmed.

SERVES 4

2 jasmine-scented green tea bags

⅔ cup granulated sugar

squeeze of lime juice, to taste

24 litchis (or lychees), peeled and pitted

Put the tea bags into a teapot or a heatproof liquid measuring cup and add 1¼ cups of boiling water. Let steep for just 90 seconds; you don't want it to get too strong and perfumed. Remove and discard the tea bags and put the tea into a pan with the sugar. Heat the contents of the pan, stirring to help the sugar dissolve. Bring to a boil and cook until reduced by one-third. Add the lime but be careful; it's just supposed to heighten the flavors, not mask the delicate jasmine. Let cool completely.

Put the litchis into a dish and pour the syrup over the top. Serve on its own. Anything else would really mask the flavors.

an alternative for warmer months...

It's difficult to get hold of litchies in the summer, so you may have to use canned litchis for this (but they are a good product). Make the syrup as above, but use rose-scented green tea. Drain a 15 oz can of litchis, put the fruit into a bowl, and add 1½ cups raspberries. Pour the syrup over the fruit. If you can't find rose-scented green tea, use green tea and add 1 teaspoon of rose water (taste as you add, because flower waters vary in strength). Raspberries, roses, and litchis are just sublime together. You could also use geranium-scented water instead of rose water. Serves 4–6.

pink rhubarb baked with star anise

Simple, not too sweet and good for breakfast as well as for dessert. Baking rhubarb is much easier than poaching (I invariably manage to let poached rhubarb fall apart, whereas, baked, the pieces stay intact and beautiful). If you want to extend it, add slices of ripe mango, or mango and litchis, or grapefruit (see below) to the cooked rhubarb; these all make a stunning looking dish.

SERVES 6

1 lb young rhubarb

½ cup superfine sugar

juice of 1 small orange

1 star anise

Preheat the oven to 340°F.

Trim the rhubarb stems at each end and cut into lengths of about 1½ inches. Put into an ovenproof dish in which the pieces can sit in a single layer. Sprinkle with the sugar and add the orange juice. Break the star anise into 3–4 pieces and add to the liquid in the dish.

Cover with a piece of aluminum foil and bake in the oven for 20–30 minutes, until the rhubarb is tender but intact. It must not be at all mushy. Let cool.

try adding … **mango or grapefruit** This is delicious—and stunningly pretty—with the addition of mango or grapefruit. Add twice the amount of orange juice and another 2 tablespoons of sugar—so you end up with more syrup—cook the rhubarb and let stand until it has completely cooled, then add 1 small mango. You need to peel it, cut the sides off from each side of the pit, then cut the side sections into slices about the thickness of a quarter Gently mix these into the rhubarb, being careful not to let the rhubarb fall apart. Pink or red grapefruit need to be segmented (see page 44). Add the segments from two fruits to the rhubarb once it's cool. Both versions serve 8 or more.

mulled quince and pear compote with cranberries

Quinces are luscious and honeyed so you don't need much to feel replete. They benefit from being mixed with pears—quinces can be almost *too* sweet on their own—and the cranberries cut this, too. Leftovers are fabulous on oatmeal.

SERVES 8

2 cups cranberry juice

⅔ cup firmly packed light brown sugar

½ cinnamon stick, broken

3 cloves

3 quinces, peeled, quartered, and cored

juice of 1 lemon

2 strips of orange zest

3 fat pears (not too ripe), peeled, quartered, and cored

1½ cups cranberries

Put the cranberry juice, sugar, cinnamon, and cloves into a wide, heavy saucepan with ⅔ cup of water and slowly bring to a boil, stirring a little to help the sugar dissolve. Reduce the heat to its lowest, add the quinces, lemon juice, and orange zest, and cook gently for 15 minutes. Add the pears and gently poach those for another 15 minutes (depending on how ripe your pears are). Turn the fruit every so often to make sure all sides get to sit in the poaching liquid.

Once the quinces and pears are almost tender, add the cranberries and gently stir them in. Cook for another 5 or 10 minutes. The cranberries should burst and color the poaching liquid and the fruit should be completely tender. You shouldn't need to reduce the poaching liquid; quinces have loads of pectin in them so it should thicken as it cools.

Transfer the fruit and juices to a serving bowl (whip out the cinnamon and the cloves). Serve at room temperature with yogurt.

pomegranates, oranges, and dates with flower water syrup

Fresh, light, scented, I get cravings for this dish. Don't assemble it too far in advance. It tastes good slightly chilled, but it's best not to put it in the refrigerator for too long as it loses its visual sparkle (and the oranges get a bit too soft).

SERVES 4–6

juice of 3 lemons

¾ cup granulated sugar

1 wide strip of lemon zest

1 wide strip of orange zest

2 tablespoons orange flower water

8 dates, pitted

5 oranges

⅔ cup pomegranate seeds

Heat 1⅓ cups of water, the lemon juice, and sugar together with the strips of zest, stirring from time to time to help the sugar dissolve. Bring to a boil, then reduce the heat and simmer for 10–12 minutes, until the mixture is syrupy. You will add oranges later and their juices will render it a bit thinner again. Let cool, then strain to remove the zests and add the flower water.

Halve the dates, then cut each half into three slices.

Cut the top and bottom off the oranges so they have a flat bottom on which to sit. Using a sharp knife, cut the peel and pith off each, working around the fruit and cutting the peel away in wide strips from top to bottom. You can either cut the oranges into slices or into segments, whichever way you cut them, catch the juice as you work and add to the syrup.

Put the oranges in a shallow bowl, layering them up with the pomegranate seeds and dates. Pour the syrup over the fruit. Chill; this is delicious and refreshing served cold. Offer Greek yogurt—slightly sweetened if you like—on the side.

the good loaf

It's much easier to get proper, handmade bread than it used to be, but beware the healthy pretender. The moniker "whole-wheat" is open to interpretation, likewise the term "natural." To think that all whole-wheat loaves are equal—and equally healthy—is like thinking a Chevy is as good as a Rolls Royce, because they're both cars.

Artisan bakeries are springing up everywhere and that's where you will find a good loaf. (And I mean *proper* artisan bakeries, not small-scale "craft" bakeries that make better-looking breads with the same cocktail of artificial additives, "improvers," and hidden processing aids as industrial bakers.) Good artisan bakeries employ slower methods to make their bread, generally use less industrial (and so more wholesome) flours, smaller quantities of yeast, and a wider range of grains. They have the skills to turn flour, water, salt, and yeast into minor works of art, and to deal with natural variations in their product. They don't always have their own shops, but you can find their stuff at farmers' markets and delis. Do an Internet search for local organic bakeries in your area. The Bread Bakers Guild of America (www.bhga.org) is a community who work together to support the principle and practice of producing the highest quality baked goods, whether professionally or at home.

I realize this sounds precious and that this kind of bread is not cheap. But why is it better not to care about what you eat, knowingly to eat inferior stuff and not to support small businesses who care about their produce? And just compare the experiences. Eat a slice of whole-wheat bread that you've bought in a supermarket alongside one from an artisan loaf. The one from the supermarket won't taste that good; in fact, it has little flavor. The slice from the artisan bakery will taste much better—nutty and deep—but here's the crunch (especially if you're watching your weight): the artisan bread will also make you feel more satisfied, so you don't want another slice, and another. I can eat three slices of supermarket bread in a row (I'm sure I'm not the only one who, in times of stress, can live on toast). But the well-made loaf? One slice. Not only has the eating been pleasurable, but I'm much more satisfied. The bread is heavier and denser. And sourdoughs, which seem expensive when you buy them, last for days (you have to toast them on the third day, but that enlivens that tangy flavor).

Is it okay to eat bread at all if you're watching your weight? All white breads and some whole-wheat breads have high glycemic indexes (GI): they cause surges in blood sugar and insulin (read more on pages 24–25). I haven't banned baguette, but eat it only occasionally. Long-fermented breads such as genuine sourdough, pumpernickel, and some other ryes have a lower GI because of their long fermentation, so I go for those, although not *just* because it's better to eat complex carbohydrates; it's mostly because they have a great, full flavor that makes you experience bread as a proper food and not a "filler." I don't buy sliced white except for nostalgic tomato sandwiches (soggy tomato sandwiches made with pappy white bread were in my childhood lunch box). You can make your own bread, too (there are recipes in this book and, once you start, you get used to it). But if you're buying bread, shop well. You'll feel better, you'll eat better … and you'll eat less of it.

black bread

This—the classic Russian bread—is from Dan Lepard's fabulous baking book *Short and Sweet*. I have changed it only slightly. It is one of the most delicious breads I make, soft and yielding with a deep, dark flavor. One slice of it seems to be much more satisfying than two of any other type of bread. Eat it with raw or smoked fish, or as part of a Scandinavian-style breakfast.

Rye bread is easy to buy, which is why I haven't given a recipe for it in the book, but black bread is much harder to find and, in any case, it is a joy to make. The dough is a gorgeous rusty color and smells heady and sweet. The whole process is invigorating.

MAKES 1 LARGE LOAF

1½ cups rye flour

2½ teaspoons active dried yeast

1 tablespoon packed brown sugar

2 tablespoons unsweetened cocoa powder

2 tablespoons instant coffee granules

¼ cup black molasses

4 teaspoons caraway seeds, plus 1 teaspoon for the top

3½ tablespoons unsalted butter

3 cups white bread flour

2 teaspoons salt

1⅓ cups finely shredded raw carrot

peanut oil for oiling

1–2 teaspoons sesame seeds

Put 1 cup of cold water into a saucepan and bring to a boil. Whisk in ⅓ cup of the rye flour with a fork—it will look like oatmeal—and let cool to lukewarm (about 15 minutes). Add the yeast and 1 teaspoon of the sugar, stir well, cover and let stand at room temperature for 45 minutes. Heat ½ cup more water and add the cocoa, coffee, molasses, 4 teaspoons of caraway seeds, the rest of the sugar, and the butter. Stir until the butter has melted. Let stand until lukewarm.

Put the white flour and the rest of the rye flour into a bowl with the salt. Make a well in the center and pour the yeast mixture into it, followed by the molasses liquid and the carrot. Mix until you have a sticky dough. Lightly oil a small area of your work surface and your hands and put the dough on to it. Knead the dough on this, or in a food mixer fitted with a dough hook. If you are doing it yourself, knead for 10 minutes; if in the food mixer, knead for 5 minutes. The dough will be glossy, taut and a rusty mud color, flecked with carrot. And it will smell delicious. Put into a lightly oiled bowl and cover with oiled plastic wrap. Let stand at room temperature for one hour (it should increase in size by about half).

Punch down the dough for 30 seconds, then shape into a round loaf with the seam underneath and put on an oiled baking sheet. Cover with the oiled plastic wrap and let stand at room temperature for about an hour. Preheat the oven to 425°F.

Remove the plastic wrap—the dough will be beautifully smooth and pillowy—and brush the surface with water. Sprinkle with the sesame and caraway seeds and cut a deep cross in the top with a serrated knife. Bake in the hot oven for 20 minutes, then reduce the heat to 350°F and bake for another 20 minutes. If you slide the loaf off and tap the underneath it should sound hollow. Slide onto a wire rack and let cool.

final thoughts

This book was finished when I started a list of guidelines (I forget things, so I love lists.) It wasn't a "diet," but a way of eating that took my newly acquired knowledge into account. This is a personal aide mémoire, but I hope you find it useful.

Why should you care how a food writer eats? Because they love food and will not suggest a way of eating, however healthy, that isn't pleasurable. Also, as they are surrounded by temptation, they know well the pitfalls facing those who love food.

After reading this book, you might end up with your own guidelines. You know better than I what is possible in your life, as well as your personal weaknesses. You might put away half a pound of cheese while preparing dinner, or find it hard to stop at one glass of wine. The following sums up what I have taken to heart during my "change of appetite."

useful mantras

Mantras are good because you can call them to mind easily. One of my favorites is from the American journalist Michael Pollan. It is, "Eat real food, mostly plants, not too much." I would simply add, "Savor it. Watch the carbs."

We don't yet understand the relationship between fruits and vegetables and health. But this seems to be the area in which there is most agreement between experts. Fruit and veg are at most incredibly beneficial and, at least, benign. Majoring on them looks like a good idea and the bigger the variety the better (though cruciferous veg and "greens" appear to offer the greatest benefits). So my second mantra is, "Eat your greens, and your reds, and your pinks."

One of the most shocking things I found was how sugar, even where it occurs naturally, is a major contributor to the growing problem of obesity. Obesity expert Robert Lustig believes fruit juice is every bit as bad as soft drinks. (As someone capable of downing half a carton of grapefruit juice in one fell swoop, I'm glad he told me.) Eating fruit is better, because it contains fiber. So one of Lustig's mantras has become mine: "Eat the fruit, not the juice."

fats

• Saturated fat, as found in butter, cheese, and red meat, may not be as bad for us as we once thought (following low-fat diets hasn't cut rates of heart disease or cancer). But it still seems sensible to keep an eye on your intake. And eating small amounts of butter is preferable to switching to a low-fat alternative that has undergone an industrial process.
• Don't eat transfats (hidden in processed foods) *at all* and look for them on food labels.
• Use olive oil, avocado oil, and canola oil freely; cold-pressed hazelnut and walnut oils are good, too (use those in dressings). Keep an eye on your intake of omega-6 oils (corn, sunflower, safflower, and grapeseed).
• Don't buy "low-fat" anything. If they've taken something *out*, there's a good chance they've put something worse (such as sugar) *in*.

eggs

It appears that there is no link between dietary cholesterol and levels of cholesterol in your blood. Eggs are back on the menu.

oily fish

Full of omega-3 fatty acids. Fill your plate. As long as they are sustainable.

carbs

• Cut refined carbs and switch to whole grains. *Watch sugar like a hawk*, especially if you have trouble with your weight. You may have to limit all carbs, even whole grains, to lose weight.
• Be careful about snacking on fruit, it contains a lot of natural sugar.
• Check the GI and GL of particular foods (especially those you like), so you know which cause insulin spikes. Check the great Australian website www.glycemicindex.com.

bread

• Eat proper whole-grain breads, based on a variety of grains, from good artisan bakers.
• Remember that not all whole-wheat breads are "healthy" (some are like white breads).

breakfast

Dump commercial breakfast cereal. Eat whole grains or protein to keep you full until lunch.

remember

• Nothing is forbidden. Healthy eating doesn't mean every meal has to be healthy. It means you should aim for *a balance overall*.
• It isn't a question of what you can't eat, more of what you can eat a lot of.
• Don't eat in a hurry, and stop eating when you're full.
• Be aware of what you've learned, but don't think slavishly about health. Food is for enjoying. When you eat delicious food you know isn't doing you good—great croissants, homemade preserves—don't angst over it. That's not what eating is about. Just *love* it.
• Plunder the healthy cuisines of the world—Middle Eastern, Mediterranean, Japanese, Thai, Burmese, Vietnamese—for dishes that are "accidentally" healthy. (There's a list of good cookbooks in the bibliography.) There are tons of bright, strong "front-of-the-mouth" flavors out there that can satisfy you (without the need for a lot of sugar or carbs).

over to you ...

This is my eighth book, and the one which has stretched me most (I prefer to think about flavors instead of food groups). It has also been the biggest surprise. In the past I groaned when people used the phrase "healthy eating" (a mountain of iceberg lettuce and cottage cheese as high as the sky would appear before my eyes). But of all my books, this is the one I keep right beside the oven. I use it all the time. My cooking has changed and developed in a delicious way. I hope it does the same for you.

bibliography

essential reading

WHAT TO EAT? 10 CHEWY
QUESTIONS ABOUT FOOD

Hattie Ellis
Portobello Books, 2012
This is the best place to start: A
personal, accessible, wide-ranging
approach to the many conflicting
ideas that are out there. Ellis is
not a nutritionist or an "expert,"
but a food lover. This will get you
thinking.

FOOD MATTERS: A GUIDE TO
CONSCIOUS EATING

Mark Bittman
Simon & Schuster, 2009
Bittman, a food writer for *The New
York Times*, changed his eating habits
because of health and environmental
concerns. Here, he tears down the
accepted wisdom on health touted
by the American government and
tackles what is wrong with the
American (increasingly the global)
diet. Unputdownable.

WHAT TO EAT: FOOD THAT'S
GOOD FOR YOUR HEALTH,
POCKET AND PLATE

Joanna Blythman
Fourth Estate, 2012
Blythman, an investigative food
journalist, goes through every
type of food looking at its health
properties and the ethics around it.
A brilliant reference. I keep it in the
kitchen.

FAT CHANCE: THE BITTER
TRUTH ABOUT SUGAR

Dr. Robert Lustig
Fourth Estate, 2013
The most persuasive, frightening
book I read during my research.
You have to get your head around
the science, but persevere. And
watch his lecture online (see
opposite).

IN DEFENCE OF FOOD:
AN EATER'S MANIFESTO

Michael Pollan
Penguin, 2009

WHY WE GET FAT: AND
WHAT TO DO ABOUT IT

Gary Taubes
Anchor Editions, 2012

ESCAPE THE DIET TRAP

Dr. John Briffa
Fourth Estate, 2013

EAT, DRINK, AND BE HEALTHY

Walter Willett
Free Press, 2003

wider reading

FOOD RULES, AN EATER'S MANUAL

Michael Pollan
Penguin, 2010

THE OMNIVORE'S DILEMMA

Michael Pollan
Bloomsbury Paperbacks, 2011

PURE, WHITE AND DEADLY

John Yudkin
Penguin, 2012

FOODS TO FIGHT CANCER

Richard Béliveau And Denis
Gingras
Dorling Kindersley, 2007

ANTICANCER: A NEW WAY OF LIFE

Dr. David Servan-Schreiber
Michael Joseph, 2011

THE DIET DELUSION

Gary Taubes
Vermilion, 2009

THE CHINA STUDY

Dr. T. Colin Campbell
Benbella, 2006

THE END OF OVEREATING

David A. Kessler
Penguin, 2010

STUFFED AND STARVED

Raj Patel
Portobello Books, 2013

FAST FOOD NATION

Eric Schlosser
Penguin, 2002

NOT ON THE LABEL

Felicity Lawrence
Penguin, 2004

EAT YOUR HEART OUT

Felicity Lawrence
Penguin, 2008

THE REVOLUTION WILL NOT
BE MICROWAVED

Sandor Ellix Katz
Chelsea Green Publishing, 2006

WHY CALORIES COUNT:
FROM SCIENCE TO POLITICS

Marion Nestle And Malden
Nesheim
University Of California Press, 2012

BAD SCIENCE

Ben Goldacre
Harper Perennial, 2009

THE FAST DIET

Dr. Michael Mosley And Mimi
Spencer
Short Books, 2013

THE DUKAN DIET

Dr. Pierre Dukan
Hodder Paperbacks, 2010

DR. ATKINS' NEW DIET
REVOLUTION

Robert C Atkins
Vermilion, 2003

THE SPECTRUM

Dean Ornish
Ballantine Books, 2008

THE PALEO DIET

Loren Cordain
John Wiley, 2002

NUTRITIONISM: THE SCIENCE AND
POLITICS OF DIETARY ADVICE

Gyorgy Scrinis
Columbia University Press, 2013

SUSHI AND BEYOND:
WHAT THE JAPANESE KNOW
ABOUT COOKING

Michael Booth
Vintage, 2010

GOOD TO THE GRAIN
Kimberley Boyce
Stewart, Tabori & Chang Inc,
2010

ANCIENT GRAINS FOR MODERN MEALS
Maria Speck
Ten Speed Press, 2011

A COOK'S GUIDE TO GRAINS
Jenni Muir
Conran Octopus, 2002

ROOTS
Diane Morgan
Chronicle Books, 2012

VEGETABLE LITERACY
Deborah Madison
Ten Speed Press, 2013

JANE GRIGSON'S VEGETABLE BOOK
Jane Grigson
Penguin Books, 1980

KNEAD TO KNOW: THE REAL BREAD STARTER
The Real Bread Campaign
Grub Street, 2013

HOW TO BAKE BREAD
Emmanuel Hadjiandreou
Ryland Peters & Small, 2011

THE BREAKFAST BIBLE
Seb Emina and Malcolm Eggs
Bloomsbury, 2013

THE GREAT BRITISH BREAKFAST
Jan Read and Maite Manjon
Michael Joseph Ltd., 1981

JAPANESE COOKING: A SIMPLE ART
Shizuo Tsuji
Kodansha America Inc., 2012

THE JAPANESE KITCHEN
Kimiko Barber
Kyle Cathie, 2004

JAPANESE FARM FOOD
Nancy Singleton Hachisu
Andrews McMeel, 2012

WASHOKU
Elizabeth Andoh
Ten Speed Press, 2005

THE ENLIGHTENED KITCHEN
Mari Fujii
Kodansha America Inc., 2012

HOT SOUR SALTY SWEET
Naomi Duguid, Jeffrey Alford
Artisan, 2000

BURMA: RIVERS OF FLAVOR
Naomi Duguid
Artisan, 2012

THE INDIAN KITCHEN
Monisha Bharadwaj
Kyle Cathie, 2010

VEGETARIAN DISHES FROM THE MIDDLE EAST
Arto Der Haroutunian
Grub Street, 2008

MIDDLE EASTERN COOKERY
Arto Der Haroutunian
Grub Street, 2010

CLASSIC VEGETARIAN COOKERY
Arto Der Haroutunian
Grub Street, 2011

THE SCANDINAVIAN KITCHEN
Camilla Plum
Kyle Cathie, 2010

THE NEW BOOK OF MIDDLE EASTERN FOOD
Claudia Roden
Penguin, 1986

VIETNAMESE: FRAGRANT AND EXOTIC
Ghillie Basan
Aquamarine, 2004

SECRETS OF THE RED LANTERN
Pauline Nguyen
Murdoch Books, 2007

THE ART OF SIMPLE FOOD
Alice Waters
Michael Joseph, 2008

broadcasts and Internet

TRANSFATS
The Food Programme, BBC
Radio 4, presented by Sheila Dillon,
transmitted 2011 (available on
BBC iPlayer)

SUGAR: THE BITTER TRUTH
Dr. Robert Lustig
University Of California Television
(available on www.youtube.com)

THE SKINNY ON OBESITY (SERIES)
University Of California Televison
(available on www.youtube.com)

THE MEN WHO MADE US FAT (SERIES)
BBC Television, reporter Jacques
Peretti, transmitted 2012

THE MEN WHO MADE US THIN (SERIES)
BBC Television, reporter Jacques
Peretti, transmitted 2013

WWW.KELLIESFOODTOGLOW.COM
Web site of health educationist
Kellie Anderson, who advises on
nutrition at Maggie's Cancer Caring
Centers, and offers fantastic food
that also happens to be good for
you. Delicious, colorful, plant-base
recipes, and information about
food's relationship to health.

index

A

agresto 178
almonds
  honeyed almonds 18
  mint and almond pesto 141
anchovies
  anchovy and caper dressing 203
  anchovy and rosemary sauce 292
  anchovy cream 48
  anchovy, olive, and caper salad
    dressing 103
  bagna cauda 300
  baby broccoli with anchovies 30
  smoked anchovies, green beans
    and egg salad 111
antioxidants 252
apples 252
  blackberry and apple rye galette
    182
  fennel and apple salad 120
  oatmeal with maple apples 240
apricots, dried
  date, apricot, and walnut loaf cake
    234
  Greek yogurt and apricot ice
    cream 22
  yogurt with honeyed saffron syrup,
    almonds, and apricot compote 266
artichoke hearts
  artichoke and ricotta salad with
    honeyed preserved lemon
    dressing 37
  Sicilian artichoke and fava bean
    salad with saffron dressing 90
artichokes, Jerusalem
  roasted pumpkin and Jerusalem
    artichokes with agresto 178
Asian hot, sour, salty, and sweet
  salad dressing 103
asparagus mimosa 28
asparagus, Veneto style 27
asparagus with shrimp and dill 27
avocados 252
  avocado "cream" 194
  avocado, raw salmon, and brown
    rice salad 306
  chilled tomato soup with cumin
    and avocado 88
  Japanese persimmon and avocado
    salad with ginger 197
  roasted tomatoes and avocado on
    toast 238

B

baby broccoli (broccolini) *see*
  broccoli
bagna cauda 300
Ballymaloe brown bread 236
barley 223
barley couscous with harissa 46
bass *see* sea bass
beans 192, *see also* cannellini,
  cranberry, edamame, fava, and
  navy beans
beans, dried 192, *see also* lentils
beef
  beef carpaccio with beluga lentils,
    horseradish, and buttermilk 313
  Japanese beef with country-style
    ponzu and wasabi 144
  tagliata 146
  Vietnamese beef with rice
    vermicelli and crispy vegetables 75
beets 253
  beet and carrot fritters 257
  beet and poppy seed relish 206
  beet and poppy seed loaf cake 80
  beet, radish, and goat cheese salad
    36
  Indian-spiced beet, pumpkin, and
    spinach 228
bell peppers
  Macedonian grilled vegetable salad
    107
  red pepper puree 64
  white beans with roasted peppers
    114
beluga lentil, roasted grape, and red
  Belgian endive salad 172
berries
  berry and hibiscus sorbet 116
  see also blackberries, blueberries,
    raspberries
black-and-white pilaf 74
black bread 324
blackberries 252
  blackberry and apple rye galette
    182
  blackberry and red wine gelatins
    233
  ricotta with summer berries 149
blueberries 252
  blueberry and gin gelatins 70
  goat curd, blueberries, and
    watercress 17
  multigrain porridge with
    blueberries and honey 239
bread 323

Ballymaloe brown bread 236
black bread 324
Clare's wheaten bread 237
flatbread 108
Middle Eastern yogurt bread 73
Persian spice bread 115
molasses bread 206
breakfasts 155–58
broccoli, baby (broccolini) 49, 253
  baby broccoli with anchovies 30
  baby broccoli with ricotta, lemon,
    and Parmesan 49
  beautiful broccoli 48
  broccoli strascinati 49
  new potatoes, baby broccoli, quail
    eggs, anchovy cream 48
  stir-fried baby broccoli with
    Chinese flavors 49
broths 168
  eastern broth with shallots 167
  broiled fish and saffron broth 171
  miso broth with greens 167
buckwheat 223
bulgur 222, 223
  cavolo nero and bulgur pilaf with
    glazed figs 180
Bulgurian grilled zucchini and
  eggplants with tarator 106
Burmese chile fish with hot-and-
  sour salad 198
Burmese melon and ginger salad
  89
Burmese-style chicken salad 216
buttermilk sauce 46

C

cabbage 253
  carrot, cabbage, and apple salad
    with caraway 175
  winter greens with crispy onion,
    tahini and sumac 259
cakes
  beet and poppy seed loaf cake 80
  date, apricot, and walnut loaf cake
    234
  gooseberry, almond, and spelt cake
    150
  orange and pomegranate cake
    305
  pistachio and lemon cake 79
Calabrian pesto 282
cannellini beans
  Middle Eastern-spiced squash and
    white beans with lemon and mint
    189

radicchio and red onions on white bean puree 288

smoked paprika sardines with white beans and roasted tomatoes 126

white beans with roasted peppers 114

carbohydrates 24, 25

cardamom-scented plum gelatins 233

carrots 272

beet and carrot fritters 257

carrot and ginger soup 169

carrot and daikon salad 274

carrot, cabbage, and apple salad 175

I-tal carrot and sweet potato soup 169

Japanese carrot and daikon salad 273

Mandalay carrot salad 277

Moroccan carrot salad 272

red lentil and carrot kofte 262

spiced carrot, date, and sesame salad 273

Uzbeki carrots 290

watercress and carrot salad 181

cavolo nero

cavolo nero and bulgur pilaf with glazed figs 180

winter greens with crispy onion, tahini, and sumac 259

celeriac, radicchio, fennel, and apple salad 174

cherries 252

goat cheese and cherry salad with almond and basil gremolata 98

see also gooseberry and spelt cake

chicken

Burmese-style chicken salad 216

chicken and fennel 74

chicken and pumpkin 219

chicken with yogurt and pomegranates 308

farareej mashri 73

Georgian chicken 302

grilled chicken, kale, and farro 225

grilled Vietnamese chicken 310

Israeli chicken 136

Japanese family rice bowl 258

Japanese ginger and garlic chicken 63

Persian saffron and mint chicken with spring couscous 20

Peruvian chicken soup 35

shawarma chicken 217

skewered chicken with lime, chile, and mint salad 139

Thai chicken and mango salad 216

see also Cornish game hens

chickpeas

chickpea puree 217

hummus 202

chocolate and rosemary sorbet 78

cholesterol 284

chutney

green chile and coconut chutney 298

citrus compote with ginger snow 200

Cornish game hens

pollo alla diavola 140

Cornish game hens with bell pepper puree 64

couscous

barley couscous with harissa 46

spring couscous 20

squid with couscous 127

white fish, saffron, and dill couscous pilaf 54

crab with chile and garlic 50

cranberry beans and kale with anchovy and rosemary sauce 292

crazy salad 230

crimson and white 250

cucumber

cucumber and yogurt soup 94

cucumber raita 169

dill and cucumber sauce 122

kachumber 89

smashed cucumber 63

sweet-and-sour cucumber 53

currants with yogurt and rye crumbs 158

D

dal 190, 192

dashi 258

dates

date and apricot loaf cake 234

eggplants with date salad 187

diets 24–26, 147

dill and cucumber sauce 122

dill and tomato sauce 118

dill and yogurt sauce 257

dressings see sauces and dressings

duck salad with plum-ginger dressing and sesame 214

E

eastern broth with shallots 167

edamame and show pea salad 63

eggplants

Bulgurian grilled zucchini and eggplants with tarator 106

grilled eggplants with date, walnut, and yogurt salad 187

Japanese eggplants with miso 188

Macedonian vegetable salad 107

eggs 56

asparagus mimosa 28

asparagus, Veneto style 27

good son-in-law eggs 56

roasted tomatoes and lentils with dukka-crumbed eggs 164

Roopa's Indian scrambled eggs 157

soft-boiled eggs with antipasti 30

Turkish poached eggs 157

espresso granita 93

F

farareej mashri 73

farro 223

farro, walnuts, grape, and fig salad 175

mustardy farro and vegetable salad 269

fat(s) 284–85

fava beans

fava bean, leek, tomato, and dill pilaf 112

fava bean puree with feta relish and cumin flatbread 108

Sicilian artichoke and fava bean salad with saffron dressing 90

fennel and apple salad 120

feta and orange salad 18

feta relish 108

figs

cavolo nero and bulgur pilaf with glazed figs 180

figs and melon 154

ricotta with figs and honey 149

fish

sashimi 210

white fish, saffron, and dill couscous pilaf 54

see also; haddock, smoked; mackerel; porgy; red snapper; salmon; sardines; sea bass; tuna

flatbread 108

freekeh 205, 224

fregola 142

fruit 25, 26, 158, 252, 253
  fruits with mint and rose 44
fruited rye grains with Gorgonzola
  287

G
gelatins
  blackberry and red wine gelatins
    233
  blueberry and gin gelatins 70
  cardamom-scented plum gelatins
    233
  rosé wine gelatin 130
Georgian chicken 302
ginger and mango relish 220
Goan baked fish with green chile
  and coconut chutney 298
goat cheese and cherry salad with
  almond and basil gremolata 98
goat curd, blueberries, and
  watercress 17
gooseberry, almond, and spelt cake
  150
granitas
  espresso 93
  ginger snow 200
  lemon and basil 93
grapefruit 252
  citrus compote with ginger snow
    200
  crimson and white 250
  grapefruit and mint sorbet 78
  warm salad of pink grapefruit,
    shrimp, and toasted coconut 97
grapes 252
  beluga lentil, roasted grape, and
    red Belgian endive salad 172
Greek yogurt and apricot ice cream
  22
gremolata 98, 254

H
haddock, smoked
  smoked haddock with Indian
    scented lentils 279
haydari 101
hibiscus flowers
  berry and hibiscus sorbet 116
hilbeh 114
hummus 202

I
ice cream
  Greek yogurt and apricot ice
    cream 22

Indian scrambled eggs, Roopa's
  157
Indian-spiced beet, pumpkin, and
  spinach 228
Indian-spiced spinach and
  mushrooms with black lentils and
  paneer 193
Israeli chicken 136

J
Japanese food 57–58
  beef with country-style ponzu 144
  carrot and daikon salad 273
  chicken, egg, and rice bowl 258
  eggplants with miso 188
  ginger and garlic chicken 63
  persimmon and avocado salad 197
  rice bowl 43
  tuna and radish salad 120

K
kachumber 89
kale
  cranberry beans and kale 292
  kale pesto with linguine 282
  kale, salmon, and barley soup 261
  see also cavolo nero
kamut 224, 307
kisir 187
kofte
  red lentil and carrot kofte 262
korma dressing 270

L
labneh 104
  roasted pumpkin, labneh, walnut
    gremolata, and pomegranates
    254
lamb
  lamb kebabs with adzhika 141
  lamb scottadito with fregola 142
  lamb with Kurdish rhubarb 309
  lamb with sekenjabin 76
leeks
  leeks with miso mustard 291
  Middle Eastern leeks with yogurt,
    dill, and sumac 38
  spelt and goat cheese risotto
    286
  warm salad of salmon, baby leeks,
    parsley, and capers 69
  see also asparagus mimosa
lemons
  lemon and basil granita 93
  pistachio and lemon cake 79

lentils
  beluga lentil, roasted grape, and
    red Belgian endive salad 172
  home-style Punjabi lentils 190
  lentil and roasted tomato soup 226
  lentilles en salade 30
  quinoa, black lentil, mango, and
    smoked chicken salad with
    korma dressing 270
  red lentil and carrot kofte 262
  roasted tomatoes and lentils with
    dukka-crumbed eggs 164
linguine
  kale pesto with whole-wheat
    linguine 282
litchis in jasmine tea 316
lunches 176–77

M
Macedonian grilled vegetable salad
  107
mackerel
  broiled summer herb mackerel
    128
  Japanese mackerel 212
  mackerel with hazelnut picada
    212
  North African spiced mackerel
    307
  smoked mackerel, beet, and poppy
    seed relish with molasses bread
    206
Madrid-style baked porgy 72
Mandalay carrot salad 277
mangoes
  ginger and mango relish 220
melon
  Burmese melon and ginger salad
    89
  figs and melon with ginger 154
  tomato, melon, and cucumber
    salad 86
Middle Eastern-spiced squash 189
Middle Eastern yogurt bread 73
mint
  fruits with mint and rose 44
  grapefruit and mint sorbet 78
  mint and almond pesto 141
  minted yogurt 194
  sekenjabin 76
miso broth with greens 167
Moroccan carrot salad 272
muesli
  toasty rye muesli with hazelnuts
    and dried cranberries 243

mushrooms
    Indian-spiced spinach and
        mushrooms 193
    soy mushrooms with egg ribbons
        244
mustardy farro and roasted winter
    vegetable salad 269

N
navy beans
    white beans with roasted peppers,
        eggs, and hilbeh 114
nectarine, tomato, and basil salad 86
new potatoes, baby broccoli, quail
    eggs, anchovy cream 48
North African spiced mackerel with
    kamut 307
nuoc cham 40

O
oats 240
    oatmeal with maple apples 240
oils 285
onions
    radicchio and red onions on white
        bean puree 288
    sumac onions 217
oranges 252
    feta and orange salad 18
    orange and cardamom sorbet 280
    orange and pomegranate cake 305
    orange and rosemary sorbet 280

P
peaches
    harissa-grilled peaches 136
    poached white peaches with rosé
        wine gelatin 130
    ricotta with peaches and honey
        149
peanut-chile dressing 274
pears
    mulled quince and pear compote
        320
    pears poached in Earl Grey 231
Persian saffron and mint chicken
    with spring couscous 20
Persian salad 14
Persian spice bread 115
persimmons
    Japanese persimmon and avocado
        salad with ginger 197
    persimmon, pomegranate, and
        red Belgian endive salad with goat
        cheese and toasted hazelnuts 184

Peruvian chicken soup 35
pestos
    Calabrian pesto 282
    kale pesto with linguine 282
    mint and almond pesto 141
    watercress pesto 282
phytochemicals 252
pilafs
    black-and-white pilaf 74
    fava bean, tomato, and dill pilaf
        112
    cavolo nero and bulgur pilaf with
        glazed figs 180
    pilaf of mixed grains, sweet potato,
        and fennel with avocado "cream"
        194
    white fish, saffron, and dill
        couscous pilaf 54
pistachio and lemon cake 79
plums 252
    cardamom-scented plum gelatins
        233
pollo alla diavola with green beans
    and Sicilian bread crumbs 140
pomegranate (molasses and seeds)
    chicken with yogurt and
        pomegranates 308
    kisir 187
    orange and pomegranate cake 305
    persimmon, pomegranate, and
        Belgian endive salad 184
    pomegranates, oranges, and dates
        322
    porridge with pomegranates 239
    spinach, pomegranate, and bulgur
        soup 260
ponzu dressing 144
porgy
    Burmese chile fish 198
    Goan baked fish with green chile
        and coconut chutney 298
    Madrid-style baked porgy 72
    porgy with ginger 209
    porgy with salsa verde 72
pork chops with ginger and mango
    relish 220
porridge with blueberries 239
porridge with pomegranates 239
probiotics 38
pumpkin and squash
    chicken and pumpkin 219
    Indian-spiced beet, pumpkin, and
        spinach 228
    Middle Eastern-spiced squash
        189

pumpkin, chestnut, and barley
    risotto 286
roasted pumpkin and Jerusalem
    artichokes with agresto 178
roasted pumpkin, labneh, walnut
    gremolata, and pomegranates
    254

Q
quail with blood orange and date
    salad 264
quinces
    mulled quince and pear compote
        with cranberries 320
    Turkish quince sorbet 232
quinoa 222, 224
quinoa, black lentil, mango, and
    smoked chicken salad with korma
    dressing 270

R
radicchio
    celeriac, radicchio, fennel, and
        apple 174
    radicchio and red onions on white
        bean puree 288
radishes
    crimson and white 250
    Japanese seared tuna and radish
        salad 120
    Persian salad 14
    radish and caper salad 30
raita, cucumber 169
raspberries 252
    raspberries with basil and
        buttermilk sherbet 153
    ricotta with summer berries and
        honey 149
    see also berries
red snapper
    baked stuffed red snapper 133
    grilled fish and saffron broth 171
    whole roasted fish with tahini
        dressing and barley tabbouleh
        135
rhubarb
    Kurdish rhubarb and split peas
        309
    pink rhubarb baked in star anise
        319
rice 223, 224
    Japanese rice bowls 43, 258
    see also pilafs
rice paper rolls with nuoc cham
    40

ricotta
  artichoke and ricotta salad 37
  baby broccoli with ricotta 49
  ricotta with summer berries and
    honey 149
risottos
  leek, spelt, and goat cheese 286
  pumpkin, chestnut, and barley
    286
rose and raspberry salad dressing
  103
rye 224
  fruited rye berries with
    Gorgonzola 287
  rye crackers 53
  toasty rye muesli with hazelnuts
    and dried cranberries 243

S
salads 102
  artichoke and ricotta 37
  avocado, salmon, and brown rice
    306
  beet and radish 96
  beet, radish, and goat cheese 36
  beluga lentil, grape, and Belgian
    endive 172
  Burmese melon and ginger 89
  Burmese-style chicken 216
  carrot and daikon 274
  carrot, cabbage, and apple 175
  carrot, date, and sesame 273
  celeriac, radicchio, and apple 174
  crazy 230
  date, walnut, and yogurt 187
  dressings for 103
  duck with plum-ginger dressing
    214
  edamame and snow pea 63
  farro, walnuts, grapes, and figs 175
  fennel and apple 120
  feta and orange 18
  goat cheese and cherry with
    almond and basil gremolata 98
  goat curd, blueberries, and
    watercress 17
  grapefruit, shrimp, and coconut 97
  hot-and-sour 198
  Japanese carrot and daikon 273
  Japanese persimmon and avocado
    197
  kachumber 89
  lentilles en salade 30
  Macedonian grilled vegetable 107
  Mandalay carrot 277

Moroccan carrot 272
mustardy farro and vegetable 269
nectarine, tomato, and basil 86
Persian 14
persimmon, pomegranate, and
  Belgian endive 184
radish and caper 30
salmon and baby leeks 69
Sicilian artichoke and fava bean 90
smoked anchovies, green beans,
  and egg 111
Thai-style chicken and mango 216
tomato, melon, and cucumber 86
tomatoes, goat curd, and basil 17
Turkish spoon 101
watercress and carrot 181
salmon
  avocado, raw salmon, and brown
    rice salad 306
  citrus-marinated salmon with
    fennel and apple salad 120
  eastern salmon carpaccio 119
  hot-smoked salmon, rye, beet, and
    radish salad 96
  kale, salmon and barley soup 261
  salmon barbecued in newspaper
    122
  salmon on the plate 119
  salmon tartare 53
  salmon with baby leeks 69
  Scandi salmon burger 118
  teriyaki salmon 60
sardines
  smoked paprika sardines with
    white beans and roasted tomatoes
    126
sashimi 210
sauces and dressings
  (*see also* pestos)
  agresto 178
  anchovy and caper 203
  anchovy and rosemary 292
  anchovy cream 48
  anchovy, olive, and caper 103
  Asian (salad) 103
  buttermilk 46
  Corfu garlic 171
  dill and cucumber 122
  dill and tomato 118
  dill and yogurt 257
  Georgian adzhika 141
  korma 270
  peanut-chile 274
  plum-ginger (salad) 214
  ponzu 144

raisin, chile, and pine nut salsa
  141
rose and raspberry (salad) 103
tahini 135, 259
walnut 302
yogurt 20
scallops with anchovy and caper
  dressing 203
scallops with ginger, soy, and
  scallion 209
Scandi salmon burger 118
sea bass ceviche with avocado and
  grapefruit 296
sea bass with spiced eggplant,
  lemon, and honey relish 124
sekenjabin 76
shallots
  eastern broth with shallots, lime,
    and cilantro 167
shawarma chicken with warm
  chickpea puree and sumac onions
  217
shrimp
  asparagus with shrimp and dill 27
  rice paper rolls with nuoc cham 40
  shrimp with lime and bok choy 213
  tofu, shrimp, and chive soup 32
  warm salad of pink grapefruit,
    shrimp, and toasted coconut 97
Sicilian artichoke and fava bean
  salad with saffron dressing 90
silken tofu, shrimp and chive soup
  32
soba noodles with chile, broccoli,
  and egg 295
sorbets
  berry and hibiscus 116
  blood orange and cardamom 280
  chocolate and rosemary 78
  grapefruit and mint 78
  orange and rosemary 280
  Turkish quince 232
soups (see also broths)
  carrot and ginger 169
  chilled tomato 88
  cucumber and yogurt 94
  I-tal carrot and sweet potato 169
  kale, salmon, and barley 261
  lentil and roasted tomato 226
  Peruvian chicken 35
  spinach, pomegranate, and bulgur
    260
  tofu, shrimp, and chive 32
soy mushrooms with egg ribbons
  and black sesame 244

spelt 224
  leek, spelt, and goat cheese
    risotto 286
  spelt and oat porridge with
    pomegranates 239
spinach 253
  Indian-spiced spinach and
    mushrooms with black lentils
    and paneer 193
  spinach, pomegranate, and bulgur
    soup 260
  Turkish poached eggs 157
split peas
  Kurdish rhubarb and split peas
    309
  tarka dal 190
squash, *see* pumpkin
squid
  hot chile-ginger stir-fried squid
    213
  squid with couscous 127
  squid with smoky almond tarator,
    bell peppers, freekeh, and
    spinach 205
sweet potatoes
  I-tal carrot and sweet potato soup
    169
  pilaf of mixed grains, sweet potato,
    and fennel with avocado "cream" 194

T
tabbouleh 135; *see also* kisir
tagliata 146
tahini dressing 135, 259
tarator 106, 205
tarka dal 190, 192
teriyaki salmon 60
Thai-style chicken and mango salad
  216
tofu, shrimp, and chive soup 32
tomatoes 252. 253
  chilled tomato soup with cumin
    and avocado 88
  kachumber 89
  kisir 187
  lentil and roasted tomato soup
    with saffron 226
  Macedonian grilled vegetable salad
    107
  nectarine, tomato, and basil salad
    with torn mozzarella 86
  roasted tomatoes and avocado on
    toast 238
  roasted tomatoes and lentils with
    dukka-crumbed eggs 164

roasted tomatoes, hummus, and
  spinach on toast 202
sweet saffron roasted tomatoes
  with labneh 104
tomato, melon, and cucumber
  salad 86
tomatoes, goat curd, and basil
  17
tuna
  Japanese seared tuna and radish
    salad 120
  seared tuna with avocado and
    wasabi puree 291
  seared tuna with chile and peanut
    dressing 132
Turkish poached eggs 157
Turkish quince sorbet 232
Turkish spoon salad 101

U
Uzbeki carrots 290

V
vegetables 12, 84, 162, 248,
  252–53,
  see also specific vegetables
  barley couscous with harissa and
    buttermilk sauce 46
  shaved vegetables with lemon and
    olive oil 66
  Turkish spoon salad 101
venison
  braised venison and beet 314
  venison with Kurdish rhubarb and
    split peas 309
Vietnamese beef with rice vermicelli
  and crispy vegetables 75

W
walnut sauce 302
wasabi 210
watercress 48, 102, 253
  goat curd, blueberries, and
    watercress 17
  watercress and carrot salad 181
  watercress pesto 282
wheat berries 224
wheaten bread 237
winter greens with crispy onions,
  tahini, and sumac 259
Y
yogurt 38
  dill and cucumber sauce 122
  dill and tomato sauce 118
  dill and yogurt sauce 257

Greek yogurt and apricot ice
  cream 22
haydari 101
labneh 104
Middle Eastern yogurt bread 73
minted yogurt 194
yogurt sauce 20
yogurt with honeyed saffron
  syrup, almonds and apricot
  compote 266

Z
zucchini
  Bulgurian grilled zucchini and
    eggplants with tarator 106

acknowledgments

For Miranda, with love.
Thank you for all the beautiful
books, and for so much else.

A Change of Appetite
by Diana Henry

An Hachette UK Company
www.hachette.co.uk

First published in Great Britain in 2014
by Mitchell Beazley, an imprint of
Octopus Publishing Group Ltd
Endeavour House, 189 Shaftesbury
Avenue London WC2H 8JY

www.octopusbooks.co.uk

Distributed in the USA by Hachette Book
Group USA, 237 Park Avenue, New York,
NY 10017 USA

Distributed in Canada by Canadian
Manda Group, 165 Dufferin Street,
Toronto, Ontario, Canada M6K 3H6

Text copyright © Diana Henry 2014
Design and layout copyright © Octopus
Publishing Group 2014
Photogrpahy copyright © Laura Edwards
2014

ISBN 978 1 84533 892 3
Printed and bound in China

10 9 8 7 6 5 4 3 2 1

Publisher: Denise Bates
Art Director: Jonathan Christie
Photographer: Laura Edwards
Design and Art Direction: Miranda Harvey
Editor: Lucy Bannell
Styling: Diana Henry and Miranda Harvey
Home Economist: Joss Herd
Assistant Production Manager: Caroline Alberti

All eggs are large unless otherwise stated.

My sons, Ted and Gillies, and my partner, Ben, ate rather a lot of "new" dishes while I was testing the recipes for this book (not all of them successful, brown rice cooked in green tea was a particular low. And no, it didn't make the cut). Thank you for patiently trying this different way of eating. And thank you Ted and Ben (the scientists in my life) for helping me to understand the material I had to digest while doing the research. I'm glad you're all on whole grains now. But I also know you love bagels, white bread, brioche … and Haribo Tangfastics. (You're a challenging lot.)

My good friend and fellow food writer Hattie Ellis gave me much guidance. I found her help—and her book *What to Eat* — invaluable. Thank you, Hattie. Enormous thanks, too, to Kellie Anderson, who read several chapters, kept me on the straight and narrow on various scientific details, and was extremely generous with her time and advice. Thanks also to Yotam Ottolenghi and to Chris Young from the Real Bread Campaign for various advice, to Yuki Sugiura for Japanese cooking lessons, and to Roopa Gulati for lessons in lentils … Xanthe Clay, Brett Barnes, Darina Allen, Roopa Gulati, Clare Henry, and Levi Roots all kindly let me use recipes. Thank you, guys.

Huge thanks to my publisher, Denise Bates at Mitchell Beazley, for completely "getting" what I was trying to do (she is so smart she can discern this even when it's in embryo and I can barely articulate it) and for letting me run with it, also for her unfailing support and fantastic judgment.

Thanks to Jonathan Christie, our talented and "can-do" art director and to the team who make sure the color is right, the ribbons are of good quality, and the damned book gets printed. Sybella Stephens, Katherine Hockley, and Caroline Alberti, without all your work on the fundamentals and your attention to detail my books wouldn't be nearly as good.

I'm very grateful to Amy Bryant from *The Sunday Telegraph* for additional research on where to buy a lot of healthy and hard-to-find stuff online.

Thanks also to Rachel Wood and Kathryn Morrissey who were total troopers and fitted into the creative chaos of the shoot days.

My greatest debt goes to the team who were at the coal-face: designer Miranda Harvey, photographer Laura Edward, editor Lucy Bannell, and cooks Joss Herd and Danny Maguire.

Laura, your photography is amazing, and you're developing so fast it leaves Miranda and I breathless. We love working with you.

Joss, I don't know anyone who can produce food that is so alive, that has such structure and movement. You are way more than a cook. You're also like sunshine in the kitchen, always laughing, ever positive. Danny, rose among thorns, we love you for being sane, a great cook, a good flirt, and for holding your own among us women. I hope we didn't shock you too often.

Lucy, you are, in my opinion, a genius editor. I can never see what you've cut, you make my voice more elegant (without changing its spirit), and you make each book as perfect as it can be. You're with me every inch of the way. I can't thank you enough.

Miranda, we are now such a long-standing team we can finish each other's sentences and completely understand each other's style. Working with you is one of the most fulfilling parts of my life.

Thanks and love to all of you. It's been bloody good fun and a creative joy.